THE ORIGINS
OF PAGAN AND
CHRISTIAN BELIEFS

THE ORIGINS
OF PAGAN AND
CHRISTIAN BELIEFS

EDWARD CARPENTER

SENATE

The Origins of Pagan & Christian Beliefs

First published in 1920 as *Pagan & Christian Creeds:
Their Origin & Meaning* by George Allen & Unwin Ltd, London.

This edition first published in 1996 by Senate, an imprint of
Random House UK Ltd, Random House, 20 Vauxhall Bridge
Road, London SW1V 2SA

ISBN 1 85958 196 X

Printed and bound in Guernsey by The Guernsey Press Co. Ltd

" *The different religions being lame attempts to represent under various guises this one root-fact of the central universal life, men have at all times clung to the religious creeds and rituals and ceremonials as symbolising in some rude way the redemption and fulfilment of their own most intimate natures—and this whether consciously understanding the interpretations, or whether (as most often) only doing so in an unconscious or quite subconscious way.*"

The Drama of Love and Death, p. 96.

CONTENTS

7

PAGAN AND CHRISTIAN CREEDS:
THEIR ORIGIN AND MEANING

I

INTRODUCTORY

THE subject of Religious Origins is a fascinating one, as
the great multitude of books upon it, published in late
years, tends to show. Indeed the great difficulty to-day
in dealing with the subject, lies in the very mass of the
material to hand—and that not only on account of the
labour involved in sorting the material, but because the
abundance itself of facts opens up temptàtion to a student
in this department of Anthropology (as happens also in
other branches of general Science) to rush in too hastily
with what seems a plausible theory. The more facts,
statistics, and so forth, there are available in any investigation, the easier it is to pick out a considerable number
which will fit a given theory. The other facts being
neglected or ignored, the views put forward enjoy for a
time a great vogue. Then inevitably, and at a later time,
new or neglected facts alter the outlook, and a new
perspective is established.

There is also in these matters of Science (though many
scientific men would doubtless deny this) a great deal of
‘ Fashion ’. Such has been notoriously the case in Poli-

tical Economy, Medicine, Geology, and even in such definite
studies as Physics and Chemistry. In a comparatively
recent science, like that with which we are now concerned,
one would naturally expect variations. A hundred and
fifty years ago, and since the time of Rousseau, the " Noble
Savage " was extremely popular ; and he lingers still in
the story books of our children. Then the reaction from
this extreme view set in, and of late years it has been
the popular cue (largely, it must be said, among " arm-
chair " travelers and explorers) to represent the religious
rites and customs of primitive folk as a senseless mass
of superstitions, and the early man as quite devoid of
decent feeling and intelligence. Again, when the study
of religious origins first began in modern times to be
seriously taken up—say in the earlier part of last century
—there was a great boom in Sungods. Every divinity
in the Pantheon was an impersonation of the Sun—unless
indeed (if feminine) of the Moon. Apollo was a sungod,
of course ; Hercules was a sungod ; Samson was a sungod ; Indra and Krishna, and even Christ, the same.
C. F. Dupuis in France (*Origine de tous les Cultes*, 1795),
F. Nork in Germany (*Biblische Mythologie*, 1842), Richard
Taylor in England (*The Devil's Pulpit*,[1] 1830), were among
the first in modern times to put forward this view. A
little later the *phallic* explanation of everything came into
fashion. The deities were all polite names for the organs
and powers of procreation. R. P. Knight (*Ancient Art
and Mythology*, 1818) and Dr. Thomas Inman (*Ancient
Faiths and Ancient Names*, 1868) popularised this idea
in England ; so did Nork in Germany. Then again there
was a period of what is sometimes called Euhemerism

---

[1] This extraordinary book, though carelessly composed and con-
taining many unproven statements, was on the whole on the right
lines. But it raised a storm of opposition—the more so because
its author was a clergyman ! He was ejected from the ministry,
of course, and was sent to prison twice.

—the theory that the gods and goddesses had actually once been men and women, historical characters round whom a halo of romance and remoteness had gathered. Later still, a school has arisen which thinks little of sun-gods, and pays more attention to Earth and Nature spirits, to gnomes and demons and vegetation-sprites, and to the processes of Magic by which these (so it was supposed) could be enlisted in man's service if friendly, or exorcised if hostile.

It is easy to see of course that there is some truth in *all* these explanations ; but naturally each school for the time being makes the most of its own contention. Mr. J. M. Robertson (*Pagan Christs* and *Christianity and Mythology*), who has done such fine work in this field,[1] relies chiefly on the solar and astronomical origins, though he does not altogether deny the others ; Dr. Frazer, on the other hand—whose great work, *The Golden Bough*, is a monumental collection of primitive customs, and will be an inexhaustible quarry for all future students—is apparently very little concerned with theories about the Sun and the stars, but concentrates his attention on the collection of innumerable details [2] of rites, chiefly magical, connected with food and vegetation. Still later writers, like S. Reinach, Jane Harrison and E. A. Crowley, being mainly occupied with customs of very primitive peoples, like the Pelasgian Greeks or the Australian aborigines, have confined themselves (necessarily) even more to Magic and Witchcraft.

Meanwhile the Christian Church from these speculations has kept itself severely apart—as of course representing a unique and divine revelation little concerned or interested in such heathenisms ; and moreover (in this country

---

[1] If only he did not waste so much time, and so needlessly, in slaughtering opponents !

[2] To such a degree, indeed, that sometimes the connecting clue of the argument seems to be lost.

at any rate) has managed to persuade the general public of its own divine uniqueness to such a degree that few people, even nowadays, realise that it has sprung from just the same root as Paganism, and that it shares by far the most part of its doctrines and rites with the latter. Till quite lately it was thought (in Britain) that only secularists and unfashionable people took any interest in sungods ; and while it was true that learned professors might point to a belief in Magic as one of the first sources of Religion, it was easy in reply to say that this obviously had nothing to do with Christianity ! The Secularists, too, rather spoilt their case by assuming, in their wrath against the Church, that all priests since the beginning of the world have been frauds and charlatans, and that all the rites of religion were merely devil's devices invented by them for the purpose of preying upon the superstitions of the ignorant, to their own enrichment. They (the Secularists) overleaped themselves by grossly exaggerating a thing that no doubt is partially true.

Thus the subject of religious origins is somewhat complex, and yields many aspects for consideration. It is only, I think, by keeping a broad course, and admitting contributions to the truth from various sides, that valuable results can be obtained. It is absurd to suppose that in this or any other science *neat systems* can be found which will cover all the facts. Nature and History do not deal in such things, or supply them for a sop to Man's vanity.

It is clear that there have been three main lines, so far, along which human speculation and study have run. One connecting religious rites and observances with the movements of the Sun and the planets in the sky, and leading to the invention of and belief in Olympian and remote gods dwelling in heaven and ruling the earth from a distance ; the second connecting religion with the changes of the season, *on* the Earth and with such practical things

as the growth of vegetation and food, and leading to or
mingled with a vague belief in earth-spirits and magical
methods of influencing such spirits ; and the third connecting religion with man's own body and the tremendous
force of sex residing in it—emblem of undying life and all
fertility and power. It is clear also—and all investigation
confirms it—that the second-mentioned phase of religion
arose on the whole *before* the first-mentioned—that is,
that men naturally thought about the very practical
questions of food and vegetation, and the magical or other
methods of encouraging the same, before they worried
themselves about the heavenly bodies and the laws of
their movements, or about the sinister or favorable influences
the stars might exert. And again it is extremely probable
that the third-mentioned aspect—that which connected
religion with the procreative desires and phenomena of
human physiology—really came *first*. These desires and
physiological phenomena must have loomed large on the
primitive mind long before the changes of the seasons or
of the sky had been at all definitely observed or considered. Thus we find it probable that, in order to understand the sequence of the actual and historical phases of
religious worship, we must approximately reverse the
order above-given in which they have been *studied*, and
conclude that in general the Phallic cults came first, the
cult of Magic and the propitiation of earth-divinities and
spirits came second, and only last came the belief in definite
God-figures residing in heaven.

At the base of the whole process by which divinities
and demons were created, and rites for their propitiation
and placation established, lay Fear—fear stimulating the
imagination to fantastic activity. *Primus in orbe deos
fecit Timor*. And fear, as we shall see, only became a
mental stimulus at the time of or after, the evolution
of *self*-consciousness. Before that time, in the period of
simple consciousness, when the human mind resembled

that of the animals, fear indeed existed, but its nature was more that of a mechanical protective instinct. There being no figure or image of *self* in the animal mind, there were correspondingly no figures or images of beings who might threaten or destroy that self. So it was that the imaginative power of fear began with Self-consciousness, and from that imaginative power was unrolled the whole panorama of the gods and rites and creeds of Religion down the centuries.

The immense force and domination of Fear in the first self-conscious stages of the human mind is a thing which can hardly be exaggerated, and which is even difficult for some of us moderns to realize. But naturally as soon as Man began to think about himself—a frail phantom and waif in the midst of tremendous forces of whose nature and mode of operation he was entirely ignorant—he was *beset* with terrors ; dangers loomed upon him on all sides. Even to-day it is noticed by doctors that one of the chief obstacles to the cure of illness among some black or native races is sheer superstitious terror ; and *Thanatomania* is the recognised word for a state of mind (" obsession of death ") which will often cause a savage to perish from a mere scratch hardly to be called a wound. The natural defence against this state of mind was the creation of an enormous number of *taboos*—such as we find among all races and on every conceivable subject—and these taboos constituted practically a great body of warnings which regulated the lives and thoughts of the community, and ultimately, after they had been weeded out and to some degree simplified, hardened down into very stringent Customs and Laws. Such taboos naturally in the beginning tended to include the avoidance not only of acts which might reasonably be considered dangerous, like touching a corpse, but also things much more remote and fanciful in their relation to danger, like merely looking at a mother-in-law, or passing a lightning-struck tree ; and (what is especially to be noticed) they tended to include acts which offered any special *pleasure* or temptation—like sex or marriage or the enjoyment of a meal. Taboos surrounded these things too, and the psychological connection is easy to divine : but I shall deal with this general subject later.

It may be guessed that so complex a system of regulations made life anything but easy to early peoples ; but, preposterous and unreasonable as some of the taboos were, they undoubtedly had the effect of compelling the growth of self-control. Fear does not seem a very worthy motive, but in the beginning it curbed the violence of the purely animal passions, and introduced order and restraint among them. Simultaneously it became itself, through the gradual increase of knowledge and observation, transmuted and etherialised into something more like wonder and awe, and (when the gods rose above the horizon) into reverence. Anyhow we seem to perceive that from the early beginnings (in the Stone Age) of self-consciousness in Man there has been a gradual development—from crass superstition, senseless and accidental, to rudimentary observation, and so to belief in Magic ; thence to Animism and personification of nature-powers in more or less human form, as earth-divinities or sky-gods or embodiments of the tribe ; and to placation of these powers by rites like Sacrifice and the Eucharist, which in their turn became the foundation of Morality. Graphic representations made for the encouragement of fertility—as on the walls of Bushmen's rock-dwellings or the ceilings of the caverns of Altamira—became the nurse of pictorial Art ; observations of plants or of the weather or the stars, carried on by tribal medicine-men for purposes of witchcraft or prophecy, supplied some of the material of Science ; and humanity emerged by faltering and hesitating steps on the borderland of those finer perceptions and reasonings which are supposed to be characteristic of Civilisation.

The process of the evolution of religious rites and cere-

monies has in its main outlines been the same all over
the world, as the reader will presently see—and this
whether in connexion with the numerous creeds of
Paganism or the supposedly unique case of Christianity ;
and now the continuity and close intermixture of these
great streams can no longer be denied—nor *is* it indeed
denied by those who have really studied the subject. It
is seen that religious evolution through the ages has been
practically One thing—that there has been in fact a World-
religion, though with various phases and branches.

And so in the present day a new problem arises, namely
how to account for the appearance of this great Phenomenon, with its orderly phases of evolution, and its own
spontaneous [1] growths in all corners of the globe—this
phenomenon which has had such a strange sway over
the hearts of men, which has attracted them with so
weird a charm, which has drawn out their devotion, love
and tenderness, which has consoled them in sorrow and
affliction, and yet which has stained their history with
such horrible sacrifices and persecutions and cruelties ?
What has been the instigating cause of it ?

The answer which I propose to this question, and which
is developed to some extent in the following chapters, is
a psychological one. It is that the phenomenon proceeds
from, and is a necessary accompaniment of, the growth
of human Consciousness itself—its growth, namely, through
the three great stages of its unfoldment. These stages
are (1) that of the simple or animal consciousness, (2) that
of *self*-consciousness, and (3) that of a third stage of consciousness which has not as yet been effectively named,
but whose indications and precursive signs we here and
there perceive in the rites and prophecies and mysteries
of the early religions, and in the poetry and art and literature generally of the later civilisations. Though I do
not expect or wish to catch Nature and History in the

[1] For the question of spontaneity see chap. x and elsewhere *infra*.

careful net of a phrase, yet I think that in the sequence
from the above-mentioned first stage to the second, and
then again in the sequence from the second to the third,
there will be found a helpful explanation of the rites and
aspirations of human religion. It is this idea, illustrated
by details of ceremonial and so forth, which forms the
main thesis of the present book. In this sequence of growth,
Christianity enters as an episode, but no more than an
episode. It does not amount to a disruption or dislocation of evolution. If it did, or if it stood as an unique
or unclassifiable phenomenon (as some of its votaries con-
tend), this would seem to be a misfortune—as it would
obviously rob us of at any rate *one* promise of progress in
the future. And the promise of something better than
Paganism and better than Christianity is very precious.
It is surely time that it should be fulfilled.

The tracing, therefore, of the part that human self-
consciousness has played, psychologically, in the evolution
of religion, runs like a thread through the following chapters,
and seeks illustration in a variety of details. The idea
has been repeated under different aspects ; sometimes,
possibly, it has been repeated too often ; but different
aspects in such a case do help, as in a stereoscope, to give
solidity to the thing seen. Though the worship of Sungods and divine figures in the sky came comparatively
late in religious evolution, I have put this subject early
in the book (chapters ii and iii), partly because (as I have
already explained) it was the phase first studied in modern
times, and therefore is the one most familiar to present-
day readers, and partly because its astronomical data
give great definiteness and ' proveability ' to it, in rebuttal
to the common accusation that the whole study of religious
origins is too vague and uncertain to have much value
Going backwards in Time, the two next chapters (iv and v)
deal with Totem-sacraments and Magic, perhaps the earliest

forms of religion. And these four lead on (in chapters vi to xi) to the consideration of rites and creeds common to Paganism and Christianity. XII and xiii deal especially with the evolution of Christianity itself ; xiv and xv explain the inner Meaning of the whole process from the beginning ; and xvi and xvii look to the Future.

The appendix on the doctrines of the Upanishads may, I hope, serve to give an idea, intimate even though in-adequate, of the third Stage—that which follows on the stage of self-consciousness ; and to portray the mental attitudes which are characteristic of that stage. Here in this third stage, it would seem, one comes upon the real *facts* of the inner life—in contradistinction to the fancies and figments of the second stage ; and so one reaches the final point of conjunction between Science and Religion.

II

SOLAR MYTHS AND CHRISTIAN FESTIVALS

To the ordinary public—notwithstanding the immense amount of work which has of late been done on this subject—the connexion between Paganism and Christianity still seems rather remote. Indeed the common notion is that Christianity was really a miraculous interposition into and dislocation of the old order of the world; and that the pagan gods (as in Milton's Hymn on the Nativity) fled away in dismay before the sign of the Cross, and at the sound of the name of Jesus. Doubtless this was a view much encouraged by the early Church itself—if only to enhance its own authority and importance; yet, as is well known to every student, it is quite misleading and contrary to fact. The main Christian doctrines and festivals, besides a great mass of affiliated legend and ceremonial, are really quite directly derived from, and related to, preceding Nature worships; and it has only been by a good deal of deliberate mystification and falsification that this derivation has been kept out of sight.

In these Nature-worships there may be discerned three fairly independent streams of religious or quasi-religious enthusiasm: (1) that connected with the phenomena of the heavens, the movements of the Sun, planets and stars, and the awe and wonderment they excited; (2) that connected with the seasons and the very important matter of the growth of vegetation and food on the Earth; and

19

(3) that connected with the mysteries of Sex and reproduction. It is obvious that these three streams would mingle and interfuse with each other a good deal ; but as far as they were separable the first would tend to create Solar heroes and Sun-myths ; the second Vegetation-gods and personifications of Nature and the earth-life ; while the third would throw its glamour over the other two and contribute to the projection of deities or dæmons worshipped with all sorts of sexual and phallic rites. All three systems would of course have their special rites and times and ceremonies ; but, as I say, the rites and ceremonies of one system would rarely be found pure and unmixed with those belonging to the two others. The whole subject is a very large one ; but for reasons given in the Introduction I shall in this and the following chapter—while not ignoring phases (2) and (3)—lay most stress on phase (1) of the question before us.

At the time of the life or recorded appearance of Jesus of Nazareth, and for some centuries before, the Mediterranean and neighbouring world had been the scene of a vast number of pagan creeds and rituals. There were Temples without end dedicated to gods like Apollo or Dionysus among the Greeks, Hercules among the Romans, Mithra among the Persians, Adonis and Attis in Syria and Phrygia, Osiris and Isis and Horus in Egypt, Baal and Astarte among the Babylonians and Carthaginians, and so forth. Societies, large or small, united believers and the devout in the service or ceremonials connected with their respective deities, and in the creeds which they confessed concerning these deities. And an extraordinarily interesting fact, for us, is that notwithstanding great geographical distances and racial differences between the adherents of these various cults, as well as differences in the details of their services, the general outlines of their creeds and ceremonials were—if not identical—so markedly similar as we find them.

I cannot of course go at length into these different cults, but I may say roughly that of all or nearly all the deities above-mentioned it was said and believed that :

(1) they were born on or very near our Christmas Day.

(2) They were born of a Virgin-Mother.

(3) And in a Cave or Underground Chamber.

(4) They led a life of toil for Mankind.

(5) And were called by the names of Light-bringer, Healer, Mediator, Saviour, Deliverer.

(6) They were however vanquished by the Powers of Darkness.

(7) And descended into Hell or the Underworld.

(8) They rose again from the dead, and became the pioneers of mankind to the Heavenly world.

(9) They founded Communions of Saints, and Churches into which disciples were received by Baptism.

(10) And they were commemorated by Eucharistic meals.

Let me give a few brief examples.

Mithra was born in a cave, and on the 25th December.[1] He was born of a Virgin.[2] He traveled far and wide as a teacher and illuminator of men. He slew the Bull (symbol of the gross Earth which the sunlight fructifies). His great festivals were the winter solstice and the Spring equinox (Christmas and Easter). He had twelve companions or disciples (the twelve months). He was buried in a tomb, from which however he rose again ; and his resurrection was celebrated yearly with great rejoicings. He was called Saviour and Mediator, and sometimes figured as a Lamb ; and sacramental feasts in remembrance of him were held by his followers. This legend is apparently

---

[1] The birthfeast of Mithra was held in Rome on the 8th day before the Kalends of January, being also the day of the Circassian games, which were sacred to the Sun. (See F. Nork, *Der Mystagog*, Leipzig.)

[2] This at any rate was reported by his later disciples (see Robertson's *Pagan Christs*, p. 338).

partly astronomical and partly vegetational; and the
same may be said of the following about Osiris.

Osiris was born (Plutarch tells us) on the 361st day of
the year, say the 27th December. He too, like Mithra
and Dionysus, was a great traveler. As King of Egypt
he taught men civil arts, and "tamed them by music
and gentleness, not by force of arms"; [1] he was the dis-
coverer of corn and wine. But he was betrayed by Typhon,
the power of darkness, and slain and dismembered. "This
happened," says Plutarch, "on the 17th of the month
Athyr, when the sun enters into the Scorpion" (the sign
of the Zodiac which indicates the oncoming of Winter).
His body was placed in a box, but afterwards, on the 19th,
came again to life, and, as in the cults of Mithra, Dionysus,
Adonis and others, so in the cult of Osiris, an image placed
in a coffin was brought out before the worshipers and
saluted with glad cries of "Osiris is risen." [1] "His
sufferings, his death and his resurrection were enacted
year by year in a great mystery-play at Abydos." [2]

The two following legends have more distinctly the
character of Vegetation myths.

Adonis or *Tammuz*, the Syrian god of vegetation, was
a very beautiful youth, born of a Virgin (Nature), and so
beautiful that Venus and Proserpine (the goddesses of
the Upper and Underworlds) both fell in love with him.
To reconcile their claims it was agreed that he should
spend half the year (summer) in the upper world, and the
winter half with Proserpine below. He was killed by a
boar (Typhon) in the autumn. And every year the maidens
"wept for Adonis" (see Ezekiel viii. 14). In the spring
a festival of his resurrection was held—the women set
out to seek him, and having found the supposed corpse
placed it (a wooden image) in a coffin or hollow tree, and
performed wild rites and lamentations, followed by even

[1] See Plutarch on *Isis and Osiris*.
[2] *Ancient Art and Ritual*, by Jane E. Harrison, chap. i.

wilder rejoicings over his supposed resurrection. At Aphaca in the North of Syria, and halfway between Byblus and Baalbec, there was a famous grove and temple of Astarte, near which was a wild romantic gorge full of trees, the birthplace of a certain river Adonis—the water rushing from a Cavern, under lofty cliffs. Here (it was said) every year the youth Adonis was again wounded to death, and the river ran red with his blood,[1] while the scarlet anemone bloomed among the cedars and the walnuts.

The story of Attis is very similar. He was a fair young shepherd or herdsman of Phrygia, beloved by Cybele (or Demeter), the Mother of the gods. He was born of a Virgin —Nana—who conceived by putting a ripe almond or pomegranate in her bosom. He died, either killed by a boar, the symbol of winter, like Adonis, or self-castrated (like his own priests) ; and he bled to death at the foot of a pine tree (the pine and pine-cone being symbols of fertility). The sacrifice of his blood renewed the fertility of the earth, and in the ritual celebration of his death and resurrection his image was fastened to the trunk of a pine-tree (compare the Crucifixion). But I shall return to this legend presently. The worship of Attis became very widespread and much honoured, and was ultimately incorporated with the established religion at Rome somewhere about the commencement of our Era.

The following two legends (dealing with Hercules and with Krishna) have rather more of the character of the solar, and less of the vegetational myth about them. Both heroes were regarded as great benefactors of humanity ; but the former more on the material plane, and the latter on the spiritual.

Hercules or *Heracles* was, like other Sun-gods and bene-

---

[1] A discoloration caused by red earth washed by rain from the mountains, and which has been observed by modern travelers. For the whole story of Adonis and of Attis see Frazer's *Golden Bough*, part iv.

factors of mankind, a great Traveler. He was known in many lands, and everywhere he was invoked as Saviour. He was miraculously conceived from a divine Father ; even in the cradle he strangled two serpents sent to destroy him. His many labours for the good of the world were ultimately epitomised into twelve, symbolised by the signs of the Zodiac. He slew the Nemæan Lion and the Hydra (offspring of Typhon) and the Boar. He overcame the Cretan Bull, and cleaned out the Stables of Augeas ; he conquered Death and, descending into Hades, brought Cerberus thence and ascended into Heaven. On all sides he was followed by the gratitude and the prayers of mortals.

As to Krishna, the Indian god, the points of agreement with the general divine career indicated above are too salient to be overlooked, and too numerous to be fully recorded. He also was born of a Virgin (Devaki) and in a Cave,[1] and his birth announced by a Star. It was sought to destroy him, and for that purpose a massacre of infants was ordered. Everywhere he performed miracles, raising the dead, healing lepers, and the deaf and the blind, and championing the poor and oppressed. He had a beloved disciple, Arjuna, (cf. John) before whom he was trans- figured.[2] His death is differently related—as being shot by an arrow, or crucified on a tree. He descended into hell ; and rose again from the dead, ascending into heaven in the sight of many people. He will return at the last day to be the judge of the quick and the dead.

Such are some of the legends concerning the pagan and pre-Christian deities—only briefly sketched now, in order that we may get something like a true perspective of the whole subject ; but to most of them, and more in detail, I shall return as the argument proceeds.

What we chiefly notice so far are two points ; on the one hand the general similarity of these stories with that

[1] Cox's *Myths of the Aryan Nations*, p. 107.
[2] *Bhagavat Gita*, ch. xi.

of Jesus Christ; on the other their analogy with the yearly phenomena of Nature as illustrated by the course of the Sun in heaven and the changes of Vegetation on the earth.

(1) The similarity of these ancient pagan legends and beliefs with Christian traditions was indeed so great that it excited the attention and the undisguised wrath of the early Christian fathers. They felt no doubt about the similarity, but not knowing how to explain it fell back upon the innocent theory that the Devil—in order to confound the Christians—had, *centuries before*, caused the pagans to adopt certain beliefs and practices! (Very crafty, we may say, of the Devil, but also very innocent of the Fathers to believe it!) Justin Martyr for instance describes [1] the institution of the Lord's Supper as narrated in the Gospels, and then goes on to say: " Which the wicked devils have *imitated* in the mysteries of Mithra, commanding the same thing to be done. For, that bread and a cup of water are placed with certain incantations in the mystic rites of one who is being initiated you either know or can learn." Tertullian also says [2] that " the devil by the mysteries of his idols imitates even the main part of the divine mysteries." . . . " He baptises his worshippers in water and makes them believe that this purifies them from their crimes." . . . " Mithra sets his mark on the forehead of his soldiers; he celebrates the oblation of bread ; he offers an image of the resurrection, and presents at once the crown and the sword ; he limits his chief priest to a single marriage ; he even has his virgins and ascetics." [3] Cortez, too, it will be remembered complained that the Devil had positively taught to the Mexicans the same things which God had taught to Christendom.

---

[1] 1 *Apol.* c. 66.

[2] *De Præscriptione Hereticorum*, c. 40, *De Bapt*, c. 5; *De Corona*, c. 15.

[3] For reference to both these examples see J. M. Robertson's *Pagan Christs*, pp. 321, 322.

Justin Martyr again, in the *Dialogue with Trypho* says that the Birth in the Stable was the prototype (!) of the birth of Mithra in the Cave of Zoroastrianism ; and boasts that Christ was born when the Sun takes its birth in the Augean Stable,[1] coming as a second Hercules to cleanse a foul world ; and St. Augustine says " we hold this (Christmas) day holy, not like the pagans because of the birth of the Sun, but because of the birth of him who made it." There are plenty of other instances in the Early Fathers of their indignant ascription of these similarities to the work of devils ; but we need not dwell over them. There is no need for *us* to be indignant. On the contrary we can now see that these animadversions of the Christian writers are the evidence of how and to what extent in the spread of Christianity over the world it had become fused with the Pagan cults previously existing.

It was not till the year A.D. 530 or so—five centuries after the supposed birth of Christ—that a Scythian Monk, Dionysius Exiguus, an abbot and astronomer of Rome, was commissioned to fix the day and the year of that birth. A nice problem, considering the historical science of the period ! For year he assigned the date which we now adopt,[2] and for day and month he adopted the 25th December—a date which had been in popular use since about 350 B.C., and the very date, within a day or two, of the supposed birth of the previous Sungods.[3] From that

[1] The Zodiacal sign of *Capricornus*, see *infra* (iii. 49).

[2] See *Encycl. Brit.* art. " Chronology."

[3] " There is however a difficulty in accepting the 25th December as the real date of the Nativity, December being the height of the rainy season in Judæa, when neither flocks nor shepherds could have been at night in the fields of Bethlehem " (!). *Encycl. Brit.* art. " Christmas Day." According to Hastings's *Encyclopædia*, art. " Christmas," " Usener says that the Feast of the Nativity was held originally on the 6th January (the Epiphany), but in 353-4 the Pope Liberius displaced it to the 25th December . . . but there is no evidence of a Feast of the Nativity taking place at all, before the fourth century A.D." It was not till 534 A.D. that Christmas Day and Epiphany were reckoned by the law-courts as *dies non*.

fact alone we may fairly conclude that by the year 530 or earlier the existing Nature-worships had become largely fused into Christianity. In fact the dates of the main pagan religious festivals had by that time become so popular that Christianity was *obliged* to accommodate itself to them.[1]

This brings us to the second point mentioned a few pages back—the analogy between the Christian festivals and the yearly phenomena of Nature in the Sun and the Vegetation.

Let us take Christmas Day first. Mithra, as we have seen, was reported to have been born on the 25th December (which in the Julian Calendar was reckoned as the day of the Winter Solstice *and* of the Nativity of the Sun) ; Plutarch says (*Isis and Osiris*, c. 12) that Osiris was born on the 361st day of the year, when a Voice rang out proclaiming him Lord of All. Horus, he says, was born on the 362nd day. Apollo on the same.

Why was all this ? Why did the Druids at Yule Tide light roaring fires ? Why was the cock supposed to crow all Christmas Eve (" The bird of dawning singeth all night long ") ? Why was Apollo born with only one hair (the young Sun with only one feeble ray) ? Why did Samson (name derived from *Shemesh*, the sun) lose all his strength when he lost his hair ? Why were so many of these gods —Mithra, Apollo, Krishna, Jesus, and others, born in caves or underground chambers ?[2] Why, at the Easter

[1] As, for instance, the festival of John the Baptist in June took the place of the pagan midsummer festival of water and bathing ; the Assumption of the Virgin in August the place of that of Diana in the same month ; and the festival of All Souls early in November, that of the world-wide pagan feasts of the dead and their ghosts at the same season.

[2] This same legend of gods (or idols) being born in caves has, curiously enough, been reported from Mexico, Guatemala, the Antilles, and other places in Central America. See C. F. P. von Martius, *Ethnographie Amerika, etc.* (Leipzig, 1867), vol. i, p. 758.

Eve festival of the Holy Sepulchre at Jerusalem is a light brought from the grave and communicated to the candles of thousands who wait outside, and who rush forth rejoicing to carry the new glory over the world ? [1]   Why indeed ? except that older than all history and all written records has been the fear and wonderment of the children of men over the failure of the Sun's strength in Autumn—the decay of their God ; and the anxiety lest by any means he should not revive or reappear ?

Think for a moment of a time far back when there were absolutely *no* Almanacs or Calendars, either nicely printed or otherwise, when all that timid mortals could see was that their great source of Light and Warmth was daily failing, daily sinking lower in the sky. As everyone now knows there are about three weeks at the fag end of the year when the days are at their shortest and there is very little change. What was happening ? Evidently the god had fallen upon evil times. Typhon, the prince of darkness, had betrayed him ; Delilah, the queen of Night, had shorn his hair ; the dreadful Boar had wounded him ; Hercules was struggling with Death itself ; he had fallen under the influence of those malign constellations—the Serpent and the Scorpion. Would the god grow weaker and weaker, and finally succumb, or would he conquer after all ? We can imagine the anxiety with which those early men and women watched for the first indication of a lengthening day ; and the universal joy when the Priest (the representative of primitive science) having made some simple observations, announced from the Temple steps that the day *was* lengthening—that the Sun was really born again to a new and glorious career.[2]

[1] Compare the Aztec ceremonial of lighting a holy fire and communicating it to the multitude from the wounded breast of a human victim, celebrated every 52 years at the end of one cycle and the beginning of another—the constellation of the Pleiades being in the Zenith (Prescott's *Conquest of Mexico*, Bk. I, ch. 4).

[2] It was such things as these which doubtless gave the Priesthood its power.

Let us look at the elementary science of those days a little closer. How without Almanacs or Calendars could the day, or probable day, of the Sun's rebirth be fixed ? Go out next Christmas Evening, and at midnight you will see the brightest of the fixed stars, Sirius, blazing in the southern sky—not however due south from you, but somewhat to the left of the Meridian line. Some three thousand years ago (owing to the Precession of the Equinoxes) that star at the winter solstice did not stand at midnight where you now see it, but almost exactly *on* the meridian line. The coming of Sirius therefore to the meridian at midnight became the sign and assurance of the Sun having reached the very lowest point of his course, and therefore of having arrived at the moment of his re-birth. Where then was the Sun at that moment ? Obviously in the underworld beneath our feet. Whatever views the ancients may have had about the shape of the earth, it was evident to the mass of people that the Sungod, after illuminating the world during the day, plunged down in the West, and remained during the hours of darkness in some cavern under the earth. Here he rested and after bathing in the great ocean renewed his garments before reappearing in the East next morning.

But in this long night of his greatest winter weakness, when all the world was hoping and praying for the renewal of his strength, it is evident that the new birth would come —if it came at all—at midnight. This then was the sacred hour when in the underworld (the Stable or the Cave or whatever it might be called) the child was born who was destined to be the Saviour of men. At that moment Sirius stood on the southern meridian (and in more southern lands than ours this would be more nearly overhead) ; and that star—there is little doubt—is the Star in the East mentioned in the Gospels

To the right, as the supposed observer looks at Sirius on the midnight of Christmas Eve, stands the magnificent

Orion, the mighty hunter. There are three stars in his belt which, as is well known, lie in a straight line pointing to Sirius. They are not so bright as Sirius, but they are sufficiently bright to attract attention. A long tradition gives them the name of the Three Kings. Dupuis [1] says : " Orion a trois belles étoiles vers le milieu, qui sont de seconde grandeur et posées en ligne droite, l'une près de l'autre, le peuple les appelle *les trois rois.* On donne aux trois rois Magis les noms de Magalat, Galgalat, Saraim ; et Athos, Satos, Paratoras. Les Catholiques les appellent Gaspard, Melchior, et Balthasar." The last-mentioned group of names comes in the Catholic Calendar in connexion with the feast of the Epiphany (6th January) ; and the name " Trois Rois " is commonly to-day given to these stars by the French and Swiss peasants.

Immediately after Midnight then, on the 25th December, the Beloved Son (or Sun-god) is born. If we go back in thought to the period, some three thousand years ago, when at that moment of the heavenly birth Sirius, coming from the East, did actually stand on the Meridian, we shall come into touch with another curious astronomical coincidence. For at that same moment we shall see the Zodiacal constellation of the Virgin in the act of rising, and becoming visible in the East divided through the middle by the line of the horizon.

The constellation Virgo is a Y-shaped group, of which a, the star at the foot, is the well-known *Spica*, a star of the first magnitude. The other principal stars, γ at the centre, and β and ε at the extremities, are of the second magnitude. The whole resembles more a *cup* than the human figure ; but when we remember the symbolic meaning of the *cup*, that seems to be an obvious explanation of the name *Virgo*, which the constellation has borne since

[1] Charles F. Dupuis (*Origine de Tous les Cultes*, Paris, 1822) was one of the earliest modern writers on these subjects

the earliest times. [The three stars β, γ and α, lie very nearly on the Ecliptic, that is, the Sun's path—a fact to which we shall return presently.]

At the moment then when Sirius, the star from the East, by coming to the Meridian at midnight signalled the Sun's new birth, the Virgin was seen just rising on the Eastern sky—the horizon line passing through her centre. And many people think that this astronomical fact is the explanation of the very widespread legend of the Virgin-birth. I

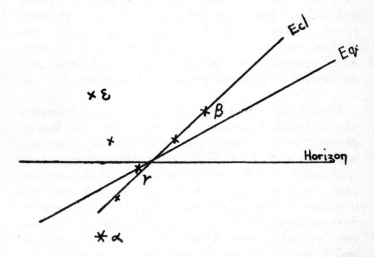

do not think that it is the sole explanation—for indeed in all or nearly all these cases the acceptance of a myth seems to depend not upon a single argument but upon the convergence of a number of meanings and reasons in the same symbol. But certainly the fact mentioned above is curious, and its importance is accentuated by the following considerations.

In the Temple of Denderah in Egypt, and on the inside of the dome, there is or *was* an elaborate circular representation of the Northern hemisphere of the sky and the

Zodiac.[1] Here Virgo the constellation is represented, as in our star-maps, by a woman with a spike of corn in her hand (Spica). But on the margin close by there is an annotating and explicatory figure—a figure of Isis with the infant Horus in her arms, and quite resembling in style the Christian Madonna and Child, except that she is sitting and the child is on her knee. This seems to show that—whatever other nations may have done in associating Virgo with Demeter, Ceres, Diana,[2] etc.—the Egyptians made no doubt of the constellation's connexion with Isis and Horus. But it is well known as a matter of history that the worship of Isis and Horus descended in the early Christian centuries to Alexandria, where it took the form of the worship of the Virgin Mary and the infant Saviour, and so passed into the European ceremonial. We have therefore the Virgin Mary connected by linear succession and descent with that remote Zodiacal cluster in the sky ! Also it may be mentioned that on the Arabian and Persian globes of Abenezra and Abuazar a Virgin and Child are figured in connexion with the same constellation.[3]

A curious confirmation of the same astronomical connexion is afforded by the Roman Catholic Calendar. For if this be consulted it will be found that the festival of the Assumption of the Virgin is placed on the 15th August, while the festival of the Birth of the Virgin is dated the 8th September. I have already pointed out that the stars, a, β and γ of Virgo are almost exactly on the Ecliptic, or Sun's path through the sky ; and a brief reference to the Zodiacal signs and the star-maps will show that the Sun each year enters the sign of *Virgo* about the first-mentioned date, and leaves it about the second date. At the present day the Zodiacal signs (owing to precession) have

---

[1] Carefully described and mapped by Dupuis, see *op. cit.*

[2] For the harvest-festival of Diana, the Virgin, and her parallelism with the Virgin Mary, see *The Golden Bough*, vol. i, 14 and ii, 121.

[3] See F. Nork, *Der Mystagog* (Leipzig, 1838).

shifted some distance from the constellations of the same name. But at the time when the Zodiac was constituted and these names were given, the first date obviously would signalise the actual disappearance of the cluster *Virgo* in the Sun's rays—i.e. the Assumption of the Virgin into the glory of the God—while the second date would signalise the reappearance of the constellation or the Birth of the Virgin. The Church of Notre Dame at Paris is supposed to be on the original site of a Temple of Isis ; and it is said (but I have not been able to verify this myself) that one of the side entrances—that, namely, on the left in entering from the North (cloister) side—is figured with the signs of the Zodiac *except* that the sign *Virgo* is replaced by the figure of the Madonna and Child.

So strange is the scripture of the sky ! Innumerable legends and customs connect the rebirth of the Sun with a Virgin parturition. Dr. J. G. Frazer in his Part IV of *The Golden Bough* [1] says : " If we may trust the evidence of an obscure scholiast the Greeks [in the worship of Mithras at Rome] used to celebrate the birth of the luminary by a midnight service, coming out of the inner shrines and crying, ' The Virgin has brought forth ! The light is waxing ! ' (Ἡ παρθένος τέτοκεν, αὔξει φῶς.)" In Elie Reclus' little book *Primitive Folk* [2] it is said of the Esquimaux that " On the longest night of the year two *angakout* (priests), of whom one is disguised as a *woman*, go from hut to hut extinguishing all the lights, rekindling them from a vestal flame, and crying out, ' From the new sun cometh a new light ! ' "

All this above-written on the Solar or Astronomical origins of the myths does not of course imply that the Vegetational origins must be denied or ignored. These latter were doubtless the earliest, but there is no reason as said in the Introduction (ch. i)—why the two elements

---

[1] Book II, ch. vi.
[2] In the *Contemporary Science Series*, p. 92.

should not to some extent have run side by side, or been fused with each other. In fact it is quite clear that they must have done so ; and to separate them out too rigidly, or treat them as antagonistic, is a mistake. The Cave or Underworld in which the New Year is born is not only the place of the Sun's winter retirement, but also the hidden chamber beneath the Earth to which the dying Vegetation goes, and from which it re-arises in Spring. The amours of Adonis with Venus and Proserpine, the lovely goddesses of the upper and under worlds, or of Attis with Cybele, the blooming Earth-mother, are obvious vegetation-symbols ; but they do not exclude the interpretation that Adonis (Adonai) may also figure as a Sun-god. The Zodiacal constellations of Aries and Taurus (to which I shall return presently) rule in heaven just when the Lamb and the Bull are in evidence on the earth ; and the yearly sacrifice of those two animals and of the growing Corn for the good of mankind runs parallel with the drama of the sky, as it affects not only the said constellations but also *Virgo* (the Earth-mother who bears the sheaf of corn in her hand).

I shall therefore continue (in the next chapter) to point out these astronomical references—which are full of significance and poetry ; but with a recommendation at the same time to the reader not to forget the poetry and significance of the terrestrial interpretations.

Between Christmas Day and Easter there are several minor festivals or holy days—such as the 28th December (the Massacre of the Innocents), the 6th January (the Epiphany), the 2nd February (Candlemas [1] Day), the period of Lent (German *Lenz*, the Spring), the Annunci-

---

[1] This festival of the Purification of the Virgin corresponds with the old Roman festival of *Juno Februata* (i.e. purified) which was held in the last month (February) of the Roman year, and which included a candle procession of Ceres, searching for Proserpine. (F. Nork, *Der Mystagog*.)

ation of the Blessed Virgin, and so forth—which have
been commonly celebrated in the pagan cults before Christianity, and in which elements of Star and Nature worship
can be traced ; but to dwell on all these would take too
long ; so let us pass at once to the period of Easter itself.

III

THE SYMBOLISM OF THE ZODIAC

THE Vernal Equinox has all over the ancient world, and from the earliest times, been a period of rejoicing and of festivals in honour of the Sungod. It is needless to labour a point which is so well known. Everyone understands and appreciates the joy of finding that the long darkness is giving way, that the Sun is growing in strength, and that the days are winning a victory over the nights. The birds and flowers reappear, and the promise of Spring is in the air. But it may be worth while to give an elementary explanation of the *astronomical* meaning of this period, because this is not always understood, and yet it is very important in its bearing on the rites and creeds of the early religions. The priests who were, as I have said, the early students and inquirers, had worked out this astronomical side, and in that way were able to fix dates and to frame for the benefit of the populace myths and legends, which were in a certain sense explanations of the order of Nature, and a kind of " popular science."

The Equator, as everyone knows, is an imaginary line or circle girdling the Earth half-way between the North and South poles. If you imagine a transparent Earth with a light at its very centre, and also imagine the *shadow* of this equatorial line to be thrown on the vast concave of the Sky, this shadow would in astronomical parlance

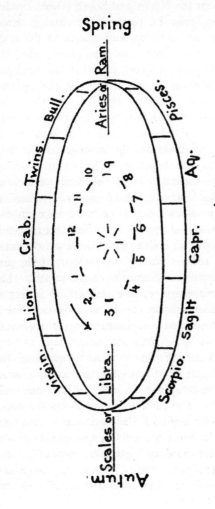

In the above illustration the signs of the Zodiac are represented by a belt which must be imagined at a practically infinite distance among the stars. The Sun is in the centre, and the dotted circle indicates the Earth's orbit—the numerals 1, 2, 3, etc., standing for the places of the Earth in the corresponding months of the year. Thus in January, to the observer at (1) the sun would appear to be in *Aquarius*; in February he would appear in *Pisces*; in March in *Aries*; and so forth. The diagram shows these relative positions fairly accurately as they were 3,000 years ago. *Now*, owing to "Precession," the place of the Spring Equinox has moved to the right, and is in *Pisces*, and not far from *Aquarius*.

coincide with the Equator of the Sky—forming an imaginary circle half-way between the North and South celestial poles.

The Equator, then, may be pictured as cutting across the sky either by day or by night, and always at the same elevation—that is, as seen from any one place. But the Ecliptic (the other important great circle of the heavens) can only be thought of as a line traversing the constellations as they are seen at *night*. It is in fact the Sun's path among the fixed stars. For (really owing to the Earth's motion in its orbit) the Sun appears to move round the heavens once a year—traveling, always to the left, from constellation to constellation. The exact path of the sun is called the Ecliptic ; and the band of sky on either side of the Ecliptic which may be supposed to include the said constellations is called the *Zodiac*. How then— it will of course be asked—seeing that the Sun and the Stars can never be seen together—were the Priests *able* to map out the path of the former among the latter ? Into that question we need not go. Sufficient to say that they succeeded ; and their success—even with the very primitive instruments they had—shows that their astronomical knowledge and acuteness of reasoning were of no mean order.

To return to our Vernal Equinox. Let us suppose that the Equator and Ecliptic of the sky, at the Spring season, are represented by the two lines *Eq.* and *Ecl.* crossing each other at the point *P*. The Sun, represented by the small circle, is moving slowly and in its annual course along the Ecliptic to the left. When it reaches the point *P* (the dotted circle) it stands on the Equator of the sky, and then for a day or two, being neither North nor South, it shines on the two terrestrial hemispheres alike, and day and night are equal. *Before* that time, when the sun is low down in the heavens, night has the advantage, and the days are short ; *afterwards*, when the Sun has traveled more to the left, the days triumph over the nights.

It will be seen then that this point *P* where the Sun's path crosses the Equator is a very critical point. It is the astronomical location of the triumph of the Sungod and of the arrival of Spring.

How was this location defined? Among what stars was the Sun moving at that critical moment? (For of course it was understood, or supposed, that the Sun was deeply influenced by the constellation through which it was, or appeared to be, moving.) It seems then that at the period when these questions were occupying men's minds—say about three thousand years ago—the point where the Ecliptic crossed the Equator was, as a matter of fact, in the region of the constellation *Aries* or the he-

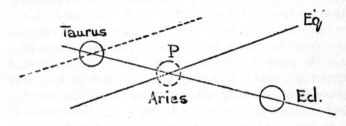

Lamb. The triumph of the Sungod was therefore, and quite naturally, ascribed to the influence of *Aries*. *The Lamb became the symbol of the risen Saviour, and of his passage from the underworld into the height of heaven.* At first such an explanation sounds hazardous; but a thousand texts and references confirm it; and it is only by the accumulation of evidence in these cases that the student becomes convinced of a theory's correctness. It must also be remembered (what I have mentioned before) that these myths and legends were commonly adopted not only for one strict reason but because they represented in a general way the convergence of various symbols and inferences.

Let me enumerate a few points with regard to the Vernal Equinox. In the Bible the festival is called the Pass-

over, and its supposed institution by Moses is related in
Exodus, ch. xii. In every house a he-lamb was to be
slain, and its blood to be sprinkled on the doorposts of
the house. Then the Lord would pass over and not smite
that house. The Hebrew word is *pasach*, to pass.[1] The
lamb slain was called the Paschal Lamb. But what was
that lamb? Evidently not an earthly lamb—(though
certainly the earthly lambs on the hillsides *were* just then
ready to be killed and eaten)—but the heavenly Lamb,
which was slain or sacrificed when the Lord ' passed over '
the equator and obliterated the constellation *Aries*. This
was the Lamb of God which was slain each year, and " slain
since the foundation of the world." This period of the
Passover (about the 25th March) was to be [2] the beginning
of a new year. The sacrifice of the Lamb, and its blood,
were to be the promise of redemption. The door-frames
of the houses—symbols of the entrance into a new life—
were to be sprinkled with blood.[3] Later, the imagery of
the saving power of the blood of the Lamb became more
popular, more highly coloured. (See St. Paul's epistles,
and the early Fathers.) And we have the expression
" washed in the blood of the Lamb " adopted into the
Christian Church.

In order fully to understand this extraordinary expression
and its origin we must turn for a moment to the worship

---

[1] It is said that *pasach* sometimes means not so much to pass over,
as to hover over and so protect. Possibly both meanings enter in
here. See Isaiah xxxi. 5.

[2] See Exodus xii. 1.

[3] It is even said (see *The Golden Bough*, vol. iii, 185) that the
doorways of houses and temples in Peru were at the Spring festival
daubed with blood of the first-born children—commuted afterwards
to the blood of the sacred animal, the Llama. And as to Mexico,
Sahagun, the great Spanish missionary, tells us that it was a custom
of the people there to " smear the outside of their houses and doors
with blood drawn from their own ears and ankles, in order to propitiate the god of Harvest " (Kingsborough's *Mexican Antiquities*,
vol. vi, p. 235).

both of Mithra, the Persian Sungod, and of Attis the Syrian god, as throwing great light on the Christian cult and ceremonies. It must be remembered that in the early centuries of our era the Mithra-cult was spread over the whole Western world. It has left many monuments of itself even here in Britain. At Rome the worship was extremely popular, and it may almost be said to have been a matter of chance whether Mithraism should over-whelm Christianity, or whether the younger religion by adopting many of the rites of the older one should establish itself (as it did) in the face of the latter.

Now we have already mentioned that in the Mithra cult the slaying of a Bull by the Sungod occupies the same sort of place as the slaying of the Lamb in the Christian cult. It took place at the Vernal Equinox and the blood of the Bull acquired in men's minds a magic virtue. Mithraism was a greatly older religion than Christianity; but its genesis was similar. In fact, owing to the Pre-cession of the Equinoxes, the crossing-place of the Ecliptic and Equator was different at the time of the establishment of Mithra-worship from what it was in the Christian period; and the Sun instead of standing in the He-lamb, or *Aries*, at the Vernal Equinox stood, about two thousand years earlier (as indicated by the dotted line in the diagram, p. 39), in this very constellation of the Bull.[1] The bull therefore became the symbol of the triumphant God, and the sacrifice of the bull a holy mystery. (Nor must we

[1] With regard to this point, see an article in the *Nineteenth Century* for September 1900, by E. W. Maunder of the Greenwich Observatory on "The Oldest Picture Book" (the Zodiac). Mr. Maunder calcu-lates that the Vernal Equinox was in the centre of the Sign of the Bull 5,000 years ago. [It would therefore be in the centre of Aries 2,845 years ago—allowing 2,155 years for the time occupied in passing from one Sign to another.] At the earlier period the Summer solstice was in the centre of Leo, the Autumnal equinox in the centre of Scorpio, and the Winter solstice in the centre of Aquarius—corre-pondingly roughly, Mr. Maunder points out, to the positions of the four ' Royal Stars,' Aldebaran, Regulus, Antares and Fomalhaut.

overlook here the agricultural appropriateness of the bull as the emblem of Spring-plowings and of service to man.)

The sacrifice of the Bull became the image of redemption. In a certain well-known Mithra-sculpture or group, the Sungod is represented as plunging his dagger into a bull, while a scorpion, a serpent, and other animals are sucking the latter's blood. From one point of view this may be taken as symbolic of the Sun fertilising the gross Earth by plunging his rays into it and so drawing forth its blood for the sustenance of all creatures ; while from another more astronomical aspect it symbolises the conquest of the Sun over winter in the moment of ' passing over ' the sign of the Bull, and the depletion of the generative power of the Bull by the *Scorpion*—which of course is the autumnal sign of the Zodiac and herald of winter. One such Mithraic group was found at Ostia, where there was a large subterranean Temple " to the invincible god Mithras."

In the worship of Attis there were (as I have already indicated) many points of resemblance to the Christian cult. On the 22nd March (the Vernal Equinox) a pine-tree was cut in the woods and brought into the Temple of Cybele. It was treated almost as a divinity, was decked with violets, and the effigy of a young man tied to the stem (cf. the Crucifixion). The 24th was called the " Day of Blood " ; the High Priest first drew blood from his own arms ; and then the others gashed and slashed themselves, and spattered the altar and the sacred tree with blood ; while novices made themselves eunuchs " for the kingdom of heaven's sake." The effigy was afterwards laid in a tomb. But when night fell, says Dr. Frazer,[1] sorrow was turned to joy. A light was brought, and the tomb was found to be empty. The next day, the 25th, was the festival of the Resurrection ; and ended in carnival and license (the *Hilaria*). Further, says Dr. Frazer, these

[1] See *Adonis, Attis* and *Osiris,* Part IV of *The Golden Bough,* by J. G. Frazer, p. 229.

mysteries "seem to have included a sacramental meal and a baptism of blood."

"In the baptism the devotee, crowned with gold and wreathed with fillets, descended into a pit, the mouth of which was covered with a wooden grating. A bull, adorned with garlands of flowers, its forehead glittering with gold leaf, was then driven on to the grating and there stabbed to death with a consecrated spear. Its hot reeking blood poured in torrents through the apertures, and was received with devout eagerness by the worshiper on every part of his person and garments, till he emerged from the pit, drenched, dripping, and scarlet from head to foot, to receive the homage, nay the adoration, of his fellows—as one who had been born again to eternal life and had washed away his sins in the blood of the bull."[1] And Frazer continuing says: "That the bath of blood derived from slaughter of the bull (*tauro-bolium*) was believed to regenerate the devotee for eternity is proved by an inscription found at Rome, which records that a certain Sextilius Agesilaus Aedesius, who dedicated an altar to Attis and the mother of the gods (Cybele) was *taurobolio criobolio que in aeternum renatus.*"[2] "In the procedure of the Taurobolia and Criobolia," says Mr. J. M. Robertson,[3] "which grew very popular in the Roman world, we have the literal and original meaning of the phrase ' washed in the blood of the lamb '; the doctrine being that resurrection and eternal life were secured by drenching or sprinkling with the actual blood of a sacrificial bull or ram." For the *popularity* of the rite we may quote Franz Cumont, who says[4] :—" Cette douche sacrée (*taurobolium*) parait avoir été administrée en Cappadoce dans un grand nombre de

[1] *Adonis, Attis and Osiris,* p. 229. References to Prudentius, and to Firmicus Maternus, *De errore* 28. 8.
[2] That is, " By the slaughter of the bull and the slaughter of the ram born again into eternity."
[3] *Pagan Christs,* p. 315.
[4] *Mystères de Mithra,* Bruxelles, 1902, p. 153.

sanctuaires, et en particulier dans ceux de Mâ la grande
divinité indigène, et dans ceux de Anahita."

Whether Mr. Robertson is right in ascribing to the
priests (as he appears to do) so materialistic a view of the
potency of the actual blood is, I should say, doubtful. I
do not myself see that there is any reason for supposing
that the priests of Mithra or Attis regarded baptism by
blood very differently from the way in which the Christian
Church has generally regarded baptism by water—namely,
as a *symbol* of some inner regeneration. There may certainly have been a little more of the *magical* view and a
little less of the symbolic, in the older religions ; but the
difference was probably on the whole more one of degree
than of essential disparity. But however that may be,
we cannot but be struck by the extraordinary analogy
between the tombstone inscriptions of that period " born
again into eternity by the blood of the Bull or the Ram,"
and the corresponding texts in our graveyards to-day.
F. Cumont in his elaborate work, *Textes et Monuments
relatifs aux Mystères de Mithra* (2 vols., Brussels, 1899)
gives a great number of texts and epitaphs of the same
character as that above-quoted,[1] and they are well worth
studying by those interested in the subject. Cumont, it
may be noted (vol. i, p. 305), thinks that the story of Mithra
and the slaying of the Bull must have originated among
some pastoral people to whom the bull was the source of
all life. The Bull in heaven—the symbol of the triumphant Sungod—and the earthly bull, sacrificed for the
good of humanity were one and the same ; the god, in
fact, *sacrificed himself or his representative*. And Mithra
was the hero who first won this conception of divinity
for mankind—though of course it is in essence quite similar
to the conception put forward by the Christian Church.

As illustrating the belief that the Baptism by Blood
was accompanied by a real regeneration of the devotee,

[1] See vol. i, pp. 334 ff.

Frazer quotes an ancient writer [1] who says that for some time after the ceremony the fiction of a new birth was kept up by dieting the devotee on *milk*, like a new-born babe. And it is interesting in that connexion to find that even in the present day a diet of *absolutely nothing but milk* for six or eight weeks is by many doctors recommended as the only means of getting rid of deep-seated illnesses and enabling a patient's organism to make a completely new start in life.

" At Rome," he further says (p. 230), " the new birth and the remission of sins by the shedding of bull's blood appear to have been carried out above all at the sanctuary of the Phrygian Goddess (Cybele) on the Vatican Hill, at or near the spot where the great basilica of St. Peter's now stands ; for many inscriptions relating to the rites were found when the church was being enlarged in 1608 or 1609. From the Vatican as a centre," he continues, " this barbarous system of superstition seems to have spread to other parts of the Roman empire. Inscriptions found in Gaul and Germany prove that provincial sanctuaries modelled their ritual on that of the Vatican."

It would appear then that at Rome in the quite early days of the Christian Church, the rites and ceremonials of Mithra and Cybele, probably much intermingled and blended, were exceedingly popular. Both religions had been recognised by the Roman State, and the Christians, persecuted and despised as they were, found it hard to make any headway against them—the more so perhaps because the Christian doctrines appeared in many respects to be merely faint *replicas* and copies of the older creeds. Robertson maintains [2] that a he-lamb was sacrificed in the Mithraic mysteries, and he quotes Porphyry as saying [3] that " a place near the equinoctial circle was assigned to Mithra as an appropriate seat ; and on this account he

[1] Sallustius philosophus. See *Adonis, Attis and Osiris*, note, p. 229.
[2] *Pagan Christs*, p. 336.   [3] *De Antro*, xxiv.

bears the sword of the Ram [Aries] which is a sign of Mars [Ares]." Similarly among the early Christians, it is said, a ram or lamb was sacrificed in the Paschal mystery.

Many people think that the association of the Lamb-god with the Cross arose from the fact that the constellation *Aries* at that time *was* on the heavenly cross (the crossways of the Ecliptic and Equator—see diagram, ch. iii, p. 39 *supra*), and in the very place through which the Sungod had to pass just before his final triumph. And it is curious to find that Justin Martyr in his *Dialogue with Trypho* [1] (a Jew) alludes to an old Jewish practice of roasting a Lamb on spits arranged in the form of a Cross. "The lamb," he says, meaning apparently the Paschal lamb, "is roasted and dressed up in the form of a cross. For one spit is transfixed right through the lower parts up to the head, and one across the back, to which are attached the legs [forelegs] of the lamb."

To-day in Morocco at the festival of Eid-el-Kebir, corresponding to the Christian Easter, the Mohammedans sacrifice a young ram and hurry it still bleeding to the precincts of the Mosque, while at the same time every household slays a lamb, as in the Biblical institution, for its family feast.

But it will perhaps be said, 'You are going too fast and proving too much. In the anxiety to show that the Lamb-god and the sacrifice of the Lamb were honoured by the devotees of Mithra and Cybele in the Rome of the Christian era, you are forgetting that the sacrifice of the Bull and the baptism in bull's blood were the salient features of the Persian and Phrygian ceremonials some centuries earlier. How can you reconcile the existence side by side of divinities belonging to such different periods, or ascribe them both to an astronomical origin?" The answer is simple enough. As I have explained before,

[1] Ch. xl.

the Precession of the Equinoxes caused the Sun, at its
moment of triumph over the powers of darkness, to stand
at one period in the constellation of the Bull, and at a
period some two thousand years later in the constellation
of the Ram.   It was perfectly natural therefore that a
change in the sacred symbols should, in the course of time,
take place ; yet perfectly natural also that these symbols,
having once been consecrated and adopted, should continue to be honoured and clung to long after the time of
their astronomical appropriateness had passed, and so
to be found side by side in later centuries.   The devotee
of Mithra or Attis on the Vatican Hill at Rome in the year
200 A.D. probably had as little notion or comprehension of
the real origin of the sacred Bull or Ram which he adored,
as the Christian in St. Peter's to-day has of the origin of
the Lamb-god whose vicegerent on earth is the Pope.

It is indeed easy to imagine that the change from the
worship of the Bull to the worship of the Lamb which
undoubtedly took place among various peoples as time
went on, was only a ritual change initiated by the priests
in order to put on record and harmonise with the astronomical alteration.   Anyhow it is curious that while Mithra
in the early times was specially associated with the bull,
his association with the lamb belonged more to the Roman
period.   Somewhat the same happened in the case of
Attis.   In the Bible we read of the indignation of Moses
at the setting up by the Israelites of a Golden Calf, *after*
the sacrifice of the ram-lamb had been instituted—as if
indeed the rebellious people were returning to the earlier
cult of Apis which they ought to have left behind them
in Egypt.   In Egypt itself, too, we find the worship of
Apis, as time went on, yielding place to that of the Ram-
headed god Amun, or Jupiter Ammon.[1]   So that both

---

[1] Tacitus (*Hist.* v. 4) speaks of a ram-sacrifice by the Jews in
honour of Jupiter Ammon. See also Herodotus (ii. 42) on the same
in Egypt.

from the Bible and from Egyptian history we may conclude that the worship of the Lamb or Ram succeeded to the worship of the Bull.

Finally it has been pointed out, and there may be some real connexion in the coincidence, that in the quite early years of Christianity the *Fish* came in as an accepted symbol of Jesus Christ. Considering that after the domination of *Taurus* and *Aries*, the Fish (*Pisces*) comes next in succession as the Zodiacal sign for the Vernal Equinox, and is now the constellation in which the Sun stands at that period, it seems not impossible that the astronomical change has been the cause of the adoption of this new symbol.

Anyhow, and allowing for possible errors or exaggerations, it becomes clear that the travels of the Sun through the belt of constellations which forms the Zodiac must have had, from earliest times, a profound influence on the generation of religious myths and legends. To say that it was the only influence would certainly be a mistake. Other causes undoubtedly contributed. But it was a main and important influence. The origins of the Zodiac are obscure ; we do not know with any certainty the reasons why the various names were given to its component sections, nor can we measure the exact antiquity of these names ; but—pre-supposing the names of the signs as once given —it is not difficult to imagine the growth of legends connected with the Sun's course among them.

Of all the ancient divinities perhaps Hercules is the one whose rôle as a Sungod is most generally admitted. The helper of gods and men, a mighty Traveler, and invoked everywhere as the *Saviour*, his labours for the good of the world became ultimately defined and systematised as twelve and corresponding in number to the signs of the Zodiac. It is true that this systematisation only took place at a late period, probably in Alexandria ; also that the identification of some of the Labours with the actual signs as we have them at present is not always clear. But considering the wide prevalence of the Hercules myth over the ancient world and the very various astronomical systems it must have been connected with in its origin, this lack of exact correspondence is hardly to be wondered at.

The Labours of Hercules which chiefly interest us are : (1) The capture of the Bull, (2) the slaughter of the Lion, (3) the destruction of the Hydra, (4) of the Boar, (5) the cleansing of the stables of Augeas, (6) the descent into Hades and the taming of Cerberus. The first of these is in line with the Mithraic conquest of the Bull ; the Lion is of course one of the most prominent constellations of the Zodiac, and its conquest is obviously the work of a Saviour of mankind ; while the last four labours connect themselves very naturally with the Solar conflict in winter against the powers of darkness. The Boar (4) we have seen already as the image of Typhon, the prince of darkness ; the Hydra (3) was said to be the offspring of Typhon ; the descent into Hades (6)—generally associated with Hercules' struggle with and victory over Death—links on to the descent of the Sun into the underworld, and its long and doubtful strife with the forces of winter ; and the cleansing of the stables of Augeas (5) has the same signification. It appears in fact that the *stables of Augeas* was another name for the sign of *Capricorn* through which the Sun passes at the Winter solstice [1]—the stable of course being an underground chamber—and the myth was that there, in this lowest tract and backwater of the Ecliptic all the malarious and evil influences of the sky were collected, and the Sungod came to wash them away (December was the height of the rainy season in Judæa) and cleanse the year towards its rebirth.

It should not be forgotten too that even as a child in the cradle Hercules slew two serpents sent for his destruction the serpent and the scorpion as autumnal constellations figuring always as enemies of the Sungod—to which

[1] See diagram of Zodiac, *supra*, p. 37.

may be compared the power given to his disciples by Jesus [1] " to tread on serpents and scorpions." Hercules also as a Sungod compares curiously with Samson (mentioned above, ii, p. 27), but we need not dwell on all the elaborate analogies that have been traced [2] between these two heroes.

The Jesus-story, it will now be seen, has a great number of correspondences with the stories of former Sungods and with the actual career of the Sun through the heavens —so many indeed that they cannot well be attributed to mere coincidence or even to the blasphemous wiles of the Devil! Let us enumerate some of these. There are (1) the birth from a Virgin mother ; (2) the birth in a stable (cave or underground chamber) ; and (3) on the 25th December (just after the winter solstice). There is (4) the Star in the East (Sirius) and (5) the arrival of the Magi (the " Three Kings ") ; there is (6) the threatened Massacre of the Innocents, and the consequent flight into a distant country (told also of Krishna and other Sungods). There are the Church festivals of (7) Candlemas (2nd February), with processions of candles to symbolise the growing light ; of (8) Lent, or the arrival of Spring ; of (9) Easter Day (normally on the 25th March) to celebrate the crossing of the Equator by the Sun ; and (10) simultaneously the outburst of lights at the Holy Sepulchre at Jerusalem. There is (11) the Crucifixion and death of the Lamb-God, on Good Friday, three days before Easter ; there are (12) the nailing to a tree, (13) the empty grave, (14) the glad Resurrection (as in the cases of Osiris, Attis and others) ; there are (15) the twelve disciples (the Zodiacal signs) ; and (16) the betrayal by one of the twelve. Then later there is (17) Midsummer Day, the 24th June, dedicated to the birth of the beloved disciple John, and corresponding

---

[1] Luke x. 19.
[2] See Doane's *Bible Myths*, ch. viii. (New York, 1882).

to Christmas Day; there are the festivals of (18) the Assumption of the Virgin (15th August) and of (19) the Nativity of the Virgin (8th September), corresponding to the movement of the god through *Virgo*; there is the conflict of Christ and his disciples with the autumnal asterisms, (20) the *Serpent* and the *Scorpion*; and finally there is the curious fact that the Church (21) dedicates the very day of the winter solstice (when any one may very naturally doubt the rebirth of the Sun) to St. Thomas, who doubted the truth of the Resurrection!

These are some of, and by no means all, the coincidences in question. But they are sufficient, I think, to prove —even allowing for possible margins of error—the truth of our general contention. To go into the parallelism of the careers of Krishna, the Indian Sungod, and Jesus would take too long; because indeed the correspondence is so extraordinarily close and elaborate.[1] I propose, however, at the close of this chapter, to dwell now for a moment on the Christian festival of the Eucharist, partly on account of its connexion with and derivation from the astronomical rites and Nature-celebrations already alluded to, and partly on account of the light which the festival generally, whether Christian or Pagan, throws on the origins of Religious Magic—a subject I shall have to deal with in the next chapter.

I have already (Ch. II, p. 25) mentioned the Eucharistic rite held in commemoration of Mithra, and the indignant ascription of this by Justin Martyr to the wiles of the Devil. Justin Martyr clearly had no doubt about the resemblance of the Mithraic to the Christian ceremony. A Sacramental meal, as mentioned a few pages back, seems to have been held by the worshipers of Attis[2] in commemoration of their god; and the 'mysteries' of the

[1] See Robertson's *Christianity and Mythology*, Part II, pp. 129–302, also Doane's *Bible Myths*, ch. xxviii, p. 278.
[2] See Frazer's *Golden Bough*, Part IV, p. 229.

Pagan cults generally appear to have included rites—
sometimes half-savage, sometimes more aesthetic—in which
a dismembered animal was eaten, or bread and wine (the
spirits of the Corn and the Vine) were consumed, as representing the body of the god whom his devotees desired
to honour. But the best example of this practice is
afforded by the rites of Dionysus, to which I will devote
a few lines. Dionysus, like other Sun or Nature deities,
was born of a Virgin (Semele or Demeter) untainted by any
earthly husband ; and born on the 25th December. He
was nurtured in a Cave, and even at that early age was
identified with the Ram or Lamb, into whose form he
was for the time being changed. At times also he was
worshiped in the form of a Bull.[1] He traveled far and
wide ; and brought the great gift of wine to mankind.[2]
He was called Liberator, and Saviour. His grave " was
shown at Delphi in the inmost shrine of the temple of
Apollo. Secret offerings were brought thither, while the
women who were celebrating the feast woke up the new-
born god. . . . Festivals of this kind in celebration of
the extinction and resurrection of the deity, were held
(by women and girls only) amid the mountains at night,
every third year, about the time of the shortest day. The
rites, intended to express the excess of grief and joy at
the death and reappearance of the god, were wild even
to savagery, and the women who performed them were
hence known by the expressive names of *Bacchae, Mœnads*,
and *Thyiades*. They wandered through woods and mountains, their flying locks crowned with ivy or snakes, brand-
ishing wands and torches, to the hollow sounds of the
drum, or the shrill notes of the flute, with wild dances
and insane cries and jubilation. The victims of the sacrifice,

---

[1] *The Golden Bough*, Part II, Book II, p. 164.

[2] " I am the *true* Vine," says the Jesus of the fourth gospel, perhaps
with an implicit and hostile reference to the cult of Dionysus—in
which Robertson suggests (*Christianity and Mythology*, p. 357) there
was a ritual miracle of turning water into wine.

oxen, goats, even fawns and roes from the forest, were killed, torn in pieces, and eaten raw. This in imitation of the treatment of Dionysus by the Titans " [1]—who it was supposed had torn the god in pieces when a child.

Dupuis, one of the earliest writers (at the beginning of last century) on this subject, says, describing the mystic rites of Dionysus [2] : " The sacred doors of the Temple in which the initiation took place were opened only once a year, and no stranger might ever enter. Night lent to these august mysteries a veil which was forbidden to be drawn aside—for whoever it might be.[3] It was the sole occasion for the representation of the passion of Bacchus [Dionysus] dead, descended into hell, and rearisen —in imitation of the representation of the sufferings of Osiris which, according to Herodotus, were commemorated at Sais in Egypt. It was in that place that the partition took place of *the body of the god*,[4] which was then eaten— the ceremony, in fact, of which our Eucharist is only a reflection ; whereas in the mysteries of Bacchus actual raw flesh was distributed, which each of those present had to consume in commemoration of the death of Bacchus dismembered by the Titans, and whose passion, in Chios and Tenedos, was renewed each year by the sacrifice of a man who represented the god.[5] Possibly it is this last fact which made people believe that the Christians (whose *hoc est corpus meum* and sharing of an Eucharistic meal were no more than a shadow of a more ancient rite) did really sacrifice a child and devour its limbs."

That Eucharistic rites were very very ancient is plain from the Totem-sacraments of savages ; and to this subject we shall now turn.

---

[1] See art. Dionysus, *Dictionary of Classical Antiquities*, Nettleship and Sandys (3rd edn., London, 1890).

[2] See Charles F. Dupuis, " *Traite des Mystéres*," ch. i.

[3] Pausan, *Corinth*, ch. 37.   [4] Clem. Prot. *Eur. Bacch.*

[5] See Porphyry, *De Abstinentia*, lii, § 56.

IV

TOTEM-SACRAMENTS AND EUCHARISTS

MUCH has been written on the origin of the Totem-system
—the system, that is, of naming a tribe or a portion of
a tribe (say a *clan*) after some *animal*—or sometimes also
after some plant or tree or Nature-element, like fire or
rain or thunder ; but at best the subject is a difficult one
for us moderns to understand. A careful study has been
made of it by Salamon Reinach in his *Cultes, Mythes et
Religions*,[1] where he formulates his conclusions in twelve
statements or definitions ; but even so—though his suggestions are helpful—he throws very little light on the
real *origin* of the system.[2]

There are three main difficulties. The first is to understand why primitive Man should name his Tribe after
an animal or object of nature at all ; the second, to understand on what principle he selected the particular name
(a lion, a crocodile, a lady bird, a certain tree) ; the third,
why he should make of the said totem a divinity, and
pay honour and worship to it. It may be worth while
to pause for a moment over these.

[1] See English translation of certain chapters (published by David
Nutt in 1912) entitled *Cults, Myths and Religions*, pp. 1–25. The
French original is in three large volumes.
[2] The same may be said of the formulated statement of the subject
in Morris Jastrow's *Handbooks of the History of Religion*, vol. iv.

(1) The fact that the Tribe was one of the early things for which Man found it necessary to have a name is interesting, because it shows how early the solidarity and psychological actuality of the tribe was recognised ; and as to the selection of a name from some animal or concrete object of Nature, that was inevitable, for the simple reason that there was *nothing else for the savage to choose from*. Plainly to call his tribe " The Wayfarers " or " The Pioneers " or the " Pacifists " or the " Invincibles," or by any of the thousand and one names which modern associations adopt, would have been impossible, since such abstract terms had little or no existence in his mind. And again to name it after an animal was the most obvious thing to do, simply because the animals were by far the most important features or accompaniments of his own life. As I am dealing in this book largely with certain psychological conditions of human evolution, it has to be pointed out that to primitive man the animal was the nearest and most closely related of all objects. Being of the same order of consciousness as himself, the animal appealed to him very closely as his mate and equal. He made with regard to it little or no distinction from himself. We see this very clearly in the case of children, who of course represent the savage mind, and who regard animals simply as their mates and equals, and come quickly into *rapport* with them, not differentiating themselves from them.

(2) As to the particular animal or other object selected in order to give a name to the Tribe, this would no doubt be largely accidental. Any unusual incident might superstitiously precipitate a name. We can hardly imagine the Tribe scratching its congregated head in the deliberate effort to think out a suitable emblem for itself. That is not the way in which nicknames are invented in a school or anywhere else to-day. At the same time the heraldic appeal of a certain object of nature, animate or inanimate, would be deeply and widely felt. The strength of the

lion, the fleetness of the deer, the food-value of a bear, the flight of a bird, the awful jaws of a crocodile, might easily mesmerise a whole tribe. Reinach points out, with great justice, that many tribes placed themselves under the protection of animals which were supposed (rightly or wrongly) to act as guides and augurs, foretelling the future. " Diodorus," he says, " distinctly states that the hawk, in Egypt, was venerated because it foretold the future." [Birds generally act as weather-prophets.]   " In Australia and Samoa the kangaroo, the crow and the owl premonish their fellow clansmen of events to come. At one time the Samoan warriors went so far as to rear owls for their prophetic qualities in war."   [The jackal, or ' pathfinder ' —whose tracks sometimes lead to the remains of a food-animal slain by a lion, and many birds and insects, have a value of this kind.]   " This use of animal totems for purposes of augury is, in all likelihood, of great antiquity. Men must soon have realised that the senses of animals were acuter than their own ; nor is it surprising that they should have expected their totems—that is to say, their natural allies—to forewarn them both of unsuspected dangers and of those provisions of nature, *wells* especially, which animals seem to scent by instinct." [1]   And again, beyond all this, I have little doubt that there are sub-conscious affinities which unite certain tribes to certain animals or plants, affinities whose origin we cannot now trace, though they are very real—the same affinities that we recognise as existing between individual *persons* and certain objects of nature. W. H. Hudson—himself in many respects having this deep and primitive relation to nature—speaks in a very interesting and autobiographical volume [2] of the extraordinary fascination exercised upon him as a boy, not only by a snake, but by certain trees, and especially by a particular flowering-plant " not more

[1] See Reinach, Eng. trans., *op. cit.*, pp. 20, 21.
[2] *Far away and Long ago* (1918) chs. xvi and xvii.

than a foot in height, with downy soft pale green leaves, and clusters of reddish blossoms, something like valerian." . . . "One of my sacred flowers," he calls it, and insists on the "inexplicable attraction" which it had for him. In various ways of this kind one can perceive how particular totems came to be selected by particular peoples.

(3) As to the tendency to divinise these totems, this arises no doubt partly out of question (2). The animal or other object admired on account of its strength or swiftness, or adopted as guardian of the tribe because of its keen sight or prophetic quality, or infinitely prized on account of its food-value, or felt for any other reason to have a peculiar relation and affinity to the tribe, is by that fact *set apart*. It becomes taboo. It must not be killed—except under necessity and by sanction of the whole tribe—nor injured ; and all dealings with it must be fenced round with regulations. It is out of this taboo or system of taboos that, according to Reinach, religion arose. "I propose (he says) to define religion as : *A sum of scruples (taboos) which impede the free exercise of our faculties.*[1] Obviously this definition is gravely deficient, simply because it is purely negative, and leaves out of account the positive aspect of the subject. In Man, the positive content of religion is the instinctive sense—whether conscious or subconscious—of an inner unity and continuity with the world around. This is the stuff out of which religion is made. The scruples or taboos which "impede the freedom" of this relation are the negative forces which give outline and form to the relation. These are the things which generate the *rites and ceremonials* of religion ; and as far as Reinach means by religion *merely* rites and ceremonies he is correct ; but clearly he only covers half the subject. The tendency to divinise the totem is at least as much dependent on the positive sense of unity with it, as on the negative scruples which limit

[1] See *Orpheus* by S. Reinach, p. 3.

the relation in each particular case. But I shall return to this subject presently, and more than once, with the view of clarifying it. Just now it will be best to illustrate the nature of Totems generally, and in some detail.

As would be gathered from what I have just said, there is found among all the more primitive peoples, and in all parts of the world, an immense variety of totem-names. The Dinkas, for instance, are a rather intelligent well-grown people inhabiting the upper reaches of the Nile in the vicinity of the great swamps. According to Dr. Seligman their clans have for totems the lion, the elephant, the crocodile, the hippopotamus, the fox, and the hyaena, as well as certain birds which infest and damage the corn, some plants and trees, and such things as rain, fire, etc. "Each clan speaks of its totem as its ancestor, and refrains [as a rule] from injuring or eating it." [1] The members of the Crocodile clan call themselves "brothers of the crocodile." The tribes of Bechuana-land have a very similar list of totem-names—the buffalo, the fish, the porcupine, the wild vine, etc. They too have a Crocodile clan, but they call the crocodile their *father*! The tribes of Australia much the same again, with the differences suitable to their country ; and the Red Indians of North America the same. Garcilasso della Vega, the Spanish historian, son of an Inca princess by one of the Spanish conquerors of Peru and author of the well-known book *Commentarias Reales*, says in that book (i, 75), speaking of the pre-Inca period, " An Indian (of Peru) was not considered honorable unless he was descended from a fountain, river or lake, or even from the sea, or from a wild animal, as a bear, lion, tiger, eagle, or the bird they call *cuntur* (condor), or some other bird of prey." [2] According

---

[1] See *The Golden Bough*, vol. iv, p. 31.
[2] See Andrew Lang, *Custom and Myth*, p. 104, also *Myth, Ritual and Religion*, vol. i, pp. 71, 76, etc.

to Lewis Morgan, the North American Indians of various tribes had for totems the wolf, bear, beaver, turtle, deer, snipe, heron, hawk, crane, loon, turkey, muskrat ; pike, catfish, carp ; buffalo, elk, reindeer, eagle, hare, rabbit, snake ; reed-grass, sand, rock, and tobacco-plant.

So we might go on rather indefinitely. I need hardly say that in more modern and civilised life, relics of the totem system are still to be found in the forms of the heraldic creatures adopted for their crests by different families, and in the bears, lions, eagles, the sun, moon and stars and so forth, which still adorn the flags and are flaunted as the *insignia* of the various nations. The names may not have been *originally* adopted from any definite belief in blood-relationship with the animal or other object in question ; but when, as Robertson says (*Pagan Christs*, p. 104), a " savage learned that he was ' a Bear ' and that his father and grandfather and forefathers were so before him, it was really impossible, after ages in which totem-names thus passed current, that he should fail to assume that his folk were *descended* from a bear."

As a rule, as may be imagined, the savage tribesman will on no account *eat* his tribal totem-animal. Such would naturally be deemed a kind of sacrilege. Also it must be remarked that some totems are hardly suitable for eating. Yet it is important to observe that occasionally, and guarding the ceremony with great precautions, it has been an almost universal custom for the tribal elders to call a feast at which an animal (either the totem or some other) *is* killed and communally eaten—and this in order that the tribesmen may absorb some virtue belonging to it, and may confirm their identity with the tribe and with each other. The eating of the bear or other animal, the sprinkling with its blood, and the general ritual in which the participants shared its flesh, or dressed and disguised themselves in its skin, or otherwise identified themselves with it, was to them a symbol of their community of life with each other, and a means of their renewal and salvation in the holy emblem. And this custom, as the reader will perceive, became the origin of the Eucharists and Holy Communions of the later religions.

Professor Robertson-Smith's celebrated *Camel* affords an instance of this.[1] It appears that St. Nilus (fifth century) has left a detailed account of the occasional sacrifice in his time of a spotless white camel among the Arabs of the Sinai region, which closely resembles a totemic communion-feast. The uncooked blood and flesh of the animal had to be entirely consumed by the faithful before daybreak. " The slaughter of the victim, the sacramental drinking of the blood, and devouring in wild haste of the pieces of still quivering flesh, recall the details of the Dionysiac and other festivals." [2]   Robertson-Smith himself says :— " The plain meaning is that the victim was devoured before its life had left the still warm blood and flesh . . . and that thus in the most literal way, all those who shared in the ceremony absorbed part of the victim's life into themselves.   One sees how much more forcibly than any ordinary meal such a rite expresses the establishment or confirmation of a bond of common life between the worshipers, and also, since the blood is shed upon the altar itself, between the worshipers and their god.   In this sacrifice, then, the significant factors are two : the conveyance of the living blood to the godhead, and the absorption of the living flesh and blood into the flesh and blood of the worshipers.   Each of these is effected in the simplest and most direct manner, so that the meaning of the ritual is perfectly transparent."

It seems strange, of course, that men should *eat* their totems ; and it must not by any means be supposed that this practice is (or was) universal ; but it undoubtedly

---

[1] See his *Religion of the Semites*, p. 320.

[2] They also recall the rites of the Passover—though in this latter the blood was no longer drunk, nor the flesh eaten raw.

obtains in some cases. As Miss Harrison says (*Themis*, p. 123), " you do not as a rule eat your relations," and *as a rule* the eating of a totem is *tabu* and forbidden, but (Miss Harrison continues) " at certain times and under certain restrictions a man not only may, but *must*, eat of his totem, though only sparingly, as of a thing sacrosanct." The ceremonial carried out in a communal way by the tribe not only identifies the tribe with the totem (animal), but is held, according to early magical ideas, and when the animal is desired for food, to favour its multiplication. The human tribe partakes of the *mana* or life-force of the animal, and is strengthened ; the animal tribe is sympathetically renewed by the ceremonial and multiplies exceedingly. The slaughter of the sacred animal and (often) the simultaneous outpouring of human blood seals the compact and confirms the magic. This is well illustrated by a ceremony of the ' Emu ' tribe referred to by Dr. Frazer :—

" In order to multiply Emus which are an important article of food, the men of the Emu totem in the Arunta tribe proceed as follows : They clear a small spot of level ground, and opening veins in their arms they let the blood stream out until the surface of the ground for a space of about three square yards is soaked with it. When the blood has dried and caked, it forms a hard and fairly impermeable surface, on which they paint the sacred design of the emu totem, especially the parts of the bird which they like best to eat, namely, the fat and the eggs. Round this painting the men sit and sing. Afterwards performers wearing long head-dresses to represent the long neck and small head of the emu, mimic the appearance of the bird as it stands aimlessly peering about in all directions." [1]

Thus blood sacrifice comes in ; and—(whether this has ever actually happened in the case of the Central Australians

---

[1] *The Golden Bough* i, 85—with reference to Spencer and Gillen's *Native Tribes of Central Australia*, pp. 179, 189.

I know not)—we can easily imagine a member of the Emu
tribe, and disguised as an actual emu, having been ceremonially slaughtered as a firstfruits and promise of the
expected and prayed-for emu-crop ; just as the same
certainly *has* happened in the case of men wearing beast-
masks of Bulls or Rams or Bears being sacrificed in propitiation of Bull-gods, Ram-gods or Bear-gods or simply in
pursuance of some kind of magic to favour the multiplication of these food-animals.

" In the light of totemistic ways of thinking we see plainly
enough the relation of man to food-animals. You need
or at least desire flesh food, yet you shrink from slaughtering
' your brother the ox ' ; you desire his *mana*, yet you
respect his *tabu*, for in you and him alike runs the common
life-blood. On your own individual responsibility you
would never kill him ; but for the common weal, on great
occasions, and in a fashion conducted with scrupulous
care, it is expedient that he die for his people, and that
they feast upon his flesh." [1]

In her little book *Ancient Art and Ritual* [2] Jane Harrison
describes the dedication of a holy Bull, as conducted in
Greece at Elis, and at Magnesia and other cities. " There
at the annual fair year by year the stewards of the city
bought a Bull ' the finest that could be got,' and at the
new moon of the month at the beginning of seed-time
[? April] they dedicated it for the city's welfare. . . . The
Bull was led in procession at the head of which went the
chief priest and priestess of the city. With them went
a herald and the sacrificer, and two bands of youths and
maidens. So holy was the Bull that nothing unlucky
might come near him. The herald pronounced aloud a
prayer for ' the safety of the city and the land, and the
citizens, and the women and children, for peace and wealth,
and for the bringing forth of grain and all other fruits,

[1] *Themis*, p. 140.
[2] Home University Library, p 87.

and of cattle.' All this longing for fertility, for food and
children, focuses round the holy Bull, whose holiness *is*
his strength and fruitfulness." The Bull is sacrificed.
The flesh is divided in solemn feast among those who
take part in the procession. " The holy flesh is not offered
to a god, it is eaten—to every man his portion—by each
and every citizen, that he may get his share of the strength
of the Bull, of the luck of the State." But at Athens the
Bouphonia, as it was called, was followed by a curious
ceremony. " The hide was stuffed with straw and sewed
up, and next the stuffed animal was set on its feet and
yoked to a plough as though it were ploughing. The Death
is followed by a Resurrection. Now this is all important.
We are so accustomed to think of sacrifice as the death,
the giving up, the renouncing of something. But *sacrifice*
does not mean ' death ' at all. It means *making holy*,
sanctifying : and holiness was to primitive man just special
strength and life. What they wanted from the Bull was
just that special life and strength which all the year long
they had put into him, and nourished and fostered. That
life was in his blood. They could not eat that flesh nor
drink that blood unless they killed him. So he must die.
But it was not to give him up to the gods that they killed
him, not to ' sacrifice ' him in our sense, but to have him,
keep him, eat him, live *by* him and through him, by his
grace."

We have already had to deal with instances of the
ceremonial eating of the sacred he-Lamb or Ram, immolated
in the Spring season of the year, and partaken of in a kind
of communal feast—not without reference (at any rate
in later times) to a supposed Lamb-god. Among the
Ainos in the North of Japan, as also among the Gilyaks
in Eastern Siberia, the Bear is the great food-animal, and
is worshiped as the supreme giver of health and strength
There also a similar ritual of sacrifice occurs. A perfect
Bear is caught and caged. He is fed up and even

pampered to the day of his death. " Fish, brandy and other delicacies are offered to him. Some of the people prostrate themselves before him ; his coming into a house brings a blessing, and if he sniffs at the food that brings a blessing too." Then he is led out and slain. A great feast takes place, the flesh is divided, cupfuls of the blood are drunk by the men ; the tribe is united and strengthened, and the Bear-god blesses the ceremony—the ideal Bear that has given its life for the people.[1]

That the eating of the flesh of an animal or a man conveys to you some of the qualities, the life-force, the *mana*, of that animal or man, is an idea which one often meets with among primitive folk. Hence the common tendency to eat enemy warriors slain in battle against your tribe. By doing so you absorb some of their valour and strength. Even the enemy scalps which an Apache Indian might hang from his belt were something magical to add to the Apache's power. As Gilbert Murray says,[2] " you devoured the holy animal to get its *mana*, its swiftness, its strength, its great endurance, just as the savage now will eat his enemy's brain or heart or hands to get some particular quality residing there." Even—as he explains on an earlier page—mere *contact* was often considered sufficient—" we have holy pillars whose holiness consists in the fact that they have been touched by the blood of a bull." And in this connexion we may note that nearly all the Christian Churches have a great belief in the virtue imparted by the mere ' laying on of hands.'

In quite a different connexion—we read[3] that among the Spartans a warrior-boy would often beg for the love of the elder warrior whom he admired (i.e. the contact with

[1] See *Art and Ritual*, pp. 92–98 ; *The Golden Bough*, ii, 375 *seq.* ; *Themis*, pp. 140, 141 ; etc.

[2] *Four Stages of Greek Religion*, p. 36.

[3] Aelian VII, iii, 12 : αὐτὸι γοῦν (οἱ παῖδες) δέονται τῶν ἐραστῶν εἰσπνεῖν αὐτοῖς. See also E. Bethe on " Die Dorische Knabenliebe " in the *Rheinisches Museum*, vol. 26, iii, 461.

his body) in order to obtain in that way a portion of the latter's courage and prowess. That through the mediation of the lips one's spirit may be united to the spirit of another person is an idea not unfamiliar to the modern mind ; while the exchange of blood, clothes, locks of hair, etc., by lovers is a custom known all over the world.[1]

To suppose that by eating another you absorb his or her soul is somewhat naïve certainly. Perhaps it *is* more native, more primitive. Yet there may be *some* truth even in that idea. Certainly the food that one eats has a psychological effect, and the flesh-eaters among the human race have a different temperament as a rule from the fruit and vegetable eaters, while among the animals (though other causes may come in here) the Carnivora are decidedly more cruel and less gentle than the Herbivora.

To return to the rites of Dionysus, Gilbert Murray, speaking of Orphism—a great wave of religious reform which swept over Greece and South Italy in the sixth century B.C.—says : [2] " A curious relic of primitive superstition and cruelty remained firmly imbedded in Orphism, a doctrine irrational and unintelligible, and for that very reason wrapped in the deepest and most sacred mystery : a belief in the *sacrifice of Dionysus himself, and the purification of man by his blood.* It seems possible that the savage Thracians, in the fury of their worship on the mountains, when they were possessed by the god and became ' wild beasts,' actually tore with their teeth and hands any hares, goats, fawns or the like that they came across. . . . The Orphic congregations of later times, in their most holy gatherings, solemnly partook of the blood of a bull, which was by a mystery the blood of Dionysus-Zagreus himself, the Bull of God, slain in sacrifice for the purification of man." [3]

[1] See Crawley's *Mystic Rose*, pp. 238, 242.
[2] See Notes to his translation of the *Bacchæ* of Euripides.
[3] For a description of this orgy see Theocritus, Idyll xxvi ; also

Such instances of early communal feasts, which fulfilled
the double part of confirming on the one hand the solidarity of the tribe, and on the other of bringing the tribe,
by the shedding of the blood of a divine Victim into close
relationship with the very source of its life, are plentiful
to find. " The sacramental rite," says Professor Robertson-
Smith,[1] " is also an atoning rite, which brings the community again into harmony with its alienated god—
atonement being simply an act of communion designed
to wipe out all memory of previous estrangement.   With
this subject I shall deal more specially in chapter vii below.
Meanwhile as instances of early Eucharists we may mention
the following cases, remembering always that as the blood
is regarded as the *Life*, the drinking or partaking of, or
sprinkling with, blood is always an acknowledgment of
the common life ; and that the juice of the grape being
regarded as the blood of the Vine, *wine* in the later ceremonials quite easily and naturally takes the place of the
blood in the early sacrifices.

Thus P. Andrada La Crozius, a French missionary,
and one of the first Christians who went to Nepaul and
Thibet, says in his *History of India* : " Their Grand Lama
celebrates a species of sacrifice with *bread* and *wine*, in
which, after taking a small quantity himself, he distributes
the rest among the Lamas present at this ceremony." [2]

---

for explanations of it, Lang's *Myth, Ritual and Religion*, vol. ii,
pp. 241-260, on Dionysus. The *Encyclopædia Brit.*, article "Orpheus,"
says :—" Orpheus, in the manner of his death, was considered to
personate the god Dionysus, and was thus representative of the god
torn to pieces every year—a ceremony enacted by the Bacchae in the
earliest times with a human victim, and afterwards with a bull, to
represent the bull-formed god.   A distinct feature of this ritual was
ὠμοφαγία (eating the flesh of the victim raw), whereby the com-
municants imagined that they consumed and assimilated the god
represented by the victim, and thus became filled with the divine
ecstasy."   Compare also the Hindu doctrine of Prajápati, the dismembered Lord of Creation.

[1] *Religion of the Semites*, p. 302.   [2] See Doane's *Bible Myths*, p. 306.

" The old Egyptians celebrated the resurrection of Osiris by a sacrament, eating the sacred cake or wafer after it had been consecrated by the priest, and thereby becoming veritable flesh of his flesh." [1] As is well known, the eating of bread or dough sacramentally (sometimes mixed with blood or seed) as an emblem of community of life with the divinity, is an extremely ancient practice or ritual. Dr. Frazer [2] says of the Aztecs, that " twice a year, in May and December, an image of the great god Huitzilopochtli was made of dough, then broken in pieces and solemnly eaten by his worshipers." And Lord Kingsborough in his *Mexican Antiquities* (vol. vi, p. 220) gives a record of a " most Holy Supper " in which these people ate the flesh of their god. It was a cake made of certain seeds, " and having made it, they blessed it in their manner, and broke it into pieces, which the high priest put into certain very clean vessels, and took a thorn of maguey which resembles a very thick needle, with which he took up with the utmost reverence single morsels, which he put into the mouth of each individual in the manner of a communion." Acosta [3] confirms this and similar accounts. The Peruvians partook of a sacrament consisting of a pudding of coarsely ground maize, of which a portion had been smeared on the idol. The priest sprinkled it with the blood of the victim before distributing it to the people." Priest and people then all took their shares in turn, " with great care that no particle should be allowed to fall to the ground—this being looked upon as a great sin." [4]

Moving from Peru to China (instead of ' from China to Peru ') we find that " the Chinese pour wine (a very

---

[1] From *The Great Law, of religious origins* : by W. Williamson (1899), p. 177.

[2] *The Golden Bough*, vol. ii, p. 79.

[3] *Natural and Moral History of the Indies*. London (1604).

[4] See Markham's *Rites and laws of the Incas*, p. 27.

general substitute for blood) on a straw image of Confucius,
and then all present drink of it, and taste the sacrificial
victim, in order to participate in the grace of Confucius."
[Here again the Corn and Wine are blended in one rite.]
And of Tartary Father Grueber thus testifies : " This only
I do affirm, that the devil so mimics the Catholic Church
there, that although no European or Christian has ever
been there, still in all essential things they agree so completely with the Roman Church, as even to celebrate the
Host with bread and wine : *with my own eyes I have seen
it.*" [1] These few instances are sufficient to show the
extraordinarily wide diffusion of Totem-sacraments and
Eucharistic rites all over the world.

[1] For these two quotations see Jevons' *Introduction to the History
of Religion*, pp. 148 and 219.

V

FOOD AND VEGETATION MAGIC

I HAVE wandered, in pursuit of Totems and the Eucharist, some way from the astronomical thread of Chapters II and III, and now it would appear that in order to understand religious origins we must wander still farther. The chapters mentioned were largely occupied with Sungods and astronomical phenomena, but now we have to consider an earlier period when there were no definite forms of gods, and when none but the vaguest astronomical knowledge existed. Sometimes in historical matters it is best and safest to move thus *backwards* in Time, from the things recent and fairly well known to things more ancient and less known. In this way we approach more securely to some understanding of the dim and remote past.

It is clear that before any definite speculations on heaven-dwelling gods or divine beings had arisen in the human mind—or any clear theories of how the sun and moon and stars might be connected with the changes of the seasons on the earth—there were still certain obvious things which appealed to everybody, learned or unlearned alike. One of these was the return of Vegetation, bringing with it the fruits or the promise of the fruits of the earth, for human food, and also bringing with it increase of animal life, for food in another form ; and the other was the return of Light and Warmth, making life easier in all ways. Food

delivering from the fear of starvation ; Light and Warmth
delivering from the fear of danger and of cold.   These
were three glorious things which returned together and
brought salvation and renewed life to man.   The period
of their return was ' Spring,' and though Spring and its
benefits might fade away in time, still there was always
the *hope* of its return—though even so it may have been
a long time in human evolution before man discovered
that it really did always return, and (with certain
allowances) at equal intervals of time.

Long then before any Sun or Star gods could be called
in, the return of the Vegetation must have enthralled
man's attention, and filled him with hope and joy.   Yet
since its return was somewhat variable and uncertain
the question, What could man do to assist that return ?
naturally became a pressing one.   It is now generally held
that the use of Magic—sympathetic magic—arose in this
way.   Sympathetic magic seems to have been generated
by a belief that your own actions cause a similar response
in things and persons around you.   Yet this belief did not
rest on any philosophy or argument, but was purely
instinctive and sometimes of the nature of a mere corporeal
reaction.   Every schoolboy knows how in watching a
comrade's high jump at the Sports he often finds himself
lifting a knee at the moment ' to help him over ' ; at football
matches quarrels sometimes arise among the spectators
by reason of an ill-placed kick coming from a too enthusiastic on-looker, behind one ; undergraduates running
on the tow-path beside their College boat in the races
will hurry even faster than the boat in order to increase
its speed ; there is in each case an automatic bodily
response increased by one's own desire.   A person *acts*
the part which he desires to be successful.   He thinks to
transfer his energy in that way.   Again, if by chance one
witnesses a painful accident, a crushed foot or what-not,
it commonly happens that one feels a pain in the same

part oneself—a sympathetic pain. What more natural than to suppose that the pain really is transferred from the one person to the other ? and how easy the inference that by tormenting a wretched scape-goat or crucifying a human victim in some cases the sufferings of people may be relieved or their sins atoned for ?

Simaetha, it will be remembered, in the second Idyll of Theocritus, curses her faithless lover Delphis, and as she melts his waxen image she prays that *he too may melt*. All this is of the nature of Magic, and is independent of and generally more primitive than Theology or Philosophy. Yet it interests us because it points to a firm instinct in early man—to which I have already alluded—the instinct of his unity and continuity with the rest of creation, and of a common life so close that his lightest actions may cause a far-reaching reaction in the world outside.

Man, then, independently of any belief in gods, may assist the arrival of Spring by magic ceremonies. If you want the Vegetation to appear you must have rain ; and the rain-maker in almost all primitive tribes has been a *most* important personage. Generally he based his rites on quite fanciful associations, as when the rain-maker among the Mandans wore a raven's skin on his head (bird of the storm) or painted his shield with red zigzags of lightning [1] ; but partly, no doubt, he had observed actual facts, or had had the knowledge of them transmitted to him—as, for instance that when rain is impending loud noises will bring about its speedy downfall, a fact we moderns have had occasion to notice on battlefields. He had observed perhaps that in a storm a specially loud clap of thunder is generally followed by a greatly increased downpour of rain. He had even noticed (a thing which I have often verified in the vicinity of Sheffield) that the copious smoke of fires will generate rain-clouds—and so quite naturally he concluded that it was his smoking

[1] See Catlin's *North American Indians*, Letter 19.

sacrifices which had that desirable effect. So far he was on the track of elementary Science. And so he made " bull-roarers " to imitate the sound of wind and the blessed rain-bringing thunder, or clashed great bronze cymbals together with the same object. Bull-voices and thunder-drums and the clashing of cymbals were used in this connexion by the Greeks, and are mentioned by Aeschylus [1] ; but the bull-roarer, in the form of a rhombus of wood whirled at the end of a string, seems to be known, or to have been known, all over the world. It is described with some care by Mr. Andrew Lang in his *Custom and Myth* (pp. 29–44), where he says " it is found always as a sacred instrument employed in religious mysteries, in New Mexico, Australia, New Zealand, ancient Greece, and Africa."

Sometimes, of course, the rain-maker was successful ; but of the inner causes of rain he knew next to nothing ; he was more ignorant even than we are ! His main idea was a more specially ' magical ' one—namely, that the sound itself would appeal to the *spirits* of rain and thunder and cause them to give a response. For of course the thunder (in Hebrew *Bath-Kol*, " the daughter of the Voice ") was everywhere regarded as the manifestation of a spirit.[2] To make sounds like thunder would therefore naturally call the attention of such a spirit; or he, the rain-maker, might make sounds like rain. He made gourd-rattles (known in ever so many parts of the world) in which he rattled dried seeds or small pebbles with a most beguiling and rain-like insistence ; or sometimes, like the priests of Baal in the Bible,[3] he would cut himself with knives

---

[1] *Themis*, p. 61.

[2] See A. Lang, *op. cit.*: " The muttering of the thunder is said to be his voice calling to the rain to fall and make the grass grow up green." Such are the very words of Umbara, the minstrel of the Tribe (Australian).

[3] I Kings xviii.

till the blood fell upon the ground in great drops suggestive of an oncoming thunder-shower. " In Mexico the rain-god was propitiated with sacrifices of children. If the children wept and shed abundant tears, they who carried them rejoiced, being convinced that rain would also be abundant." [1] Sometimes he, the rain-maker, would *whistle* for the wind, or, like the Omaha Indians, flap his blankets for the same purpose.

In the ancient myth of Demeter and Persephone—which has been adopted by so many peoples under so many forms—Demeter the Earth-mother loses her daughter Persephone (who represents of course the Vegetation), carried down into the underworld by the evil powers of Darkness and Winter. And in Greece there was a yearly ceremonial and ritual of magic for the purpose of restoring the lost one and bringing her back to the world again. Women carried certain charms, " fir-cones and snakes and unnameable objects made of paste, to ensure fertility ; there was a sacrifice of pigs, who were thrown into a deep cleft of the earth, and their remains afterwards collected and scattered as a charm over the fields." [2] Fir-cones and snakes from their very forms were emblems of male fertility ; snakes, too, from their habit of gliding out of their own skins with renewed brightness and colour were suggestive of resurrection and re-vivification ; pigs and sows by their exceeding fruitfulness would in their hour of sacrifice remind old mother Earth of what was expected from her ! Moreover, no doubt it had been observed that the scattering of dead flesh over the ground or mixed with the seed, did bless the ground to greater fertility ; and so by a strange mixture of primitive observation with a certain child-like belief that by means of symbols and

[1] Quoted from Sahagun ll, 2, 3 by A. Lang in *Myth, Ritual and Religion*, vol. ii, p. 102.
[2] See Gilbert Murray's *Four Stages of Greek Religion*, p. 29.

suggestions Nature could be appealed to and induced to answer to the desires and needs of her children this sort of ceremonial Magic arose. It was not exactly Science, and it was not exactly Religion ; but it was a naïve, and perhaps not altogether mistaken, sense of the bond between Nature and Man.

For we can perceive that earliest man was not yet consciously differentiated from Nature. Not only do we see that the tribal life was so strong that the individual seldom regarded himself as different or separate or opposed to the rest of the tribe ; but that something of the same kind was true with regard to his relation to the Animals and to Nature at large. This outer world was part of himself, *was* also himself. His sub-conscious sense of unity was so great that it largely dominated his life. That brain-cleverness and brain-activity which causes modern man to perceive such a gulf between him and the animals, or between himself and Nature, did not exist in the early man. Hence it was no difficulty to him to believe that he was a Bear or an Emu. Sub-consciously he was wiser than we are. He knew that he *was* a bear or an emu, or any other such animal as his totem-creed led him to fix his mind upon. Hence we find that a familiarity and common consent existed between primitive man and many of his companion animals such as has been lost or much attenuated in modern times. Elisée Reclus in his very interesting paper *La Grande Famille* [1] gives support to the idea that the so-called domestication of animals did not originally arise from any forcible subjugation of them by man, but from a natural amity with them which grew up in the beginning from common interests, pursuits and affections. Thus the chetah of India (and probably the puma of Brazil) from far-back times took to hunting in the company of his two-legged and bow-and-arrow-armed

[1] Published originally in *Le Magazine Internationale*, January 1896.

friend, with whom he divided the spoil. W. H. Hudson [1] declares that the Puma, wild and fierce though it is, and capable of killing the largest game, will never even to-day attack man, but when maltreated by the latter submits to the outrage, unresisting, with mournful cries and every sign of grief. The Llama, though domesticated in a sense, has never allowed the domination of the whip or the bit, but may still be seen walking by the side of the Brazilian peasant and carrying his burdens in a kind of proud companionship. The mutual relations of Woman and the Cow, or of Man and the Horse [2] (also the Elephant) reach so far into the past that their origin cannot be traced. The Swallow still loves to make its home under the cottage eaves and still is welcomed by the inmates as the bringer of good fortune. Elisée Reclus assures us that the Dinka man on the Nile calls to certain snakes by name and shares with them the milk of his cows.

And so with Nature. The communal sense, or subconscious perception, which made primitive men feel their unity with other members of their tribe, and their obvious kinship with the animals around them, brought them also so close to general Nature that they looked upon the trees, the vegetation, the rain, the warmth of the sun, as part of their bodies, part of themselves. Conscious differentiation had not yet set in. To cause rain or thunder you had to make rain- or thunder-like noises ; to encourage Vegetation and the crops to leap out of the ground, you had to leap and dance. " In Swabia and among the Transylvanian Saxons it is a common custom (says Dr. Frazer) for a man who has some hemp to leap high in the field in the belief that this will make the hemp grow tall." [3]

[1] See *The Naturalist in La Plata*. ch. ii.

[2] " It is certain that the primitive Indo-European reared droves of tame or half-tame horses for generations, if not centuries, before it ever occurred to him to ride or drive them" (F. B. Jevons, *Introd. to Hist. Religion*, p. 119).

[3] See *The Golden Bough*, i, 139 *seq*. Also *Art and Ritual*, p. 31.

Native May-pole dances and Jacks in the Green have hardly yet died out—even in this most civilized England. The bower of green boughs, the music of pipes, the leaping and the twirling, were all an encouragement to the arrival of Spring, and an expression of Sympathetic Magic. When you felt full of life and energy and virility in yourself you naturally leapt and danced, so why should you not sympathetically do this for the energising of the crops? In every country of the world the vernal season and the resurrection of the Sun has been greeted with dances and the sound of music. But if you wanted success in hunting or in warfare then you danced before-hand mimic dances suggesting the successful hunt or battle. It was no more than our children do to-day, and it all was, and is, part of a natural-magic tendency in human thought.

Let me pause here for a moment. It is difficult for us with our academical and somewhat school-boardy minds to enter into all this, and to understand the sense of (unconscious or sub-conscious) identification with the world around which characterised the primitive man—or to look upon Nature with his eyes. A Tree, a Snake, a Bull, an Ear of Corn. *We* know so well from our botany and natural history books what these things are. Why should our minds dwell on them any longer or harbour a doubt as to our perfect comprehension of them?

And yet (one cannot help asking the question): Has any one of us really ever *seen* a Tree? I certainly do not think that I have—except most superficially. That very penetrating observer and naturalist, Henry D. Thoreau, tells us that he would often make an appointment to visit a certain tree, miles away—but what or whom he saw when he got there, he does not say. Walt Whitman, also a keen observer, speaks of a tulip-tree near which he sometimes sat—" the Apollo of the woods—tall and graceful, yet robust and sinewy, inimitable in hang of foliage and

throwing-out of limb ; as if the beauteous, vital, leafy
creature could walk, if it only would " ; and mentions that
in a dream-trance he actually once saw his " favorite trees
step out and promenade up, down and around, *very
curiously.*" [1] Once the present writer seemed to have a
partial vision of a tree. It was a beech, standing somewhat
isolated, and still leafless in quite early Spring. Suddenly
I was aware of its skyward-reaching arms and up-turned
finger-tips, as if some vivid life (or electricity) was streaming
through them far into the spaces of heaven, and of its
roots plunged in the earth and drawing the same energies
from below. The day was quite still and there was no
movement in the branches, but in that moment the tree
was no longer a separate or separable organism, but a vast
being ramifying far into space, sharing and uniting the
life of Earth and Sky, and full of a most amazing
activity.

The reader of this will probably have had some similar
experiences. Perhaps he will have seen a full-foliaged
Lombardy poplar swaying in half a gale in June—the
wind and the sun streaming over every little twig and
leaf, the tree throwing out its branches in a kind of
ecstasy and bathing them in the passionately boisterous
caresses of its two visitants ; or he will have heard the
deep glad murmur of some huge sycamore with ripening
seed clusters when after weeks of drought the steady warm
rain brings relief to its thirst ; and he will have known that
these creatures are but likenesses of himself, intimately
and deeply-related to him in their love and hunger longing,
and, like himself too, unfathomed and unfathomable.

It would be absurd to credit early man with conscious
speculations like these, belonging more properly to the
twentieth century ; yet it is incontrovertible, I think, that
in some ways the primitive peoples, with their swift sub
conscious intuitions and their minds unclouded by mere

[1] *Specimen Days*, 1882-3 Edition, p. 111.

book knowledge, perceived truths to which we moderns are blind. Like the animals they arrived at their perceptions without (individual) brain effort; they knew things without thinking. When they did *think* of course they went wrong. Their budding science easily went astray. Religion with them had as yet taken no definite shape; science was equally protoplasmic; and all they had was a queer jumble of the two in the form of Magic. When at a later time Science gradually defined its outlook and its observations, and Religion, from being a vague subconscious feeling, took clear shape in the form of gods and creeds, then mankind gradually emerged into the stage of evolution *in which we now are*. *Our* scientific laws and doctrines are of course only temporary formulæ, and so also are the gods and the creeds of our own and other religions; but these things, with their set and angular outlines, have served in the past and will serve in the future as stepping-stones towards another kind of knowledge of which at present we only dream, and will lead us on to a renewed power of perception which again will not be the laborious product of thought but a direct and instantaneous intuition like that of the animals —and the angels.

To return to our Tree. Though primitive man did not speculate in modern style on these things, I yet have no reasonable doubt that he felt (and *feels*, in those cases where we can still trace the workings of his mind) his essential relationship to the creatures of the forest more intimately, if less analytically, than we do to-day. If the animals with all their wonderful gifts are (as we readily admit) a veritable part of Nature—so that they live and move and have their being more or less submerged in the spirit of the great world around them—then Man, when he first began to differentiate himself from them, must for a long time have remained in this *sub*conscious unity, becoming only distinctly *conscious* of it when he was already beginning to lose it. That early dawn of distinct consciousness corresponded to the period of belief in Magic. In that first mystic illumination almost every object was invested with a halo of mystery or terror or adoration. Things were either *tabu*, in which case they were dangerous, and often not to be touched or even looked upon—or they were overflowing with magic grace and influence, in which case they were holy, and any rite which released their influence was also holy. William Blake, that modern prophetic child, beheld a Tree full of angels ; the Central Australian native believes certain bushes to be the abode of spirits which leap into the bodies of passing women and are the cause of the conception of children ; Moses saw in the desert a bush (perhaps the *mimosa*) like a flame of fire, with Jehovah dwelling in the midst of it, and he put off his shoes for he felt that the place was holy ; Osiris was at times regarded as a Tree-spirit [1] ; and in inscriptions is referred to as " the solitary one in the acacia "—which reminds us curiously of the " burning bush." The same is true of others of the gods ; in the old Norse mythology Ygdrasil was the great branching World-Ash, abode of the soul of the universe ; the Peepul or Bo-tree in India is very sacred and must on no account be cut down, seeing that gods and spirits dwell among its branches. It is of the nature of an Aspen, and of little or no practical use,[2] but so holy that the poorest peasant will not disturb it. The Burmese believe the things of nature, but especially the trees, to be the abode of spirits. " To the Burman of to-day, not less than to the Greek of long ago, all nature is alive. The forest and the river and the mountains are full of spirits, whom the Burmans call Nats. There are all kinds of Nats, good and bad, great and little, male and female, now living round about us. Some of them live

---

[1] *The Golden Bough*, iv, 339.
[2] Though its sap is said to contain caoutchouc.

in the trees, especially in the huge figtree that shades
half-an-acre without the village ; or among the fern-like
fronds of the tamarind." [1]

There are also in India and elsewhere popular rites of
marriage of women (and men) to Trees ; which suggest
that trees were regarded as very near akin to human
beings ! *The Golden Bough* [2] mentions many of these,
including the idea that some trees are male and others
female. The well-known Assyrian emblem of a Pine
cone being presented by a priest to a Palm-tree is supposed
by E. B. Tylor to symbolise fertilisation—the Pine cone
being masculine and the Palm feminine. The ceremony
of the god Krishna's marriage to a Basil plant is still celebrated in India down to the present day ; and certain
trees are clasped and hugged by pregnant women—the
idea no doubt being that they bestow fertility on those
who embrace them. In other cases apparently it is the
trees which are benefited, since it is said that men sometimes go naked into the Clove plantations at night in order
by a sort of sexual intercourse to fertilise them.[3]

One might go on multiplying examples in this direction
quite indefinitely. There is no end to them. They all
indicate—what was instinctively felt by early man, and
is perfectly obvious to all to-day who are not blinded by
' civilisation ' (and Herbert Spencer !) that the world
outside us *is* really most deeply akin to ourselves, that
it is not dead and senseless but intensely alive and instinct
with feeling and intelligence resembling our own. It is
this perception, this conviction of our essential unity with
the whole of creation, which lay from the first at the base
of all Religion ; yet at first, as I have said, was hardly a
conscious perception. Only later, when it gradually became

[1] *The Soul of a People*, by H. Fielding (1902), p. 250.
[2] Vol. i, p. 40, vol. ii, pp. 24 sq.
[3] *Ibid.*, vol. ii, p. 98.

more conscious, did it evolve itself into the definite forms of the gods and the creeds—but of that process I will speak more in detail presently.

The Tree therefore was a most intimate presence to the Man. It grew in the very midst of his Garden of Eden. It had a magical virtue, which his tentative science could only explain by chance analogies and assimilations. Attractive and beloved and worshiped by reason of its many gifts to mankind—its grateful shelter, its abounding fruits, its timber, and other invaluable products—why should it not become the natural emblem of the female, to whom through sex man's worship is ever drawn? If the Snake has an unmistakable resemblance to the male organ in its active state, the foliage of the tree or bush is equally remindful of the female. What more clear than that the conjunction of Tree and Serpent is the fulfilment in nature of that sex-mystery which is so potent in the life of man and the animals? and that the magic ritual most obviously fitted to induce fertility in the tribe or the herds (or even the crops) is to set up an image of the Tree and the Serpent combined, and for all the tribe-folk in common to worship and pay it reverence. In the Bible with more or less veiled sexual significance we have this combination in the Eden-garden, and again in the brazen Serpent and Pole which Moses set up in the wilderness (as a cure for the fiery serpents of lust); illustrations of the same are said to be found in the temples of Egypt and of South India, and even in the ancient temples of Central America.[1] In the myth of Hercules the golden apples of the Hesperides garden are guarded by a dragon. The Etruscans, the Persians and the Babylonians had also legends of the Fall of man through a serpent tempting him to taste of the fruit of a holy Tree. And De Gubernatis,[2]

[1] See *Ancient Pagan and Modern Christian Symbolism*, by Thomas Inman (Trübner, 1874), p. 55.
[2] *Zoological Mythology*, vol. ii, pp. 410 *sq.*

pointing out the phallic meaning of these stories, says
" the legends concerning the tree of golden apples or figs
which yields honey or ambrosia, guarded by dragons,
in which the life, the fortune, the glory, the strength and
the riches of the hero have their beginning, are numerous
among every people of Aryan origin : in India, Persia,
Russia, Poland, Sweden, Germany, Greece and Italy."

Thus we see the natural-magic tendency of the human
mind asserting itself. To some of us indeed this tendency
is even greater in the case of the Snake than in that of the
Tree. W. H. Hudson, in *Far Away and Long Ago*, speaks
of " that sense of something supernatural in the serpent,
which appears to have been universal among peoples in
a primitive state of culture, and still survives in
some barbarous or semi-barbarous countries." The
fascination of the Snake—the fascination of its mysteriously
gliding movement, of its vivid energy, its glittering eye,
its intensity of life, combined with its fatal dart of Death
—is a thing felt even more by women than by men—and
for a reason (from what we have already said) not far to
seek. It was the Woman who in the story of the Fall
was the first to listen to its suggestions. No wonder that,
as Professor Murray says,[1] the Greeks worshiped a gigantic
Snake (Meilichios) the lord of Death and Life, with ceremonies of appeasement, and sacrifices, long before they
arrived at the worship of Zeus and the Olympian gods.

Or let us take the example of an Ear of Corn. Some
people wonder—hearing nowadays that the folk of old
used to worship a Corn-spirit or Corn-god—wonder that
any human beings could have been so foolish. But probably
the good people who wonder thus have never *really looked*
(with their town-dazed eyes) at a growing spike of wheat. [2]

[1] *Four Stages of Greek Religion*, p. 28.
[2] Even the thrice-learned Dr. Farnell quotes apparently with
ap proval the scornful words of Hippolytus, who (he says) " speaks

Of all the wonderful things in Nature I hardly know any that thrills one more with a sense of wizardry than just this very thing—to observe, each year, this disclosure of the Ear within the Blade—first a swelling of the sheath, then a transparency and a whitey-green face within a hooded shroud, and then the perfect spike of grain disengaging itself and spiring upward towards the sky—" the resurrection of the wheat with pale visage appearing out of the ground."

If this spectacle amazes one to-day, what emotions must it not have aroused in the breasts of the earlier folk, whose outlook on the world was so much more direct than ours —more ' animistic ' if you like ! What wonderment, what gratitude, what deliverance from fear (of starvation), what certainty that this being who had been ruthlessly cut down and sacrificed last year for human food had indeed arisen again as a saviour of men, what readiness to make some human sacrifice in return, both as an acknowledgment of the debt, and as a gift of something which would no doubt be graciously accepted !—(for was it not well known that where blood had been spilt on the ground the future crop was so much the more generous ?)—what readiness to adopt some magic ritual likely to propitiate the unseen power—even though the outline and form of the latter were vague and uncertain in the extreme ! Dr. Frazer, speaking of the Egyptian Osiris as one out of many corn-gods of the above character, says [1] : " The primitive conception of him as the corn-god comes clearly out in the festival of his death and resurrection, which was celebrated in the month of Cholak, and at a later period in the month of Athyr. That festival appears to have been essentially a festival of sowing, which properly fell at the time when the husbandman actually committed the seed

of the Athenians imitating people at the Eleusinian mysteries and showing to the epoptæ (initiates) that great and marvellous mystery of perfect revelation—in solemn silence—a *cut cornstalk* (τεθερισμένον στάχον)."—*Cults of the Greek States*, vol. iii, p. 182.

[1] *The Golden Bough*, iv, p. 330.

to the earth. On that occasion an effigy of the corn-god, moulded of earth and corn, was buried with funeral rites in the ground in order that, dying there, he might come to life again with the new crops. The ceremony was in fact a charm to ensure the growth of the corn by sympathetic magic, and we may conjecture that as such it was practised in a simple form by every Egyptian farmer on his fields long before it was adopted and transfigured by the priests in the stately ritual of the temple." [1]

The magic in this case was of a gentle description ; the clay image of Osiris sprouting all over with the young green blade was pathetically poetic ; but, as has been suggested, bloodthirsty ceremonies were also common enough. Human sacrifices, it is said, had at one time been offered at the grave of Osiris. We hear that the Indians in Ecuador used to sacrifice men's hearts and pour out human blood on their fields when they sowed them ; the Pawnee Indians used a human victim the same, allowing his blood to drop on the seed-corn. It is said that in Mexico girls were sacrificed, and that the Mexicans would sometimes *grind* their (male) victim, like corn, between two stones. (" I'll grind his bones to make me bread.") Among the Khonds of East India—who were particularly given to this kind of ritual—the very *tears* of the sufferer were an incitement to more cruelties, for tears of course were magic for Rain.[2]

And so on. We have referred to the Bull many times, both in his astronomical aspect as pioneer of the Spring-Sun, and in his more direct rôle as plougher of the fields, and provider of food from his own body. " The tremendous *mana* of the wild bull," says Gilbert Murray, " occupies almost half the stage of pre-Olympic ritual." [3] Even to us there is something mesmeric and overwhelming in the

[1] See ch. xv *infra*, p. 5.
[2] *The Golden Bough*, vol. vii, " The Corn-Spirit," pp. 236 *sq.*
[3] *Four Stages*, p. 34.

sense of this animal's glory of strength and fury and sexual power. No wonder the primitives worshiped him, or that they devised rituals which should convey his power and vitality by mere contact, or that in sacramental feasts they ate his flesh and drank his blood as a magic symbol and means of salvation.

VI

MAGICIANS, KINGS AND GODS

It is perhaps necessary, at the commencement of this chapter, to say a few more words about the nature and origin of the belief in Magic. Magic represented on one side, and clearly enough, the beginnings of Religion—i.e. the instinctive sense of Man's inner continuity with the world around him, *taking shape* : a fanciful shape it is true, but with very real reaction on his practical life and feelings.[1] On the other side it represented the beginnings of Science. It was his first attempt not merely to *feel* but to *understand* the mystery of things.

Inevitably these first efforts to understand were very puerile, very superficial. As E. B. Tylor says[2] of primitive folk in general, "they mistook an imaginary for a real connexion." And he instances the case of the inhabitants of the City of Ephesus, who laid down a rope, seven furlongs in length, from the City to the temple of Artemis, in order to place the former under the protection of the latter ! *We* should lay down a telephone wire, and consider that we had established a much more efficient connexion ; but in the beginning, and quite naturally, men, like children, rely on surface associations. Among the Dyaks of Borneo,[3] when the men are away fighting,

[1] For an excellent account of the relation of Magic to Religion see W. McDougall, *Social Psychology* (1908), pp. 317-320.
[2] *Primitive Culture*, vol. i, p. 106.
[3] See *The Golden Bough*, i, 127.

the *women* must use a sort of telepathic magic in order
to safeguard them—that is, they must themselves rise
early and keep awake all day (lest darkness and sleep
should give advantage to the enemy) ; they must not
oil their hair (lest their husbands should make any *slips*) ;
they must eat sparingly and put aside rice at every meal
(so that the men may not want for food). And so on.
Similar superstitions are common. But they gradually
lead to a little thought, and then to a little more, and so
to the discovery of actual and proveable influences.
Perhaps one day the cord connecting the temple with
Ephesus was drawn *tight* and it was found that messages
could be, by tapping, transmitted along it. That way
lay the discovery of a fact. In an age which worshiped
fertility, whether in mankind or animals, *Twins* were
ever counted especially blest, and were credited with a
magic power. (The Constellation of the Twins was thought
peculiarly lucky.) Perhaps after a time it was discovered
that twins sometimes run in families, and in such cases
really do bring fertility with them. In cattle it is known
nowadays that there are more twins of the female sex
than of the male sex.[1]

Observations of this kind were naturally made by the
ablest members of the tribe—who were in all probability
the medicine-men and wizards—and brought in consequence power into their hands. The road to power in
fact—and especially was this the case in societies which
had not yet developed wealth and property—lay through
Magic. As far as magic represented early superstition
and religion it laid hold of the *hearts* of men—their hopes
and fears ; as far as it represented science and the beginnings of actual knowledge, it inspired their minds with
a sense of power, and gave form to their lives and customs.
We have no reason to suppose that the early magicians

---

[1] See *Evolution of Sex*, by Geddes and Thomson (1901), p. 41,
note.

and medicine-men were peculiarly wicked or bent on mere self-aggrandisement—any more than we have to think the same of the average country vicar or country doctor of to-day. They were merely men a trifle wiser or more instructed than their flocks. But though probably in most cases their original intentions were decent enough, they were not proof against the temptations which the possession of power always brings, and as time went on they became liable to trade more and more upon this power for their own advancement. In the matter of Religion the history of the Christian priesthood through the centuries shows sufficiently to what misuse such power can be put ; and in the matter of Science it is a warning to us of the dangers attending the formation of a scientific priesthood, such as we see growing up around us to-day. In both cases—whether Science or Religion—vanity, personal ambition, lust of domination and a hundred other vices, unless corrected by a real devotion to the public good, may easily bring as many evils in their train as those they profess to cure.

The Medicine-man, or Wizard, or Magician, or Priest, slowly but necessarily gathered power into his hands, and there is much evidence to show that in the case of many tribes at any rate, it was *he* who became ultimate chief and leader and laid the foundations of Kingship. The *Basileus* was always a sacred personality, and often united in himself as head of the clan the offices of chief in warfare and leader in priestly rites—like Agamemnon in Homer, or Saul or David in the Bible. As a magician he had influence over the fertility of the earth and, like the blameless king in the Odyssey, under his sway

> " the dark earth beareth in season
> Barley and wheat, and the trees are laden with fruitage, and alway
> Yean unfailing the flocks, and the sea gives fish in abundance." [1]

[1] Odyssey xix, 109 *sq.* Translation by H. B. Cotterill.

As a magician too he was trusted for success in warfare ;
and Schoolcraft, in a passage quoted by Andrew Lang,[1]
says of the Dacotah Indians " the war-chief who leads
the party to war is always one of these medicine-men."
This connexion, however, by which the magician is transformed into the king has been abundantly studied, and
need not be further dwelt upon here.

And what of the transformation of the king into a god—
or of the Magician or Priest directly into the same ?
Perhaps in order to appreciate this, one must make a
further digression.

For the early peoples there were, as it would appear,
two main objects in life : (1) to promote fertility in cattle
and crops, for food ; and (2) to placate or ward off Death ;
and it seemed very obvious—even before any distinct
figures of gods, or any idea of prayer, had arisen—to attain
these objects by magic ritual. The rites of Baptism, of
Initiation (or Confirmation) and the many ceremonies
of a Second Birth, which we associate with fully-formed
religions, did belong also to the age of Magic ; and they
all implied a belief in some kind of re-incarnation—in a
life going forward continually and being renewed in birth
again and again. It is curious that we find such a belief
among the lowest savages even to-day. Dr. Frazer,
speaking of the Central Australian tribes, says the belief
is firmly rooted among them " that the human soul undergoes an endless series of re-incarnations—the living men
and women of one generation being nothing but the spirits
of their ancestors come to life again, and destined themselves to be reborn in the persons of their descendants.
During the interval between two re-incarnations the souls
live in their *nanja* spots, or local totem-centres, which
are always natural objects such as trees or rocks. Each
totem clan has a number of such totem-centres scattered
over the country. There the souls of the dead men and

[1] *Myth, Ritual and Religion*, vol. i, p. 113.

women of the totem, but no others, congregate, and are
born again in human form when a favorable opportunity
presents itself." [1]

And what the early people believed of the human spirit,
they believed of the corn-spirits and the tree and vegetation
spirits also. At the great Spring-ritual among the primitive Greeks "the tribe and the growing earth were
renovated together : the earth arises afresh from her dead
seeds, the tribe from its dead ancestors." And the whole
process projects itself in the idea of a spirit of the year,
who "in the first stage is living, then dies with each year,
and thirdly rises again from the dead, raising the whole
dead world with him. The Greeks called him in this stage
'The Third One' [*Tritos Sotêr*] or the 'Saviour'; and
the renovation ceremonies were accompanied by a casting-
off of the old year, the old garments, and everything that
is polluted by the infection of death." [2] Thus the multiplication of the crops and the renovation of the tribe, and
at the same time the evasion and placation of death,
were all assured by similar rites and befitting ceremonial
magic.[3]

In all these cases, and many others that I have not
mentioned—of the magical worship of Bulls and Bears
and Rams and Cats and Emus and Kangaroos, of Trees
and Snakes, of Sun and Moon and Stars, and the spirit of
the Corn in its yearly and miraculous resurrection out of
the ground—there is still the same idea or moving inspiration, the sense mentioned in the foregoing chapter, the
feeling (hardly yet conscious of its own meaning) of

---

[1] *The Golden Bough*, vol. i, p. 96.
[2] Gilbert Murray, *Four Stages*, p. 46.
[3] It is interesting to find, with regard to the renovation of the
tribe, that among the Central Australians the foreskins or male
members of those who died were deposited in the above-mentioned
nanja spots—the idea evidently being that like the seeds of the corn
the seeds of the human crop must be carefully and ceremonially
preserved for their re-incarnation.

intimate relationship and unity with all this outer world, the instinctive conviction that the world can be swayed by the spirit of Man, if the man can only find the right ritual, the right word, the right *spell*, wherewith to move it. An *aura* of emotion surrounded everything—of terror, of *tabu*, of fascination, of desire. The world, to these people, was transparent with presences related to themselves; and though hunger and sex may have been the dominant and overwhelmingly practical needs of their life, yet their outlook on the world was essentially poetic and imaginative.

Moreover it will be seen that in this age of magic and the belief in spirits, though there was an intense sense of every thing being alive, the gods, in the more modern sense of the world, hardly existed [1]—that is, there was no very clear vision, to these people, of supra-mundane beings, sitting apart and ordaining the affairs of earth, as it were from a distance. Doubtless this conception was slowly evolving, but it was only incipient. For the time being—though there might be orders and degrees of spirits (and of gods)—every such being was only conceived of, and could only be conceived of, as actually a part of Nature, dwelling in and interlaced with some phenomenon of Earth and Sky, and having no separate existence.

How was it then, it will be asked, that the belief in separate and separable gods and goddesses—each with his or her well-marked outline and character and function, like the divinities of Greece, or of India, or of the Egyptian or Christian religions, ultimately arose? To this question Jane Harrison (in her *Themis* and other books) gives an ingenious answer, which as it chimes in with my own speculations (in the *Art of Creation* and elsewhere) I am inclined to adopt. It is that the figures of the supra-

[1] For a discussion of the evolution of *religion* out of *magic*, see Westermarck's *Origin of Moral Ideas*, ch. 47.

natural gods arose from a process in the human mind similar to that which the photographer adopts when by photographing a number of faces on the same plate, and so superposing their images on one another, he produces a so-called " composite " photograph or image. Thus, in the photographic sphere, the portraits of a lot of members of the same family superposed upon one another may produce a composite image or ideal of that family type, or the portraits of a number of Aztecs or of a number of Apache Indians the ideals respectively of the Aztec or of the Apache types. And so in the mental sphere of each member of a tribe the many images of the well-known Warriors or Priests or wise and gracious Women of that tribe did inevitably combine at last to composite figures of gods and goddesses—on whom the enthusiasm and adoration of the tribe was concentrated.[1] Miss Harrison has ingeniously suggested how the leading figures in the magic rituals of the past—being the figures on which all eyes would be concentrated ; and whose importance would be imprinted on every mind—lent themselves to this process. The suffering Victim, bound and scourged and crucified, recurring year after year as the centre-figure of a thousand ritual processions, would at last be drama-tised and idealised in the general race-consciousness into the form of a Suffering God—a Jesus Christ or a Dionysus or Osiris—dismembered or crucified for the salvation of mankind. The Priest or Medicine-Man—or rather the succession of Priests or Medicine-Men—whose figures would recur again and again as leaders and ordainers of the ceremonies, would be glorified at last into the composite-image of a God in whom were concentrated all magic powers. " Recent researches," says Gilbert Murray, " have shown us in abundance the early Greek medicine-chiefs making thunder and lightning and rain." Here is the

[1] See *The Art of Creation*, ch. viii, " The Gods as Apparitions of the Race-Life."

germ of a Zeus or a Jupiter. The particular medicine-man
may fail; that does not so much matter; he is only the
individual representative of the glorified and composite
being who exists in the mind of the tribe (just as a present-
day King may be unworthy, but is surrounded all the
same by the agelong glamour of Royalty). " The real
Θεός, tremendous, infallible, is somewhere far away, hidden
in clouds perhaps, on the summit of some inaccessible
mountain. If the mountain is once climbed the god will
move to the upper sky. The medicine-chief meanwhile
stays on earth, still influential. He has some connexion
with the great god more intimate than that of other
men . . . he knows the rules for approaching him and
making prayers to him." [1] Thus did the Medicine-man,
or Priest, or Magician (for these are but three names
for one figure) represent one step in the evolution of
the god.

And farther back still in the evolutionary process we
may trace (as in chapter iv above) the divinisation or
deification of four-footed animals and birds and snakes
and trees and the like, from the personification of the
collective emotion of the tribe towards these creatures.
For people whose chief food was bear-meat, for instance,
whose totem was a bear, and who believed themselves
descended from an ursine ancestor, there would grow up
in the tribal mind an image surrounded by a halo of
emotions—emotions of hungry desire, of reverence, fear,
gratitude and so forth—an image of a *divine Bear* in whom
they lived and moved and had their being. For another
tribe or group in whose yearly ritual a Bull or a Lamb or
a Kangaroo played a leading part there would in the same
way spring up the image of a holy bull, a divine lamb, or
a sacred kangaroo. Another group again might come
to worship a Serpent as its presiding genius, or a particular
kind of Tree, simply because these objects were and had

[1] *The Four Stages*, p. 140.

been for centuries prominent factors in its yearly and
seasonal Magic. As Reinach and others suggest, it was
the Taboo (bred by Fear) which by first forbidding contact
with the totem-animal or priest or magician-chief gradually
invested him with Awe and Divinity.

According to this theory the god—the full-grown god in
human shape, dwelling apart and beyond the earth—did
not come first, but was a late and more finished product
of evolution. He grew up by degrees and out of the
preceding animal-worships and totem-systems. And this
theory is much supported and corroborated by the fact
that in a vast number of early cults the gods are represented by human figures with animal heads. The Egyptian
religion was full of such divinities—the jackal-headed
Anubis, the ram-headed Ammon, the bull-fronted Osiris,
or Muth, queen of darkness, clad in a vulture's skin ; Minos
and the Minotaur in Crete ; in Greece, Athena with an
owl's head, or Herakles masked in the hide and jaws of
a monstrous lion. What could be more obvious than that,
following on the tribal worship of any totem-animal, the
priest or medicine-man or actual king in leading the magic
ritual should don the skin and head of that animal, and
wear the same as a kind of mask—this partly in order to
appear to the people as the true representative of the
totem, and partly also in order to obtain from the skin
the magic virtues and *mana* of the beast, which he could
then duly impart to the crowd ? Zeus, it must be remembered, wears the *ægis*, or *goat-skin*—said to be the hide
of the goat Amaltheia who suckled him in his infancy ;
there are a number of legends which connected the Arcadian
Artemis with the worship of the *bear*, Apollo with the
wolf, and so forth. And, most curious as showing similarity of rites between the Old and New Worlds, there are
found plenty of examples of the wearing of beast-masks
in religious processions among the native tribes of both
North and South America. In the *Atlas of Spix and*

Martius (who travelled together in the Amazonian forests about 1820) there is an interesting and characteristic picture of the men (and some women) of the tribe of the Tecunas moving in procession through the woods, mostly naked, except for wearing animal heads and masks—the masks representing Cranes of various kinds, Ducks, the Opossum, the Jaguar, the Parrot, etc., probably symbolic of their respective clans.

By some such process as this, it may fairly be supposed, the forms of the Gods were slowly exhaled from the actual figures of men and women, of youths and girls, who year after year took part in the ancient rituals. Just as the Queen of the May or Father Christmas with us are idealised forms derived from the many happy maidens or white-bearded old men who took leading parts in the May or December mummings and thus gained their apotheosis in our literature and tradition—so doubtless Zeus with his thunderbolts and arrows of lightning is the idealisation into Heaven of the Priestly rain-maker and storm-controller ; Ares the god of War, the similar idealisation of the leading warrior in the ritual war-dance preceding an attack on a neighboring tribe ; and Mercury of the foot-running Messenger whose swiftness in those days (devoid of steam or electricity) was so precious a tribal possession.

And here it must be remembered that this explanation of the genesis of the gods only applies to the *shapes* and *figures* of the various deities. It does not apply to the genesis of the widespread belief in spirits or a Great Spirit generally ; that, as I think will become clear, has quite another source. Some people have jeered at the ' animistic ' or ' anthropomorphic ' tendency of primitive man in his contemplation of the forces of Nature or his imaginations of religion and the gods. With a kind of superior pity they speak of " the poor Indian whose untutored mind sees God in clouds and hears him in the wind." But I must confess that to me the " poor Indian " seems on the

whole to show more good sense than his critics, and to
have aimed his rude arrows at the philosophic mark more
successfully than a vast number of his learned and scientific successors. A consideration of what we have said
above would show that early people felt their unity with
Nature so deeply and intimately that—like the animals
themselves—they did not think consciously or theorise
about it. It was just their life to be—like the beasts of
the field and the trees of the forest—a part of the whole
flux of things, non-differentiated so to speak. What more
natural or indeed more logically correct than for them to
assume (when they first began to think or differentiate
themselves) that these other creatures, these birds, beasts
and plants, and even the sun and moon, were of the same
blood as themselves, their first cousins, so to speak, and
having the same interior nature ? What more reasonable
(if indeed they credited *themselves* with having some kind
of soul or spirit) than to credit these other creatures with
a similar soul or spirit ? Im Thurn, speaking of the Guiana
Indians, says that for them " the whole world swarms with
beings." Surely this could not be taken to indicate an
untutored mind—unless indeed a mind untutored in the
nonsense of the Schools—but rather a very directly per-
ceptive mind. And again what more reasonable (seeing
that these people themselves were in the animal stage of
evolution) than that they should pay great reverence to
some ideal animal—first cousin or ancestor—who played
an important part in their tribal existence, and make of
this animal a totem emblem and a symbol of their common
life ?

And, further still, what more natural than that when
the tribe passed to some degree beyond the animal stage
and began to realise a life more intelligent and emotional
—more specially human in fact—than that of the beasts
of the field, that it should then in its rituals and ceremonies
throw off the beast-mask and pay reverence to the interior

and more human spirit. Rising to a more enlightened consciousness of its own intimate quality, and still deeply penetrated with the sense of its kinship to external nature, it would inevitably and perfectly logically credit the latter with an inner life and intelligence, more distinctly human than before. Its religion in fact would become *more* ' anthropomorphic ' instead of less so ; and one sees that this is a process that is inevitable ; and inevitable not-withstanding a certain parenthesis in the process, due to obvious elements in our ' Civilisation ' and to the temporary and fallacious domination of a leaden-eyed so-called ' Science.' According to this view the true evolution of Religion and Man's outlook on the world has proceeded not by the denial by man of his unity with the world, but by his seeing and understanding that unity more deeply. And the more deeply he understands himself the more certainly he will recognise in the external world a Being or beings resembling himself.

W. H. Hudson—whose mind is certainly not of a quality to be jeered at—speaks of Animism as " the projection of ourselves into nature : the sense and apprehension of an intelligence like our own, but more powerful, in all visible things " ; and continues, " old as I am this same primitive faculty which manifested itself in my early boyhood, still persists, and in those early years was so powerful that I am almost afraid to say how deeply I was moved by it." [1]   Nor will it be *quite* forgotten that Shelley once said :—

> The moveless pillar of a mountain's weight
> Is active living spirit.   Every grain
> Is sentient both in unity and part,
> And the minutest atom comprehends
> A world of loves and hatreds.

The tendency to animism and later to anthropomorphism

[1] *Far Away and Long Ago*, ch. xiii, p. 225.

is I say inevitable, and perfectly logical. But the great
value of the work done by some of those investigators
whom I have quoted has been to show that among quite
primitive people (whose interior life and ' soul-sense '
was only very feeble) their projections of intelligence into
Nature were correspondingly feeble. The reflections of
themselves projected into the world beyond could not
reach the stature of eternal ' gods,' but were rather of the
quality of ephemeral phantoms and ghosts ; and the
ceremonials and creeds of that period are consequently
more properly described as Magic than as Religion. There
have indeed been great controversies as to whether there
has or has not been, in the course of religious evolution,
a *pre*-animistic stage. Probably of course human evolution in this matter must have been perfectly continuous
from stages presenting the very feeblest or an absolutely
deficient animistic sense to the very highest manifestations
of anthropomorphism ; but as there is a good deal of
evidence to show that *animals* (notably dogs and horses)
see ghosts, the inquiry ought certainly to be enlarged so
far as to include the pre-human species. Anyhow it must
be remembered that the question is one of *consciousness*
— that is, of how far and to what degree consciousness of
self has been developed in the animal or the primitive man
or the civilised man, and therefore how far and to what
degree the animal or human creature has credited the outside world with a similar consciousness. It is not a question
of whether there *is* an inner life and *sub*-consciousness
common to all these creatures of the earth and sky, because
that, I take it, is a fact beyond question ; they all emerge
or have emerged from the same matrix, and are rooted in
identity ; but it is a question of how far they are *aware*
of this, and how far by separation (which is the genius
of evolution) each individual creature has become conscious of the interior nature both of itself and of the other
creatures *and* of the great whole which includes them all.

Finally, and to avoid misunderstanding, let me say that Anthropomorphism, in man's conception of the gods, is itself of course only a stage and destined to pass away. In so far, that is, as the term indicates a belief in divine beings corresponding to our *present* conception of ourselves —that is as separate personalities having each a separate and limited character and function, and animated by the separatist motives of ambition, possession, power, vainglory, superiority, patronage, self-greed, self-satisfaction, etc.—in so far as anthropomorphism is the expression of that kind of belief it is of course destined, with the illusion from which it springs, to pass away. When man arrives at the final consciousness in which the idea of such a self, superior or inferior or in any way antagonistic to others, ceases to operate, then he will return to his first and primal condition, and will cease to need *any* special religion or gods, knowing himself and all his fellows to be divine and the origin and perfect fruition of all.

VII

RITES OF EXPIATION AND REDEMPTION

THERE is a passage in Richard Jefferies' imperishably beautiful book *The Story of my Heart*—a passage well-known to all lovers of that prose-poet—in which he figures himself standing " in front of the Royal Exchange where the wide pavement reaches out like a promontory," and pondering on the vast crowd and the mystery of life. " Is there any theory, philosophy, or creed," he says, " is there any system of culture, any formulated method, able to meet and satisfy each separate item of this agitated pool of human life ? By which they may be guided, by which they may hope, by which look forward ? Not a mere illusion of the craving heart—something real, as real as the solid walls of fact against which, like seaweed, they are dashed ; something to give each separate personality sunshine and a flower in its own existence now ; something to shape this million-handed labour to an end and outcome that will leave more sunshine and more flowers to those who must succeed ? Something real now, and not in the spirit-land ; in this hour now, as I stand and the sun burns. . . . Full well aware that all has failed, yet, side by side with the sadness of that knowledge, there lives on in me an unquenchable belief, thought burning like the sun, that there is yet something to be

found. . . . It must be dragged forth by the might of
thought from the immense forces of the universe."

In answer to this passage we may say " No—a thousand
times No! there is *no* theory, philosophy, creed, system
or formulated method which will meet or ever satisfy
the demand of each separate item of the human whirlpool." And happy are we to know there is no such thing!
How terrible if one of these bloodless ' systems ' which
strew the history of religion and philosophy and the political
and social paths of human endeavour *had* been found
absolutely correct and universally applicable—so that
every human being would be compelled to pass through
its machine-like maw, every personality to be crushed
under its Juggernath wheels! No, thank Heaven! there
is no theory or creed or system ; and yet there is something—as Jefferies prophetically felt and with a great
longing desired—that *can* satisfy ; and that, the root of
all religion, has been hinted at in the last chapter. It
is the *consciousness* of the world-life burning, blazing, deep
down within us : it is the Soul's intuition of its roots in
Omnipresence and Eternity.

The gods and the creeds of the past, as shown in the
last chapter—whatever they may have been, animistic
or anthropomorphic or transcendental, whether grossly
brutish or serenely ideal and abstract—are essentially
projections of the human mind ; and no doubt those who
are anxious to discredit the religious impulse generally
will catch at this, saying " Yes, they are mere forms and
phantoms of the mind, ephemeral dreams, projected on
the background of Nature, and having no real substance
or solid value. The history of Religion (they will say)
is a history of delusion and illusion ; why waste time over
it ? These divine grizzly Bears or Aesculapian Snakes,
these cat faced Pachtr, this Isis, queen of heaven, and
Astarte and Baal and Indra and Agni and Kali and
Demeter and the Virgin Mary and Apollo and Jesus Christ

and Satan and the Holy Ghost, are only shadows cast
outwards onto a screen ; the constitution of the human
mind makes them all tend to be anthropomorphic ; but
that is all ; they each and all inevitably pass away. Why
waste time over them ? "

And this is in a sense a perfectly fair way of looking
at the matter. The gods and creeds *are* only projections
of the human mind. But all the same it misses, does
this view, the essential fact. It misses the fact that there
is no shadow without a fire, that the very existence of
a shadow argues a light somewhere (though we may not
directly see it) as well as the existence of a solid form which
intercepts that light. Deep, deep in the human mind
there is that burning blazing light of the world-consciousness—so deep indeed that the vast majority of individuals
are hardly aware of its existence. Their gaze turned
outwards is held and riveted by the gigantic figures and
processions passing across their sky ; they are unaware
that the latter are only shadows—silhouettes of the forms
inhabiting their own minds.[1] The vast majority of people
have never observed their own minds ; their own mental
forms. They have only observed the reflections cast
by these. Thus it may be said, in this matter, that there
are three degrees of reality. There are the mere shadows
—the least real and most evanescent ; there are the actual
mental outlines of humanity (and of the individual), much
more real, but themselves also of course slowly changing ;
and most real of all, and permanent, there is the light
" which lighteth every man that cometh into the world "
—the glorious light of the world-consciousness. Of this
last it may be said that it never changes. Every thing
is known to it—even the very impediments to its shining.
But as it is from the *impediments* to the shining of a light
that shadows are cast, so we now may understand that

[1] See, in the same connexion, Plato's allegory of the Cave, *Republic,*
Book vii.

the things of this world and of humanity, though real in their degree, have chiefly a kind of negative value ; they are opaquenesses, clouds, materialisms, ignorances, and the inner light falling upon them gradually reveals their negative character and gradually dissolves them away till they are lost in the extreme and eternal Splendour. I think Jefferies, when he asked that question with which I have begun this chapter, was in some sense subconsciously, if not quite consciously, aware of the answer. His frequent references to the burning blazing sun throughout *The Story of my Heart* seem to be an indication of his real deep-down attitude of mind.

The shadow-figures of the creeds and theogonies pass away truly like ephemeral dreams ; but to say that time spent in their study is wasted, is a mistake, for they have value as being indications of things much more real than themselves, namely, of the stages of evolution of the human mind. The fact that a certain god-figure, however grotesque and queer, or a certain creed, however childish, cruel, and illogical, held sway for a considerable time over the hearts of men in any corner or continent of the world is good evidence that it represented a real formative urge at the time in the hearts of those good people, and a definite stage in their evolution and the evolution of humanity. Certainly it was destined to pass away, but it was a step, and a necessary step in the great process ; and certainly it was opaque and brutish, but it is through the opaque things of the world, and not through the transparent, that we become aware of the light.

It may be worth while to give instances of how some early rituals and creeds, in themselves apparently barbarous or preposterous, were really the indications of important moral and social conceptions evolving in the heart of man. Let us take, first, the religious customs connected with the ideas of Sacrifice and of Sin, of which such innumerable examples are now to be found in the

modern books on Anthropology. If we assume, as I have
done more than once, that the earliest state of Man wàs
one in which he did not consciously separate himself from
the world, animate and inanimate, which surrounded
him, then (as I have also said) it was perfectly natural
for him to take some animal which bulked large on his
horizon—some food-animal for instance—and to pay
respect to it as the benefactor of his tribe, its far-back
ancestor and totem-symbol ; or, seeing the boundless
blessing of the cornfields, to believe in some kind of spirit
of the corn (not exactly a god but rather a magical ghost)
which, reincarnated every year, sprang up to save mankind from famine. But then no sooner had he done this
than he was bound to perceive that in cutting down the
corn or in eating his totem-bear or kangaroo he was slaying
his own best self and benefactor. In that instant the
consciousness of *disunity*, the sense of sin in some undefined
yet no less disturbing and alarming form would come in.
If, before, his ritual magic had been concentrated on the
simple purpose of multiplying the animal or vegetable
forms of his food, now in addition his magical endeavour
would be turned to averting the just wrath of the spirits
who animated these forms—just indeed, for the rudest
savage would perceive the wrong done and the probability
of its retribution. Clearly the wrong done could only be
expiated by an equivalent sacrifice of some kind on the
part of the man, or the tribe—that is by the offering to
the totem-animal or to the corn-spirit of some victim
whom these nature powers in their turn could feed upon
and assimilate. In this way the nature-powers would
be appeased, the sense of unity would be restored, and
the first At-one-ment effected.

It is hardly necessary to recite in any detail the cruel
and hideous sacrifices which have been perpetrated in
this sense all over the world, sometimes in appeasement
of a wrong committed or supposed to have been com-

mitted by the tribe or some member of it, sometimes in
placation or for the averting of death, or defeat, or plague,
sometimes merely in fulfilment of some long-standing
custom of forgotten origin—the flayings and floggings
and burnings and crucifixions of victims without end,
carried out in all deliberation and solemnity of established
ritual. I have mentioned some cases connected with the
sowing of the corn.   The Bible is full of such things, from
the intended sacrifice of Isaac by his father Abraham,
to the actual crucifixion of Jesus by the Jews.   The first-
born sons were claimed by a god who called himself
" jealous," and were only to be redeemed by a substitute.[1]
Of the Canaanites it was said that " even their daughters
they have *burnt* in the fire to their gods " ; [2] and of the
King of Moab, that when he saw his army in danger of
defeat, " he took his eldest son that should have reigned
in his stead and offered him for a burnt-offering on the
wall ! "[3]   Dr. Frazer[4] mentions the similar case of the
Carthaginians (about B.C. 300) sacrificing two hundred
children of good family as a propitiation to Baal and to
save their beloved city from the assaults of the Sicilian
tyrant Agathocles.   And even so we hear that on that
occasion three hundred more young folk *volunteered* to
die for the fatherland.

The awful sacrifices made by the Aztecs in Mexico to
their gods Huitzilopochtli, Texcatlipoca, and others are
described in much detail by Sahagun, the Spanish missionary of the sixteenth century.   The victims were mostly
prisoners of war or young children ; they were numbered
by thousands.   In one case Sahagun describes the huge
Idol or figure of the god as largely plated with gold and
holding his hands palm upward and in a downward sloping
position over a cauldron or furnace placed below.   The

[1] Exodus xxxiv. 20.
[2] Deut. xii. 31.   [3] 2 Kings iii. 27.
[4] *The Golden Bough*, vol. " The Dying God," p. 167.

children, who had previously been borne in triumphal
state on litters over the crowd and decorated with every
ornamental device of feathers and flowers and wings, were
placed one by one on the vast hands and *rolled down* into
the flames—as if the god were himself offering them.[1]
As the procession approached the temple, the members
of it wept and danced and sang, and here again the abundance of tears was taken for a good augury of rain.[2]

Bernal Diaz describes how he saw one of these monstrous
figures—that of Huitzilopochtli, the god of war, all inlaid
with gold and precious stones; and beside it were
" braziers, wherein burned the hearts of three Indians,
torn from their bodies that very day, and the smoke of
them and the savour of incense were the sacrifice."

Sahagun again (in Book II, ch. 5) gives a long account
of the sacrifice of a perfect youth at Easter-time—which
date Sahagun connects with the Christian festival of the
Resurrection. For a whole year the youth had been held
in honour and adored by the people as the very image
of the god (Tetzcatlipoca) to whom he was to be sacrificed.
Every luxury and the fulfilment of his last wish (including
such four courtesans as he desired) had been granted him.
At the last and on the fatal day, leaving his companions
and his worshipers behind, he slowly ascended the Temple
staircase, stripping on each step the ornaments from his
body, and breaking and casting away his flutes and other

---

[1] It is curious to find that exactly the same story (of the sloping
hands and the children rolled down into the flames) is related concerning the above-mentioned Baal image at Carthage (see Diodorus
Siculus, xx. 14 ; also Baring Gould's *Religious Belief,* vol i, p. 375).

[2] " A los niños que mataban, componianlos en muchos atavios
para llevarlos al sacrificio, y llevábanlos en unas literas sobre los
hombros, estas literas iban adornadas con plumages y con flores :
iban tañendo, cantando y bailando delante de ellos . . . Cuando
llevában los niños a matar, si llevában y echaban muchos lagrimas,
alegrabansi los que los llevában porque tomaban pronostico de que
habian de tener muchas aguas en aquel año." Sahagun, *Historia
Nueva España,* Bk. II, ch. i.

musical instruments; till, reaching the summit, he was stretched, curved on his back, and belly upwards, over the altar stone, while the priest with obsidian knife cut his breast open and, snatching the heart out, held it up, yet beating, as an offering to the Sun. In the meantime, and while the heart still lived, his successor for the next year was chosen.

In Book II, ch. 7 of the same work Sahagun describes the similar offering of a woman to a goddess. In both cases (he explains) of young man or young woman, the victims were richly adorned in the guise of the god or goddess to whom they were offered, and at the same time great largesse of food was distributed to all who needed. [Here we see the connexion in the general mind between the gift of food (by the gods) and the sacrifice of precious blood (by the people).] More than once Sahagun mentions that the victims in these Mexican ceremonials not infrequently offered *themselves* as a voluntary sacrifice; and Prescott says [1] that the offering of one's life to the gods was " sometimes voluntarily embraced, as a most glorious death opening a sure passage into Paradise."

Dr. Frazer describes [2] the far-back Babylonian festival of the Sacaea in which " a prisoner, condemned to death, was dressed in the king's robes, seated on the king's throne, allowed to issue whatever commands he pleased, to eat, drink and enjoy himself, and even to lie with the king's concubines." But at the end of the five days he was stripped of his royal robes, scourged, and hanged or impaled. It is certainly astonishing to find customs so similar prevailing among peoples so far removed in space and time as the Aztecs of the sixteenth century A.D. and the Babylonians perhaps of the sixteenth century B.C. But we know that this subject of the yearly sacrifice of

---

[1] *Conquest of Mexico*, Bk. I, ch. 3.

[2] *Golden Bough*, " The Dying God," p. 114. See also S. Reinach, *Cults, Myths and Religion*, p. 94, on the martyrdom of St. Dasius.

a victim attired as a king or god is one that Dr. Frazer
has especially made his own, and for further information
on it his classic work should be consulted.

Andrew Lang also, with regard to the Aztecs, quotes
largely from Sahagun, and summarises his conclusions
in the following passage : " The general theory of worship
was the adoration of a deity, first by innumerable human
sacrifices, next by the special sacrifice of a *man* for the
male gods, of a *woman* for each goddess.[1] The latter
victims were regarded as the living images or incarnations
of the divinities in each case ; for no system of worship
carried farther the identification of the god with the
sacrifice [? victim], and of both with the officiating priest.
The connexion was emphasized by the priests wearing
the newly-flayed skins of the victims—just as in Greece,
Egypt and Assyria, the fawn-skin or bull-hide or goat-skin
or fish-skin of the victims is worn by the celebrants.
Finally, an image of the god was made out of paste, and
this was divided into morsels and eaten in a hideous
sacrament by those who communicated."[2]
Revolting as this whole picture is, it represents as we
know a mere thumbnail sketch of the awful practices of
human sacrifice all over the world.   We hold up our hands
in horror at the thought of Huitzilopochtli dropping children
from his fingers into the flames, but we have to remember
that our own most Christian Saint Augustine was content
to describe unbaptized infants as crawling for ever about
the floor of Hell !   What sort of god, we may ask, did

[1] Compare the festival of *Thargelia* at Athens, originally connected
with the ripening of the crops.   A procession was formed and the
firstfruits of the year offered to Apollo, Artemis and the Horae.   It
was an expiatory feast, to purify the State from all guilt and avert
the wrath of the god [the Sun].   A man and a woman, as representing
the male and female population, were led about with a garland of
figs [fertility] round their necks, to the sound of flutes and singing.
They were then scourged, sacrificed, and their bodies burned by the
seashore.   (Nettleship and Sandys.)

[2] A. Lang, *Myth, Ritual and Religion*, vol. ii, p. 97.

Augustine worship? The Being who could condemn children to such a fate was certainly no better than the Mexican Idol.

And yet Augustine was a great and noble man, with some by no means unworthy conceptions of the greatness of his God. In the same way the Aztecs were in many respects a refined and artistic people, and their religion was not all superstition and bloodshed. Prescott says of them [1] that they believed in a supreme Creator and Lord " omnipresent, knowing all thoughts, giving all gifts, without whom Man is as nothing—invisible, incorporeal, one God, of perfect perfection and purity, under whose wings we find repose and a sure defence." How can we reconcile St. Augustine with his own devilish creed, or the religious belief of the Aztecs with their unspeakable cruelties? Perhaps we can only reconcile them by remembering out of what deeps of barbarism and what nightmares of haunting Fear, man has slowly emerged— and is even now only slowly emerging; by remembering also that the ancient ceremonies and rituals of Magic and Fear remained on and were cultivated by the multitude in each nation long after the bolder and nobler spirits had attained to breathe a purer air; by remembering that even to the present day in each individual the Old and the New are for a long period thus intricately intertangled. It is hard to believe that the practice of human and animal sacrifice (with whatever revolting details) should have been cultivated by nine-tenths of the human race over the globe out of sheer perversity and without some reason which at any rate to the perpetrators themselves appeared commanding and convincing. To-day [1918] we are witnessing in the Great European War a carnival of human slaughter which in magnitude and barbarity eclipses in one stroke all the accumulated ceremonial sacrifices of historical ages; and when we ask the why and wherefore of this

[1] *Conquest of Mexico*, Bk. I, ch. 3.

horrid spectacle we are told, apparently in all sincerity, and by both the parties engaged, of the noble objects and commanding moralities which inspire and compel it. We can hardly, in this last case, disbelieve altogether in the genuineness of the plea, so why should we do so in the former case ?   In both cases we perceive that underneath the surface pretexts and moralities Fear is and was the great urging and commanding force.

The truth is that Sin and Sacrifice represent—if you once allow for the overwhelming sway of fear—perfectly reasonable views of human conduct, adopted instinctively by mankind since the earliest times. If in a moment of danger or an access of selfish greed you deserted your brother tribesman or took a mean advantage of him, you ' sinned' against him ; and naturally you expiated the sin by an equivalent sacrifice of some kind made to the one you had wronged. Such an idea and such a practice were the very foundation of social life and human morality, and must have sprung up as soon as ever, in the course of evolution, man became *capable* of differentiating himself from his fellows and regarding his own conduct as that of a ' separate self.' It was in the very conception of a separate self that ' sin ' and disunity first began ; and it was by ' sacrifice ' that unity and harmony were restored, appeasement and atonement effected.

But in those earliest times, as I have already indicated more than once, man felt himself intimately related not only to his brother tribesman, but to the animals and to general Nature. It was not so much that he *thought* thus as that he never thought *otherwise* ! He *felt* subconsciously that he was a part of all this outer world. And so he adopted for his totems or presiding spirits every possible animal, as we have seen, and all sorts of nature-phenomena, such as rain and fire and water and clouds, and sun, moon and stars—which *we* consider quite senseless and inanimate. Towards these apparently senseless things therefore he felt the same compunction as I have described him feeling towards his brother tribesmen. He could sin against them too. He could sin against his totem-animal by eating it ; he could sin against his ' brother the ox ' by consuming its strength in the labour of the plough ; he could sin against the corn by cutting it down and grinding it into flour, or against the precious and beautiful pine-tree by laying his axe to its roots and converting it into mere timber for his house. Further still, no doubt he could sin against elemental nature. This might be more difficult to be certain of, but when the signs of elemental displeasure were not to be mistaken—when the rain withheld itself for months, or the storms and lightning dealt death and destruction, when the crops failed or evil plagues afflicted mankind—then there could be little uncertainty that he had sinned ; and Fear, which had haunted him like a demon from the first day when he became conscious of his separation from his fellows and from Nature, stood over him and urged to dreadful propitiations.

In all these cases some sacrifice in reparation was the obvious thing. We have seen that to atone for the cutting-down of the corn a human victim would often be slaughtered. The corn-spirit clearly approved of this, for wherever the blood and the remains of the victim were strewn the corn always sprang up more plentifully. The tribe or human group made reparation thus to the corn ; the corn-spirit signified approval. The ' sin ' was expiated and harmony restored. Sometimes the sacrifice was voluntarily offered by a tribesman ; sometimes it was enforced, by lot or otherwise ; sometimes the victim was a slave, or a captive enemy ; sometimes even an animal. All that did not so much matter. The main thing was that the formal expiation had been carried out, and the wrath of the spirits averted.

It is known that tribes whose chief food-animal was the bear felt it necessary to kill and eat a bear occasionally ;

but they could not do this without a sense of guilt, and some fear of vengeance from the great Bear-spirit. So they ate the slain bear at a communal feast in which the tribesmen shared the guilt and celebrated their community with their totem and with each other. And since they could not make any reparation directly to the slain animal itself *after* its death, they made their reparation *before*, bringing all sorts of presents and food to it for a long anterior period, and paying every kind of worship and respect to it. The same with the bull and the ox. At the festival of the Bouphonia, in some of the cities of Greece as I have already mentioned, the actual bull sacrificed was the handsomest and most carefully nurtured that could be obtained ; it was crowned with flowers and led in procession with every mark of reverence and worship. And when—as I have already pointed out—at the great Spring festival, instead of a bull or a goat or a ram, a *human* victim was immolated, it was a custom (which can be traced very widely over the world) to feed and indulge and honour the victim to the last degree for a *whole year* before the final ceremony, arraying him often as a king and placing a crown upon his head, by way of acknowledgment of the noble and necessary work he was doing for the general good.

What a touching and beautiful ceremony was that—belonging especially to the North of Syria, and lands where the pine is so beneficent and beloved a tree—the mourning ceremony of the death and burial of Attis ! when a pine-tree, felled by the axe, was hollowed out, and in the hollow an image (often itself carved out of pinewood) of the young Attis was placed. Could any symbolism express more tenderly the idea that the gracious youth—who represented Spring, too soon slain by the rude tusk of Winter—was himself the very human soul of the pine-tree ?[1] At

---

[1] See Julius Firmicus, who says (*De Errore*, c. 28): " In sacris Phrygiis, quæ Matris deum dicunt, per annos singulos arbor pinea

some earlier period, no doubt, a real youth had been sacrificed and his body bound within the pine ; but now it was
deemed sufficient for the maidens to sing their wild songs
of lamentation ; and for the priests and male enthusiasts
to cut and gash themselves with knives, or to sacrifice
(as they did) to the Earth-mother the precious blood
offering of their virile organs—symbols of fertility in
return for the promised and expected renewal of Nature
and the crops in the coming Spring. For the ceremony,
as we have already seen, did not end with death and
lamentation, but led on, perfectly naturally, after a day or
two to a festival of resurrection, when it was discovered
—just as in the case of Osiris—that the pine-tree coffin
was empty, and the immortal life had flown. How strange
the similarity and parallelism of all these things to the
story of Jesus in the Gospels—the sacrifice of a life made
in order to bring salvation to men and expiation of sins,
the crowning of the victim, and arraying in royal attire,
the scourging and the mockery, the binding or nailing to
a tree, the tears of Mary, and the resurrection and the
empty coffin !—or how not at all strange when we consider
in what numerous forms and among how many peoples,
this same parable and ritual had as a matter of fact been
celebrated, and how it had ultimately come down to
bring its message of redemption into a somewhat obscure
Syrian city, in the special shape with which we are
familiar.

Though the parable or legend in its special Christian
form bears with it the consciousness of the presence of
beings whom we may call gods, it is important to remember

caeditur, et in media arbore simulacrum juvenis subligatur. In
Isiacis sacris de pinea arbore caeditur truncus ; hujus trunci media
pars subtiliter excavatur, illis de segminibus factum idolum Osiridis
sepelitur. In Proserpinæ sacris cæsa arbor in effigiem virginis
formamque componitur, et cum intra civitatem fuerit illata,
quadraginta noctibus plangitur, quadragesima vero nocte
comburitur.''

that in many or most of its earlier forms, though it dealt in ' spirits '—the spirit of the corn, or the spirit of the Spring, or the spirits of the rain and the thunder, or the spirits of totem-animals—it had not yet quite risen to the idea of gods. It had not risen to the conception of eternal deities sitting apart and governing the world in solemn conclave—as from the slopes of Olympus or the recesses of the Christian Heaven. It belonged, in fact, in its inception, to the age of Magic. The creed of Sin and Sacrifice, or of Guilt and Expiation—whatever we like to call it—was evolved perfectly naturally out of the human mind (when brought face to face with Life and Nature) at some early stage of its self-consciousness. It was essentially the result of man's deep, original and instinctive sense of solidarity with Nature, now denied and belied and to some degree broken up by the growth and conscious insistence of the self-regarding impulses. It was the consciousness of disharmony and disunity, causing men to feel all the more poignantly the desire and the need of reconciliation. It was a realisation of union made clear by its very loss. It assumed of course, in a subconscious way as I have already indicated, that the external world was the *habitat* of a mind or minds similar to man's own ; but *that* being granted, it is evident that the particular theories current in this or that place about the nature of the world—the theories, as we should say, of science or theology—did not alter the general outlines of the creed ; they only coloured its details and gave its ritual different dramatic settings. The mental attitudes, for instance, of Abraham sacrificing the ram, or of the Siberian *angakout* slaughtering a totem-bear, or of a modern and pious Christian contemplating the Saviour on the Cross are really almost exactly the same. I mention this because in tracing the origins or the evolution of religions it is important to distinguish clearly what is essential and universal from that which is merely local and temporary.

Some people, no doubt, would be shocked at the comparisons just made ; but surely it is much more inspiriting and encouraging to think that whatever progress *has* been made in the religious outlook of the world has come about through the gradual mental growth and consent of the peoples, rather than through some unique and miraculous event of a rather arbitrary and unexplained character— which indeed might never be repeated, and concerning which it would perhaps be impious to suggest that it *should* be repeated.

The consciousness then of Sin (or of alienation from the life of the whole), and of restoration or redemption through Sacrifice, seems to have disclosed itself in the human race in very very far-back times, and to have symbolised itself in some most ancient rituals ; and if we are shocked sometimes at the barbarities which accompanied those rituals, yet we must allow that these barbarities show how intensely the early people felt the solemnity and importance of the whole matter ; and we must allow too that the barbarities did sear and burn themselves into rude and ignorant minds with the sense of the *need* of Sacrifice, and with a result perhaps which could not have been compassed in any other way.

For after all we see now that sacrifice is of the very essence of social life. " It is expedient that one man should die for the people " ; and not only that *one* man should actually die, but (what is far more important) that each man should be ready and *willing* to die in that cause, when the occasion and the need arises. Taken in its larger meanings and implications Sacrifice, as conceived in the ancient world, was a perfectly reasonable thing. It *should* pervade modern life more than it does. All we have or enjoy flows from, or is implicated with, pain and suffering in others, and—if there is any justice in Nature or Humanity – it demands an equivalent readiness to suffer on our part. If Christianity has any real essence, that essence is perhaps expressed in some such ritual or practice of Sacrifice, and we see that the dim beginnings of this idea date from the far-back customs of savages coming down from a time anterior to all recorded history.

VIII

PAGAN INITIATIONS AND THE SECOND BIRTH

WE have suggested in the last chapter how the conceptions of Sin and Sacrifice coming down to us from an extremely remote past, and embodied among the various peoples of the world sometimes in crude and bloodthirsty rites, sometimes in symbols and rituals of a gentler and more gracious character, descended at last into Christianity and became a part of its creed and of the creed of the modern world. On the whole perhaps we may trace a slow amelioration in this process and may flatter ourselves that the Christian centuries exhibit a more philosophical understanding of what Sin is, and a more humane conception of what Sacrifice *should* be, than the centuries preceding. But I fear that any very decided statement or sweeping generalisation to that effect would be—to say the least—rash. Perhaps there *is* a very slow amelioration ; but the briefest glance at the history of the Christian churches—the horrible rancours and revenges of the clergy and the sects against each other in the fourth and fifth centuries A.D., the heresy-hunting crusades at Beziers and other places and the massacres of the Albigenses in the twelfth and thirteenth centuries, the witch-findings and burnings of the sixteenth and seventeenth, the hideous science-urged and bishop-blessed warfare of the twentieth —horrors fully as great as any we can charge to the account

of the Aztecs or the Babylonians—must give us pause.
Nor must we forget that if there is by chance a substantial
amelioration in our modern outlook with regard to these
matters the same had begun already before the advent
of Christianity and can by no means be ascribed to any
miraculous influence of that religion. Abraham was
prompted to slay a ram as a substitute for his son, long
before the Christians were thought of; the rather savage
Artemis of the old Greek rites was (according to Pausanias) [1]
honoured by the yearly sacrifice of a perfect boy and girl,
but later it was deemed sufficient to draw a knife across
their throats as a symbol, with the result of spilling only
a few drops of their blood, or to flog the boys (with the
same result) upon her altar. Among the Khonds in old
days many victims (*meriahs*) were sacrificed to the gods,
" but in time the man was replaced by a horse, the horse
by a bull, the bull by a ram, the ram by a kid, the kid
by fowls, and the fowls by many flowers." [2]   At one time,
according to the Yajur-Veda, there was a festival at which
one hundred and twenty-five victims, men and women,
boys and girls, were sacrificed ; " but reform supervened,
and now the victims were bound as before to the stake,
but afterwards amid litanies to the immolated (god)
Narayana, the sacrificing priest brandished a knife and
—severed the bonds of the captives ! " [3]   At the Athenian
festival of the Thargelia, to which I referred in the last
chapter, it appears that the victims, in later times, instead
of being slain, were tossed from a height into the sea, and
after being rescued were then simply banished ; while
at Leucatas at a similar festival the fall of the victim was
graciously broken by tying feathers and even living birds
to his body.[4]

With the lapse of time and the general progress of man-

[1] vii. 19, and iii. 8, 16.
[2] *Primitive Folk*, by Elie Reclus (Contemp. Science Series), p. 330.
[3] *Ibid.*
[4] Muller's *Dorians*, Book II, ch. ii, par 10.

kind we may, I think, perceive some such slow ameliorations in the matter of the brutality and superstition of the old religions. How far any later ameliorations were due to the direct influence of Christianity might be a difficult question ; but what I think we can clearly see—and what especially interests us here—is that in respect to its main religious ideas, and the matter underlying them (exclusive of the *manner* of their treatment, which necessarily has varied among different peoples) Christianity is of one piece with the earlier pagan creeds and is for the most part a re-statement and renewed expression of world-old doctrines whose first genesis is lost in the haze of the past, beyond all recorded history.

I have illustrated this view with regard to the doctrine of Sin and Sacrifice. Let us take two or three other illustrations. Let us take the doctrine of Re-birth or Regeneration. The first few verses of St. John's Gospel are occupied with the subject of salvation through rebirth or regeneration. " Except a man be born again, he cannot see the kingdom of God." . . . " Except a man be born of water and the Spirit, he cannot enter into the kingdom of God." Our Baptismal Service begins by saying that " forasmuch as all men are conceived and born in sin ; and that our Saviour Christ saith, None can enter into the kingdom of God except he be regenerate and born anew of water and the Holy Ghost " ; therefore it is desirable that this child should be baptised, " received into Christ's Holy Church, and be made a lively member of the same." That is to say, there is one birth, after the flesh, but a second birth is necessary, a birth after the Spirit and into the Church of Christ. Our Confirmation Service is simply a service repeating and confirming these views, at an age (fourteen to sixteen or so) when the boy or girl is capable of understanding what is being done.

But our Baptismal and Confirmation ceremonies com-

bined are clearly the exact correspondence and parallel
of the old pagan ceremonies of Initiation, which are or
have been observed in almost every primitive tribe over
the world. "The rite of the second birth," says Jane
Harrison,[1] " is widespread, universal, over half the savage
world. With the savage to be twice-born is the rule. By
his first birth he comes into the world ; by his second he
is born into his tribe. At his first birth he belongs to his
mother and the women-folk ; at his second he becomes
a full-fledged man and passes into the society of the
warriors of his tribe." . . . " These rites are very various,
but they all point one moral, that the former things are
passed away and that the new-born man has entered upon
a new life. Simplest of all, and most instructive, is the
rite practised by the Kikuyu tribe of British East Africa,
who require that every boy, just before circumcision,
must be born again. The mother stands up with the boy
crouching at her feet ; she pretends to go through all the
labour pains, and the boy on being reborn cries like a babe
and is washed."[2]

Let us pause for a moment. An Initiate is of course
one who " enters in." He enters into the Tribe ; he enters
into the revelation of certain Mysteries ; he becomes an
associate of a certain Totem, a certain God ; a member
of a new Society, or Church—a church of Mithra, or
Dionysus or Christ. To do any of these things he must
be born again ; he must die to the old life ; he must pass
through ceremonials which symbolise the change. One
of these ceremonials is washing. As the new-born babe
is washed, so must the new-born initiate be washed ; and
as by primitive man (and not without reason) *blood* was
considered the most vital and regenerative of fluids, the
very elixir of life, so in earliest times it was common to
wash the initiate in blood. If the initiate had to be born

[1] *Ancient Art and Ritual*, p. 104.
[2] See also *Themis*, p. 21.

anew, it would seem reasonable to suppose that he must first die. So, not unfrequently, he was wounded, or scourged, and baptised with his own blood, or, in cases, one of the candidates was really killed and his blood used as a substitute for the blood of the others. No doubt *human* sacrifice attended the earliest initiations. But later it was sufficient to be half-drowned in the blood of a Bull as in the Mithra cult,[1] or ' washed in the blood of the Lamb ' as in the Christian phraseology. Finally, with a growing sense of decency and aesthetic perception among the various peoples, washing with pure water came in the initiation-ceremonies to take the place of blood ; and our baptismal service has reduced the ceremony to a mere sprinkling with water.[2]

To continue the quotation from Miss Harrison : " More often the new birth is simulated, or imagined, as a death and a resurrection, either of the boys themselves or of some one else in their presence. Thus at initiation among some tribes of South-east Australia, when the boys are assembled an old man dressed in stringy bark-fibre lies down in a grave. He is covered up lightly with sticks and earth, and the grave is smoothed over. The buried man holds in his hand a small bush which seems to be growing from the ground, and other bushes are stuck in the ground round about. The novices are then brought to the edge of the grave and a song is sung. Gradually, as the song goes on, the bush held by the buried man begins to quiver. It moves more and more, and bit by bit the man himself starts up from the grave."

Strange ! in our own Baptismal Service and just before the actual christening we read these words, " *Then shall the Priest say :* O merciful God, grant that the old Adam in this child may be so *buried* that the new man may be

[1] See *supra*, ch. iii. p. 43.
[2] For the virtue supposed to reside in blood see Westermarck's *Moral Ideas*, ch. 46.

raised up in him : grant that all carnal affections may
die in him, and that all things belonging to the Spirit may
live and grow in him ! " Can we doubt that the Australian
medicine-man, standing at the graveside of the re-arisen
old black-fellow, pointed the same moral to the young
initiates as the priest does to-day to those assembled before
him in church—-for indeed we know that among savage
tribes initiations have always been before all things the
occasions of moral and social teaching ? Can we doubt
that he said, in substance if not in actual words : " As
this man has arisen from the grave, so you must also arise
from your old childish life of amusement and self-gratification and *enter into* the life of the tribe, the life of the
Spirit of the tribe." " In totemistic societies," to quote
Miss Harrison again, " and in the animal secret societies
that seem to grow out of them, the novice is born again
as the sacred animal. Thus among the Carrier Indians [1]
when a man wants to become a *Lulem* or ' Bear,' however
cold the season he tears off his clothes, puts on a bear-skin
and dashes into the woods, where he will stay for three
or four days. Every night his fellow-villagers will go
out in search parties to find him. They cry out *Yi !*
Kelulem (come on, Bear), and he answers with angry growls.
Usually they fail to find him, but he comes back at last
himself. He is met, and conducted to the ceremonial
lodge, and there in company with the rest of the Bears
dances solemnly his first appearance. Disappearance and
reappearance is as common a rite in initiation as simulated
killing and resurrection, and has the same object. Both
are rites of transition, of passing from one state to another."
In the Christian ceremonies the boy or girl puts away
childish things and puts on the new man, but instead of
putting on a bear-skin he puts on Christ. There is not so
much difference as may appear on the surface. To be
identified with your Totem is to be identified with the

[1] *Golden Bough* [2], III, p. 438.

sacred being who watches over your tribe, who has given his life for your tribe; it is to be born again, to be washed not only with water but with the Holy Spirit of all your fellows. To be baptized into Christ ought to mean to be regenerated in the Holy Spirit of all humanity; and no doubt in cases it does mean this, but too often unfortunately it has only amounted to a pretence of religious sanction given to the meanest and bitterest quarrels of the Churches and the States.

This idea of a New Birth at initiation explains the prevalent pagan custom of subjecting the initiates to serious ordeals, often painful and even dangerous. If one is to be born again, obviously one must be ready to face death; the one thing cannot be without the other. One must be able to endure pain, like the Red Indian braves; to go long periods fasting and without food or drink, like the *choupan* among the Western Inoits—who wanders for whole nights over the ice-fields under the moon, scantily clothed and braving the intense cold; to overcome the very fear of death and danger, like the Australian novices who, at first terrified by the sound of the bull-roarer and threats of fire and the knife, learn finally to cast their fears away.[1] By so doing one puts off the old childish things, and qualifies oneself by firmness and courage to become a worthy member of the society

---

[1] According to accounts of the Wiradthuri tribe of Western Australia, in their initiations, the lads were frightened by a large fire being lighted near them, and hearing the awful sound of the bull roarers, while they were told that Dhuramoolan was about to burn them; the legend being that Dhuramoolan, a powerful being, whose voice sounded like thunder, would take the boys away into the bush and instruct them in all the laws, traditions and customs of the community. So he pretended that he always killed the boys, cut them up, and burnt them to ashes, after which he moulded the ashes into human shape, and restored them to life as new beings. (See R. H. Matthews, " The Wiradthuri tribes," *Journal Anthrop. Inst.*, vol. xxv, 1896, pp. 297 *sq.*)

into which one is called.[1] The rules of social life are taught—the duty to one's tribe, and to oneself, truth-speaking, defence of women and children, the care of cattle, the meaning of sex and marriage, and even the mysteries of such religious ideas and rudimentary science as the tribe possesses. And by so doing one really enters into a new life. Things of the spiritual world begin to dawn. Julius Firmicus, in describing the mysteries of the resurrection of Osiris,[2] says that when the worshipers had satiated themselves with lamentations over the death of the god then the priest would go round anointing them with oil and whispering, " Be of good cheer, O Neophytes of the new-arisen God, for to us too from our pains shall come salvation." [3]

It would seem that at some very early time in the history of tribal and priestly initiations an attempt was made to impress upon the neophytes the existence and over-shadowing presence of spiritual and ghostly beings. Perhaps the pains endured in the various ordeals, the long fastings, the silences in the depth of the forests or on the mountains or among the ice-floes, helped to rouse the visionary faculty. The developments of this faculty among the black and coloured peoples—East-Indian, Burmese, African, American-Indian, etc.—are well known. Miss Alice Fletcher, who lived among the Omaha Indians for thirty years, gives a most interesting account [4] of the general philosophy of that people and their rites of initiation. " The Omahas regard all animate and inanimate forms, all phenomena, as pervaded by a common life, which was continuous with and similar to the will-power they were conscious of in

[1] See Catlin's *North-American Indians*, vol. i, for initiations and ordeals among the Mandans.
[2] *De Errore*, c. 22.
[3] Θαρρεῖτε, μύσται τοῦ θεοῦ σεσωσμένου,
Εσται γὰρ ἡμῖν εκ πονῶν σωτηρία.
[4] Summarised in *Themis*, pp. 68–71.

themselves. This mysterious power in all things they called *Wakonda*, and through it all things were related to man and to each other. In the idea of the continuity of life a relation was maintained between the seen and the unseen, the dead and the living, and also between the fragment of anything and its entirety." [1] Thus an Omaha novice might at any time seek to obtain *Wakonda* by what was called *the rite of the vision*. He would go out alone, fast, chant incantations, and finally fall into a trance (much resembling what in modern times has been called *cosmic consciousness*) in which he would perceive the inner relations of all things and the solidarity of the least object with the rest of the universe.

Another rite in connexion with initiation, and common all over the pagan world—in Greece, America, Africa, Australia, New Mexico, etc.—was the daubing of the novice all over with clay or chalk or even dung, and then after a while removing the same. [2] The novice must have looked a sufficiently ugly and uncomfortable object in this state ; but later, when he was thoroughly *washed*, the ceremony must have afforded a thrilling illustration of the idea of a new birth, and one which would dwell in the minds of the spectators. When the daubing was done as not infrequently happened with white clay or gypsum, and the ritual took place at night, it can easily be imagined that the figures of young men and boys moving about in the darkness would lend support to the idea that they were spirits belonging to some intermediate world—who had already passed through death and were now waiting for their second birth on earth (or into the tribe) which would be signalised by their thorough and ceremonial washing. It will be remembered that Herodotus (viii, 27) gives a circumstantial account of how the Phocians in

[1] A. C. Fletcher, *The Significance of the Scalp-lock*, Journal of Anthropological Studies, xxvii (1897-8), p. 436.
[2] See A. Lang's *Myth, Ritual and Religion*, i, 274 *sq.*

a battle with the Thessalians smeared six hundred of their bravest warriors with white clay so that, looking like supernatural beings, and falling upon the Thessalians by night, they terrified the latter and put them to instant flight.

Such then—though very scantily described—were some of the rites of Initiation and Second Birth celebrated in the old Pagan world. The subject is far too large for adequate treatment within the present limits ; but even so we cannot but be struck by the appropriateness in many cases of the teaching thus giving to the young, the concreteness of the illustrations, the effectiveness of the symbols used, the dramatic character of the rites, the strong enforcement of lessons on the nature and duties of the life into which the candidates were about to enter. Christianity followed on, and inherited these traditions, but one feels that in its ceremonies of Baptism and Confirmation, which of course correspond to the Pagan Initiations, it falls far short of the latter. Its ceremonies (certainly as we have them to-day in Protestant countries) are of a very milk-and-watery character ; all allusion to and teaching on the immensely important subject of Sex is omitted, the details of social and industrial morality are passed by, and instruction is limited to a few rather commonplace lessons in general morality and religion.

It may be appropriate here, before leaving the subject of the Second Birth, to inquire how it has come about that this doctrine—so remote and metaphysical as it might appear—has been taken up and embodied in their creeds and rituals by quite *primitive* people all over the world, to such a degree indeed that it has ultimately been adopted and built into the foundations of the later and more intellectual religions, like Hinduism, Mithraism, and the Egyptian and Christian cults. I think the answer to this question must be found in the now-familiar fact that the earliest peoples felt themselves so much a part of Nature and the animal and vegetable world around them that (whenever they thought about these matters at all) they never for a moment doubted that the things which were happening all round them in the external world were also happening within themselves. They saw the Sun, overclouded and nigh to death in winter, come to its birth again each year; they saw the Vegetation shoot forth anew in spring—the revival of the spirit of the Earth; the endless breeding of the Animals, the strange transformations of Worms and Insects; the obviously new life taken on by boys and girls at puberty; the same at a later age when the novice was transformed into the medicine-man—the *choupan* into the *angakok* among the Esquimaux, the Dacotah youth into the *wakan* among the Red Indians; and they felt in their sub-conscious way the same everlasting forces of rebirth and transformation working within themselves. In some of the Greek Mysteries the newly admitted Initiates were fed for some time after on milk only " as though we were being born again." (See Sallustius, quoted by Gilbert Murray.) When sub-conscious knowledge began to glimmer into direct consciousness one of the first aspects (and no doubt one of the truest) under which people saw life was just thus : as a series of rebirths and transformations.[1] The most modern science, I need hardly say, in biology as well as in chemistry and the field of inorganic Nature, supports that view. The savage in earliest times *felt* the truth of some things which we to-day are only beginning intellectually to perceive and analyse.

Christianity adopted and absorbed—as it was bound to do—this world-wide doctrine of the second birth. Passing over its physiological and biological applications, it gave to it a fine spiritual significance or rather it insisted

[1] The fervent and widespread belief in animal metamorphoses among early peoples is well-known.

especially on its spiritual significance, which (as we have seen) had been widely recognised before. Only—as I suppose must happen with all local religions—it narrowed the application and outlook of the doctrine down to a special case—" As in Adam all die, so in *Christ* shall all be made alive." The Universal Spirit which can give rebirth and salvation to *every* child of man to whom it comes, was offered only under a very special form—that of Jesus Christ.[1] In this respect it was no better than the religions which preceded it. In some respects—that is, where it was especially fanatical, blinkered, and hostile to other sects—it was *worse*. But to those who perceive that the Great Spirit may bring new birth and salvation to some under the form of Osiris, equally well as to others under the form of Jesus, or again to some under the form of a Siberian totem-Bear equally as to others under the form of Osiris, these questionings and narrowings fall away as of no importance. We in this latter day can see the main thing, namely that Christianity was and is just one phase of a world-old religion, slowly perhaps expanding its scope, but whose chief attitudes and orientations have been the same through the centuries.

Many other illustrations might be taken of the truth of this view, but I will confine myself to two or three more. There is the instance of the *Eucharist*, and its exceedingly widespread celebration (under very various forms) among the pagans all over the world—as well as among Christians. I have already said enough on this subject, and need not delay over it. By partaking of the sacramental meal, even in its wildest and crudest shapes, as in the mysteries of Dionysus, one was identified with and united to the

[1] The same happened with regard to another great Pagan doctrine (to which I have just alluded), the doctrine of transformations and metamorphoses ; and whereas the pagans believed in these things, as the common and possible heritage of *every* man, the Christians only allowed themselves to entertain the idea in the special and unique instance of the Transfiguration of Christ.

god ; in its milder and more spiritual aspects as in the Mithraic, Egyptian, Hindu and Christian cults, one passed behind the veil of *maya* and this ever-changing world, and entered into the region of divine peace and power.[1]

Or again the doctrine of the *Saviour*. That also is one on which I need not add much to what has been said already. The number of pagan deities (mostly virgin-born and done to death in some way or other in their efforts to save mankind) is so great [2] as to be difficult to keep account of. The god *Krishna* in India, the god *Indra* in Nepaul and Thibet, spilt their blood for the salvation of men ; *Buddha* said, according to Max Müller,[3] " Let all the sins that were in the world fall on me, that the world may be delivered " ; the Chinese *Tien*, the Holy One— " one with God and existing with him from all eternity " —died to save the world ; the Egyptian *Osiris* was called Saviour, so was *Horus* ; so was the Persian *Mithras* ; so was the Greek *Hercules* who overcame Death though his body was consumed in the burning garment of mortality, out of which he rose into heaven. So also was the Phrygian *Attis* called Saviour, and the Syrian *Tammuz* or *Adonis* likewise—both of whom, as we have seen, were nailed or tied to a tree, and afterwards rose again from their biers or coffins. *Prometheus*, the greatest and earliest benefactor of the human race, was *nailed by the hands and feet, and with arms extended*, to the rocks of Mount Caucasus. *Bacchus* or *Dionysus*, born of the virgin Semele

---

[1] Baring Gould in his *Orig. Relig. Belief*, 1. 401, says :—" Among the ancient Hindus *Soma* was a chief deity ; he is called the Giver of Life and Health. . . . He became incarnate among men, was taken by them and slain, and brayed in a mortar [a god of corn and wine apparently]. But he rose in flame to heaven to be ' the Bene-factor of the World ' and the ' Mediator between God and Man.' Through communion with him in his sacrifice, man (who partook of this god) has an assurance of immortality, for by that sacrament he obtains union with his divinity."

[2] See for a considerable list Doane's *Bible Myths*, ch. xx.

[3] *Hist. Sanskrit Literature*, p. 80.

to be the Liberator of mankind (Dionysus Eleutherios as
he was called), was torn to pieces, not unlike Osiris. Even
in far Mexico *Quetzalcoatl*, the Saviour, was born of a virgin,
was tempted, and fasted forty days, was done to death,
and his second coming looked for so eagerly that (as is well
known) when Cortes appeared, the Mexicans, poor things,
greeted *him* as the returning god ! [1]   In Peru and among
the American Indians, North and South of the Equator,
similar legends are, or were, to be found.

Briefly sketched as all this is, it is enough to prove quite
abundantly that the doctrine of the Saviour is world-wide
and world-old, and that Christianity merely appropriated
the same and (as the other cults did) gave it a special
colour. Probably the wide range of this doctrine would
have been far better and more generally known, had not
the Christian Church, all through, made the greatest of
efforts and taken the greatest precautions to extinguish
and snuff out all evidence of pagan claims on the subject.
There is much to show that the early Church took this
line with regard to pre-Christian saviours [2] ; and in later
times the same policy is remarkably illustrated by the
treatment in the sixteenth century of the writings of
Sahagun the Spanish missionary—to whose work I have
already referred. Sahagun was a wonderfully broad-
minded and fine man who, while he did not conceal the
barbarities of the Aztec religion, was truthful enough to
point out redeeming traits in the manners and customs
of the people and some resemblances to Christian doctrine
and practice. This infuriated the bigoted Catholics of
the newly formed Mexican Church. They purloined the
manuscripts of Sahagun's *Historia* and scattered and hid
them about the country, and it was only after infinite
labour and an appeal to the Spanish Court that he got them
together again. Finally, at the age of eighty, having

---

[1] See Kingsborough, *Mexican Antiquities*, vol. vi.
[2] See Tertullian's *Apologia*, c. 16 ; Ad Nationes, c. xii.

translated them into Spanish (from the original Mexican) he sent them in two big volumes home to Spain for safety ; but there almost immediately *they disappeared*, and could not be found ! It was only after *two centuries* that they ultimately turned up (1790) in a Convent at Tolosa in Navarre. Lord Kingsborough published them in England in 1830.

I have thus dwelt upon several of the main doctrines of Christianity—namely, those of Sin and Sacrifice, the Eucharist, the Saviour, the Second Birth, and Trans-figuration—as showing that they are by no means unique in our religion, but were common to nearly all the religions of the ancient world. The list might be much further extended, but there is no need to delay over a subject which is now very generally understood. I will, however, devote a page or two to one instance, which I think is very remarkable, and full of deep suggestion.

There is no doctrine in Christianity which is more reverenced by the adherents of that religion, or held in higher estimation, than that God sacrificed his only Son for the salvation of the world ; also that since the Son was not only of like nature but of the *same* nature with the Father, and equal to him as being the second Person of the Divine Trinity, the sacrifice amounted to an immolation of Himself for the good of mankind. The doctrine is so mystical, so remote, and in a sense so absurd and impossible, that it has been a favorite mark through the centuries for the ridicule of the scoffers and enemies of the Church ; and here, it might easily be thought, is a belief which—whether it be considered glorious or whether contemptible—is at any rate unique, and peculiar to that Church.

And yet the extraordinary fact is that a similar belief ranges all through the ancient religions, and can be traced back to the earliest times. The word *host* which is used in the Catholic Mass for the bread and wine on the Altar, supposed to be the transubstantiated body and blood of Christ, is from the Latin *Hostia* which the dictionary interprets as " an animal slain in sacrifice, a sin-offering." It takes us far far back to the Totem stage of folk-life, when the tribe, as I have already explained, crowned a victim-bull or bear or other animal with flowers, and honoring it with every offering of food and worship, sacrificed the victim to the Totem spirit of the tribe, and consumed it in an Eucharistic feast—the medicine-man or priest who conducted the ritual wearing a skin of the same beast as a sign that he represented the Totem-divinity, taking part in the sacrifice of ' himself to himself.' It reminds us of the Khonds of Bengal sacrificing their *meriahs* crowned and decorated as gods and goddesses ; of the Aztecs doing the same ; of Quetzalcoatl pricking his elbows and fingers so as to draw blood, which he offered on his own altar ; or of Odin hanging by his own desire upon a tree. " I know I was hanged upon the tree shaken by the winds for nine long nights. I was transfixed by a spear ; I was vowed to Odin, myself to myself." And so on. The instances are endless. " I am the oblation," says the Lord Krishna in the Bhagavad Gita,[1] " I am the sacrifice, I the ancestral offering." " In the truly orthodox conception of sacrifice," says Elie Reclus,[2] " the consecrated offering, be it man, woman or virgin, lamb or heifer, cock or dove, represents *the deity himself.* . . . Brahma is the ' imperishable sacrifice ' ; Indra, Soma, Hari and the other gods, became incarnate in animals to the sole end that they might be immolated. Purusha, the Universal Being, caused himself to be slain by the Immortals, and from his substance were born the birds of the air, wild and domestic animals, the offerings of butter and curds. The world, declared the Rishis, is a series of sacrifices disclosing other sacrifices. To stop

[1] Ch. ix, v. 16.   [2] *Primitive Folk*, ch. vi.

them would be to suspend the life of Nature. The god Siva, to whom the Tipperahs of Bengal are supposed to have sacrificed as many as a thousand human victims a year, said to the Brahmins : ' It is I that am the actual offering ; it is I that you butcher upon my altars.' "

It was in allusion to this doctrine that R. W. Emerson, paraphrasing the Katha-Upanishad, wrote that immortal verse of his :—

> If the red slayer thinks he slays,
> Or the slain thinks he is slain,
> They know not well the subtle ways
> I take, and pass, and turn again.

I say it is an astonishing thing to think and realise that this profound and mystic doctrine of the eternal sacrifice of Himself, ordained by the Great Spirit for the creation and salvation of the world—a doctrine which has attracted and fascinated many of the great thinkers and nobler minds of Europe, which has also inspired the religious teachings of the Indian sages and to a less philosophical degree the writings of the Christian Saints—should have been seized in its general outline and essence by rude and primitive people before the dawn of history, and embodied in their rites and ceremonials. What is the explanation of this fact ?

It is very puzzling. The whole subject is puzzling. The world-wide adoption of similar creeds and rituals (and, we may add, legends and fairy tales) among early peoples, and in far-sundered places and times is so remarkable that it has given the students of these subjects ' furiously to think ' [1]—yet for the most part without great success in the way of finding a solution. The supposition that (1) the creed, rite or legend in question has sprung up, so to speak, accidentally, in one place, and

[1] See A. Lang's *Myth, Ritual and Religion*, vol. ii.

then has traveled (owing to some inherent plausibility) over the rest of the world, is of course one that commends itself readily at first ; but on closer examination the practical difficulties it presents are certainly very great. These include the migrations of customs and myths in quite early ages of the earth across trackless oceans and continents, and between races and peoples absolutely incapable of understanding each other. And if to avoid these difficulties it is assumed that the present human race all proceeds from one original stock which radiating from one centre—say in South-Eastern Asia [1]—overspread the world, carrying its rites and customs with it, why, then we are compelled to face the difficulty of supposing this radiation to have taken place at an enormous time ago (the continents being then all more or less conjoined) and at a period when it is doubtful if any religious rites and customs at all existed ; not to mention the further difficulty of supposing all the four or five hundred languages now existing to be descended from one common source. The far tradition of the Island of Atlantis seems to afford a possible explanation of the community of rites and customs between the Old and New World, and this without assuming in any way that Atlantis (if it existed) was the original and *sole* cradle of the human race.[2] Anyhow it is clear that these origins of human culture must be of extreme antiquity, and that it would not be wise to be put off the track of the investigation of a possible common source merely by that fact of antiquity.

A second supposition, however, is (2) that the natural psychological evolution of the human mind has in the

---

[1] See Hastings, *Encycl. Religion and Ethics*, art. " Ethnology."
[2] E. J. Payne, *History of the New World called America* (vol. i, p. 93) says : " It is certain that Europe and America once formed a single continent," but inroads of the sea " left a vast island or peninsula stretching from Iceland to the Azores—which gradually disappeared." Also he speaks (i. 93) of the " Miocene Bridge " between Siberia and the New World.

various times and climes led folk of the most diverse surroundings and heredity—and perhaps even sprung from separate anthropoid stocks—to develop their social and religious ideas along the same general lines—and that even to the extent of exhibiting at times a remarkable similarity in minute details. This is a theory which commends itself greatly to a deeper and more philosophical consideration ; but it brings us up point-blank against another most difficult question (which we have already raised), namely, how to account for extremely rude and primitive peoples in the far past, and on the very border-land of the animal life, having been *susceptible* to the germs of great religious ideas (such as we have mentioned) and having been instinctively—though not of course by any process of conscious reasoning—moved to express them in symbols and rites and ceremonials, and (later no doubt) in myths and legends, which satisfied their *feelings* and sense of fitness—though they may not have known *why*— and afterwards were capable of being taken up and embodied in the great philosophical religions.

This difficulty almost compels us to a view of human knowledge which has found supporters among some able thinkers—the view, namely, that a vast store of knowledge is already contained in the subconscious mind of man (and the animals) and only needs the provocation of outer experience to bring it to the surface ; and that in the second stage of human psychology this process of crude and piecemeal externalisation *is* taking place, in preparation for the final or third stage in which the knowledge will be re-absorbed and become direct and intuitional on a high and harmonious plane—something like the present intuition of the animals as we perceive it on the animal plane. However this general subject is one on which I shall touch again, and I do not propose to dwell on it at any length now.

There is a third alternative theory (3)—a combination

of (1) and (2)—namely, that if one accepts (2) and the idea that at any given stage of human development there is a *predisposition* to certain symbols and rites belonging to that stage, then it is much more easy to accept theory (1) as an important factor in the spread of such symbols and rites ; for clearly, then, the smallest germ of a custom or practice, transported from one country or people to another at the right time, would be sufficient to wake the development or growth in question and stimulate it into activity. It will be seen, therefore, that the important point towards the solution of this whole puzzling question is the discussion of theory (2)—and to this theory, as illustrated by the world-wide myth of the Golden Age, I will now turn.

IX

MYTH OF THE GOLDEN AGE

THE tradition of a "Golden Age" is widespread over the world, and it is not necessary to go at any length into the story of the *Garden of Eden* and the other legends which in almost every country illustrate this tradition. Without indulging in sentiment on the subject we may hold it not unlikely that the tradition *is* justified by the remembrance, among the people of every race, of a pre-civilisation period of comparative harmony and happiness when two things, which to-day we perceive to be the prolific causes of discord and misery, were absent or only weakly developed—namely, *property* and *self-consciousness.*[1]

During the first century B.C. there was a great spread of Messianic Ideas over the Roman world, and Virgil's 4th Eclogue, commonly called the Messianic Eclogue, reflects very clearly this state of the public mind. The expected babe in the poem was to be the son of Octavian (Augustus) the first Roman emperor, and a messianic halo surrounded it in Virgil's verse. Unfortunately it turned out to be a *girl*! However there is little doubt that Virgil did—in that very sad age of the world, an age of " misery and massacre," and in common with thousands of others —look for the coming of a great 'redeemer.' It was only

[1] For a fuller working out of this, see *Civilisation : its Cause and Cure*, by E. Carpenter, ch. i.

137

a few years earlier—about B.C. 70—that the great revolt
of the shamefully maltreated Roman slaves occurred,
and that in revenge six thousand prisoners from Spartacus'
army were nailed on crosses all the way from Rome to
Capua (150 miles).   But long before this Hesiod had
recorded a past Golden Age when life had been gracious
in communal fraternity and joyful in peace, when human
beings and animals spoke the same language, when death
had followed on sleep, without old age or disease, and
after death men had moved as good *daimones* or *genii*
over the lands.   Pindar, three hundred years after Hesiod,
had confirmed the existence of the Islands of the Blest,
where the good led a blameless, tearless, life.   Plato the
same,[1] with further references to the fabled island of
Atlantis ; the Egyptians believed in a former golden age
under the god Râ to which they looked back with regret
and envy ; the Persians had a garden of Eden similar to
that of the Hebrews ; the Greeks a garden of the Hesperides,
in which dwelt the serpent whose head was ultimately
crushed beneath the heel of Hercules ; and so on.   The
references to a supposed far-back state of peace and
happiness are indeed numerous.

So much so that latterly, and partly to explain their
prevalence, a theory has been advanced which may be
worth while mentioning.   It is called the " Theory of
intra-uterine Blessedness," and, remote as it may at first
appear, it certainly has some claim for attention.   The
theory is that in the minds of mature people there still
remain certain vague memories of their *pre-natal* days
in the maternal womb—memories of a life which, though
full of growing vigour and vitality, was yet at that time
one of absolute harmony with the surroundings, and of
perfect peace and contentment, spent within the body of
the mother—the embryo indeed standing in the same

---

[1] See arts. by Margaret Scholes, *Socialist Review*, Nov. and Dec.
1912.

relation to the mother as St. Paul says *we* stand to God, " *in* whom we live and move and have our being "; and that these vague memories of the intra-uterine life in the individual are referred back by the mature mind to a past age in the life of the *race*. Though it would not be easy at present to positively confirm this theory, yet one may say that it is neither improbable nor unworthy of consideration ; also that it bears a certain likeness to the former ones about the Eden-gardens, etc. The well-known parallelism of the Individual history with the Race-history, the " recapitulation " by the embryo of the development of the race, does in fact afford an additional argument for its favorable reception.

These considerations, and what we have said so often in the foregoing chapters about the unity of the Animals (and Early Man) with Nature, and their instinctive and agelong adjustment to the conditions of the world around them, bring us up hard and fast against the following conclusions, which I think we shall find difficult to avoid.

We all recognise the extraordinary grace and beauty, in their different ways, of the (wild) animals ; and not only their beauty but the extreme fitness of their actions and habits to their surroundings—their subtle and penetrating Intelligence in fact. Only we do not generally use the word " Intelligence." We use another word (Instinct)—and rightly perhaps, because their actions are plainly not the result of definite self-conscious reasoning, such as we use, carried out by each individual ; but are (as has been abundantly proved by Samuel Butler and others) the systematic expression of experiences gathered up and sorted out and handed down from generation to generation in the bosom of the race—an Intelligence in fact, or Insight, of larger subtler scope than the other, and belonging to the tribal or racial Being rather than to the isolated individual—a super-consciousness in fact, ramifying afar in space and time.

But if we allow (as we must) this unity and perfection of nature, and this somewhat cosmic character of the mind, to exist among the Animals, we can hardly refuse to believe that there must have been a period when Man, too, hardly as yet differentiated from them, did himself possess these same qualities—perhaps even in greater degree than the animals—of grace and beauty of body, perfection of movement and action, instinctive perception and knowledge (of course in limited spheres) ; and a period when he possessed above all a sense of unity with his fellows and with surrounding Nature which became the ground of a common consciousness between himself and his tribe, similar to that which Maeterlinck, in the case of the Bees, calls the Spirit of the Hive.[1] It would be difficult, nay impossible, to suppose that human beings on their first appearance formed an entire exception in the process of evolution, or that they were completely lacking in the very graces and faculties which we so admire in the animals—only of course we see that (*like* the animals) they would not be *self*-conscious in these matters, and what perception they had of their relations to each other or to the world around them would be largely inarticulate and *sub*-conscious—though none the less real for that.

Let us then grant this preliminary assumption—and it clearly is not a large or hazardous one—and what follows ? It follows—since to-day discord is the rule, and Man has certainly lost the grace, both physical and mental, of the animals—that at some period a break must have occurred in the evolution-process, a discontinuity— similar perhaps to that which occurs in the life of a child at the moment when it is born into the world. Humanity took a new departure ; but a departure which for the moment was signalised as a *loss*—the loss of its former

[1] See *The Life of the Bee* by Maurice Maeterlinck , and for numerous similar cases among other animals, P. Kropotkin's *Mutual Aid : a actor in Evolution.*

harmony and self-adjustment. And the cause or accompaniment of this change was the growth of Self-consciousness. Into the general consciousness of the tribe (in relation to its environment) which, in fact, had constituted the mentality of the animals and of man up to this stage, there now was intruded another kind of consciousness, a consciousness centering round each little individual self and concerned almost entirely with the interests of the latter. Here was evidently a threat to the continuance of the former happy conditions. It was like the appearance of innumerable little ulcers in a human body—a menace which if continued would inevitably lead to the break-up of the body. It meant the loss of tribal harmony and nature-adjustment. It meant instead of unity a myriad conflicting centres; it meant alienation from the spirit of the tribe, the separation of man from man, discord, recrimination, and the fatal unfolding of the sense of sin. The process symbolised itself in the legend of the Fall. Man ate of the Tree of the knowledge of good and evil. Sometimes people wonder why knowledge of any kind —and especially the knowledge of good and evil—should have brought a curse. But the reason is obvious. Into the placid and harmonious life of the animal and human tribes fulfilling their days in obedience to the slow evolutions and age-long mandates of nature, Self-consciousness broke with its inconvenient and impossible query: "How do these arrangements suit *me*? Are they good for me, are they evil for me? I want to know. I *will know*." Evidently knowledge (such knowledge as we understand by the word) only began, and could only begin, by queries relating to the little local self. There was no other way for it to begin. Knowledge and self-consciousness were born, as twins, together. Knowledge therefore meant Sin; for self consciousness meant sin

---

[1] Compare also other myths, like *Cupid and Psyche, Lohengrin*, etc., in which a fatal curiosity leads to tragedy.

142 PAGAN AND CHRISTIAN CREEDS

(and it means sin to-day). Sin is Separation. That is
probably (though disputed) the etymology of the word—
that which *sunders*.[1] The essence of sin is one's separation
from the whole (the tribe or the god) of which one is
a part. And knowledge—which separates subject from
object, and in its inception is necessarily occupied with
the 'good and evil' of the little local self, is the great
engine of this separation. [Mark! I say nothing *against*
this association of Self-consciousness with 'Sin' (so-called)
and 'Knowledge' (so-called). The growth of all three
together is an absolutely necessary part of human evolution,
and to rail against it would be absurd. But we may as
well open our eyes and see the fact straight instead of
blinking it.] The culmination of the process and the
fulfilment of the 'curse' we may watch to-day in the
towering expansion of the self-conscious individualised
Intellect—science as the handmaid of human Greed
devastating the habitable world and destroying its unworthy civilisation. And the process must go on—
necessarily must go on—until Self-consciousness, ceasing
its vain quest (vain in both senses) for the separate domination of life, surrenders itself back again into the arms
of the Mother-consciousness from which it originally sprang
—surrenders itself back, not to be merged in nonentity,
but to be affiliated in loving dependence on and harmony
with the cosmic life.

All this I have dealt with in far more detail in *Civilisation :
its Cause and Cure*, and in *The Art of Creation* ; but I have
only repeated the outline of it as above, because some
such outline is necessary for the proper ordering and
understanding of the points which follow.

We are not concerned now with the ultimate effects of
the 'Fall' of Man or with the present-day fulfilment of

[1] German *Sünde*, sin, and *sonder*, separated ; Dutch *zonde*, sin ;
Latin *sons*, guilty. Not unlikely that the German root *Sühn*, expiation, is connected ; *Sühn-bock*, a scape-goat

the Eden-curse. What we want to understand is how the 'Fall' into self-consciousness led to that great panorama of Ritual and Religion which we have very briefly described and summarised in the preceding chapters of this book. We want for the present to fix our attention on the *commencement* of that process by which man lapsed away from his living community with Nature and his fellows into the desert of discord and toil, while the angels of the flaming sword closed the gates of Paradise behind him.

It is evident I think that in that 'golden' stage when man was simply the crown and perfection of the animals —and it is hardly possible to refuse the belief in such a stage--he possessed in reality all the essentials of Religion.[1] It is not necessary to sentimentalise over him ; he was probably raw and crude in his lusts of hunger and of sex ; he was certainly ignorant and superstitious ; he loved fighting with and persecuting 'enemies' (which things of course all religions to-day—except perhaps the Buddhist —love to do) ; he was dominated often by unreasoning Fear, and was consequently cruel. Yet he was full of that Faith which the animals have to such an admirable degree —unhesitating faith in the inner promptings of his *own* nature ; he had the joy which comes of abounding vitality, springing up like a fountain whose outlet is free and un-hindered ; he rejoiced in an untroubled and unbroken sense of unity with his Tribe, and in elaborate social and friendly institutions within its borders ; he had a marvelous sense-acuteness towards Nature and a gift in that direction verging towards "second-sight" ; strengthened by a conviction—which had never become *conscious* because it had never been *questioned*—of his own personal relation

[1] See S. Reinach, *Cultes, Mythes, etc.*, introduction : " The primitive life of humanity, in so far as it is not purely animal, is religious. Religion is the parent stem which has thrown off, one by one, art, agriculture, law, morality, politics, etc."

to the things outside him, the Earth, the Sky, the Vegetation, the Animals. Of such a Man we get glimpses in
the far past—though indeed only glimpses, for the simple
reason that all our knowledge of him comes through civilised
channels ; and wherever civilisation has touched these
early peoples it has already withered and corrupted them,
even before it has had the sense to properly observe them.
It is sufficient, however, just to mention peoples like some
of the early Pacific Islanders, the Zulus and Kafirs of
South Africa, the Fans of the Congo Region (of whom
Winwood Reade [1] speaks so highly), some of the Malaysian
and Himalayan tribes, the primitive Chinese, and even
the evidence with regard to the neolithic peoples of Europe,[2]
in order to show what I mean.

Perhaps one of the best ideas of the gulf of difference
between the semi-civilised and the quite primal man is
given by A. R. Wallace in his *Life* (vol. i, p. 288) : " A most
unexpected sensation of surprise and delight was my first
meeting and living with man in a state of nature—with
absolute uncontaminated savages ! This was on the
Uaupes river. . . . They were all going about their own
work or pleasure, which had nothing to do with the white
men or their ways ; they walked with the free step of
the independent forest-dweller . . . original and self-sus-
taining as the wild animals of the forests, absolutely independent of civilisation . . . living their own lives in their
own way, as they had done for countless generations before
America was discovered. Indeed the true denizen of the
Amazonian forests, like the forest itself, is unique and
not to be forgotten." Elsewhere [3] Wallace speaks of
the quiet, good-natured, inoffensive character of these
copper-coloured peoples, and of their quickness of hand
and skill, and continues : " their figures are generally

---

[1] *Savage Africa*, ch. xxxvii.
[2] See Kropotkin's *Mutual Aid*, ch. iii.
[3] *Travels on the Amazon* (1853), ch. xvii.

superb; and I have never felt so much pleasure in gazing at the finest statue as at these living illustrations of the beauty of the human form."

Though some of the peoples just mentioned may be said to belong to different grades or stages of human evolution and physically some no doubt were far superior to others, yet they mostly exhibit this simple grace of the bodily and mental organism, as well as that closeness of tribal solidarity of which I have spoken. The immense antiquity of the *clan organisation*, as shown by investigations into early marriage, points to the latter conclusion. Travelers among Bushmen, Hottentots, Fuegians, Esquimaux, Papuans and other peoples—peoples who have been pushed aside into unfavorable areas by the invasion of more warlike and better-equipped races, and who have suffered physically in consequence—confirm this. Kropotkin, speaking of the Hottentots, quotes the German author P. Kolben who traveled among them in 1725 or so. "He knew the Hottentots well and did not pass by their defects in silence, but could not praise their tribal morality highly enough. Their word is sacred, he wrote, they know nothing of the corruption and faithless arts of Europe. They live in great tranquillity and are seldom at war with their neighbours, and are all kindness and goodwill to one another." [1] Kropotkin further says: "Let me remark that when Kolben says 'they are certainly the most friendly, the most liberal and the most benevolent people to one another that ever appeared on the earth' he wrote a sentence which has continually appeared since in the description of savages. When first meeting with primitive races, the Europeans usually make a caricature of their life; but when an intelligent man has stayed among them

[1] P. Kropotkin, *Mutual Aid*, p. 90. W. J. Sollas also speaks in terms of the highest praise of the Bushmen—"their energy, patience, courage, loyalty, affection, good manners and artistic sense" (*Ancient Hunters*, 1915, p. 425).

for a longer time he generally describes them as the 'kindest' or the 'gentlest' race on the earth. These very same words have been applied to the Ostyaks, the Samoyedes, the Eskimos, the Dayaks, the Aleoutes, the Papuas, and so on, by the highest authorities. I also remember having read them applied to the Tunguses, the Tchuktchis, the Sioux, and several others. The very frequency of that high commendation already speaks volumes in itself." [1]

Many of the tribes, like the Aleonts, Eskimos, Dyaks, Papuans, Fuegians, etc., are themselves in the Neolithic stage of culture—though for the reason given above probably degenerated physically from the standard of their neolithic ancestors ; and so the conclusion is forced upon one that there must have been an *immense period*, [2] prior to the first beginnings of ' civilisation,' in which the human tribes in general led a peaceful and friendly life on the earth, comparatively little broken up by dissensions, in close contact with Nature and in that degree of sympathy with and understanding of the Animals which led to the establishment of the Totem system. Though it would be absurd to credit these tribes with any great degree of comfort and well-being according to our modern standards, yet we may well suppose that the memory of this long period lingered on for generations and generations and was ultimately idealised into the Golden Age, in contrast to the succeeding period of everlasting warfare, rancour and strife, which came in with the growth of Property with its greeds and jealousies, and the accen-

[1] *Ibid*, p. 91.
[2] See for estimates of periods *infra* ch. xiii ; also, for the peacefulness of these early peoples, Havelock Ellis on " The Origin of War," where he says " We do not find the *weapons* of warfare or the *wounds* of warfare among these Palaeolithic remains . . . it was with civilisation that the art of killing developed, i.e. within the last 10,000 or 12,000 years when Neolithic men (who became our ancestors) were just arriving."

ERRATUM P. 146 footnote : *instead of* ch. xiii *read* ch. xiv

tuation of Self-consciousness with all its vanities and ambitions.

I say that each tribe at this early stage of development had within it the *essentials* of what we call Religion—namely a bedrock sense of its community with Nature, and of the Common life among its members—a sense so intimate and fundamental that it was hardly aware of itself (any more than the fish is aware of the sea in which it lives), but yet was really the matrix of tribal thought and the spring of tribal action. It was this sense of unity which was destined by the growth of *self-consciousness* to come to light and evidence in the shape of all manner of rituals and ceremonials ; and by the growth of the *imaginative intellect* to embody itself in the figures and forms of all manner of deities.

Let us examine into this a little more closely. A lark soaring in the eye of the sun, and singing rapt between its " heaven and home " realises no doubt in actual fact all that those two words mean to us ; yet its realisation is quite subconscious. It does not define its own experience : it *feels* but it does not *think*. In order to come to the stage of *thinking* it would perhaps be necessary that the lark should be exiled from the earth and the sky, and confined in a cage. Early Man *felt* the great truths and realities of Life--often I believe more purely than we do —but he could not give form to his experience. *That* stage came when he began to lose touch with these realities ; and it showed itself in rites and ceremonials. The inbreak of self-consciousness brought *out* the facts of his inner life into ritualistic and afterwards into intellectual forms.

Let me give examples. For a long time the Tribe is all in all ; the individual is completely subject to the ' Spirit of the Hive ' ; he does not even *think* of contravening it Then the day comes when self interest, as apart from the Tribe, becomes sufficiently strong to drive him against some tribal custom. He breaks the *tabu* ;

he eats the forbidden apple ; he sins against the tribe, and is cast out. Suddenly he finds himself an exile, lonely, contemned and deserted. A horrible sense of distress seizes him—something of which he had no experience before. He tries to think about it all, to understand the situation, but is dazed and cannot arrive at any conclusion. His one *necessity* is Reconciliation, Atonement. He finds he cannot *live* outside of and alienated from his tribe. He makes a Sacrifice, an offering to his fellows, as a seal of sincerity—an offering of his own bodily suffering or precious blood, or the blood of some food-animal, or some valuable gift or other—if only he may be allowed to return. The offering is accepted. The ritual is performed ; and he is received back. I have already spoken of this perfectly natural evolution of the twin-ideas of Sin and Sacrifice, so I need not enlarge upon the subject. But two things we may note here : (1) that the ritual, being so concrete (and often severe), graves itself on the minds of those concerned, and expresses the feelings of the tribe, with an intensity and sharpness of outline which no words could rival, and (2) that such rituals may have, and probably did, come into use even while language itself was in an infantile condition and incapable of dealing with the psychological situation except by symbols. They, the rituals, were the first effort of the primitive mind to get beyond subconscious feeling and emerge into a world of forms and definite thought.

Let us carry the particular instance, given above, a stage farther, even to the confines of abstract Thought and Philosophy. I have spoken of " The Spirit of the Hive " as if the term were applicable to the Human as well as to the Bee tribe. The individual bee obviously has never *thought* about that ' Spirit,' nor mentally understood what Maeterlinck means by it ; and yet in terms of actual experience it is an intense reality to the bee (ordaining for instance on some fateful day the slaughter of all the drones), controlling bee-movements and bee-morality generally. The individual tribesman similarly steeped in the age-long human life of his fellows has never thought of the Tribe as an ordaining being or Spirit, separate from himself—*till* that day when he is exiled and outcast from it. *Then* he sees himself and the tribe as two opposing beings, himself of course an Intelligence or Spirit in his own limited degree, the Tribe as a much greater Intelligence or Spirit, standing against and over him. From that day the conception of a god arises on him. It may be only a totem-god—a divine Grizzly-Bear or what not—but still a god or supernatural Presence, embodied in the life of the tribe. This is what Sin has taught him.[1] This is what Fear, founded on self-consciousness, has revealed to him. The revelation may be true, or it may be fallacious (I do not prejudge it) ; but there it is—the beginning of that long series of human evolutions which we call Religion.

[For when the human mind has reached that stage of consciousness in which each man realises his own 'self' as a rational and consistent being, "looking before and after," then, as I have said already, the mind projects on the background of Nature similarly rational Presences which we may call 'Gods' ; and at that stage 'Religion' begins. Before that, when the mind is quite unformed and dream-like, and consists chiefly of broken and scattered rays, and when distinct self-consciousness is hardly yet developed, then the presences imagined in Nature are merely flickering and intermittent phantoms, and their propitiation and placation comes more properly under the head of 'Magic.']

So much for the genesis of the religious ideas of Sin

[1] It is to be noted, in that charming idyll of the Eden garden, that it is only *after* eating of the forbidden fruit that Adam and Eve perceive the Lord God walking in the garden, and converse with him Genesis iii. 8).

and Sacrifice, and the rites connected with these ideas—
their genesis through the in-break of self-consciousness
upon the corporate *sub*-consciousness of the life of the
Community. But an exactly similar process may be
observed in the case of the other religious ideas.

I spoke of the doctrine of the *second birth*, and the rites
connected with it both in Paganism and in Christianity.
There is much to show that among quite primitive peoples
there is less of shrinking from death and more of certainty
about a continued life after death than we generally find
among more intellectual and civilised folk. It is, or has
been, quite common among many tribes for the old and
decrepit, who are becoming a burden to their fellows,
to offer themselves for happy dispatch, and to take willing
part in the ceremonial preparations for their own extinction ; and this readiness is encouraged by their naïve
and untroubled belief in a speedy transference to " happy
hunting-grounds " beyond the grave. The truth is that
when, as in such cases, the tribal life is very whole and
unbroken—each individual identifying himself completely
with the tribe—the idea of the individual's being dropped
out at death, and left behind by the tribe, hardly arises.
The individual is the tribe, has no other existence. The
tribe goes on, living a life which is eternal, and only changes
its hunting-grounds ; and the individual, identified with
the tribe, feels in some subconscious way the same about
himself.

But when one member has broken faith with the tribe,
when he has sinned against it and become an outcast—
ah ! then the terrors of death and extinction loom large
upon him. " The wages of sin is death." There comes
a period in the evolution of tribal life when the primitive
bonds are loosening, when the tendency towards *self*-will
and *self*-determination (so necessary of course in the long
run for the evolution of humanity) becomes a real danger
to the tribe, and a terror to the wise men and elders of

the community. It is seen that the children inherit this
tendency—even from their infancy. They are no longer
mere animals, easily herded ; it seems that they are born
in sin—or at least in ignorance and neglect of their tribal
life and calling. The only cure is that they *must be born
again*. They must deliberately and of set purpose be
adopted into the tribe, and be made to realise, even severely,
in their own persons what is happening. They must go
through the initiations necessary to impress this upon
them. Thus a whole series of solemn rites spring up,
different no doubt in every locality, but all having the
same object and purpose. [And one can understand how
the necessity of such initiations and second birth may
easily have made itself felt in every race, at some stage
of its evolution—and *that* quite as a spontaneous growth,
and independently of any contagion of example caught
from other races.]

The same may be said about the world-wide practice
of the Eucharist. No more effective method exists for
impressing on the members of a body their community
of life with each other, and causing them to forget their
jangling self-interests, than to hold a feast in common.
It is a method which has been honoured in all ages as well
as to-day. But when the flesh partaken of at the feast
is that of the Totem—the guardian and presiding genius
of the tribe—or perhaps of one of its chief food-animals—
then clearly the feast takes on a holy and solemn character.
It becomes a sacrament of unity—of the unity of all with
the tribe, and with each other. Self-interests and self-
consciousnesses are for the time submerged, and the
common life asserts itself ; but here again we see that a
custom like this would not come into being as a deliberate
rite until self-consciousness and the divisions consequent
thereon had grown to be an obvious evil. The herd-
animals (cows, sheep, and so forth) do not have Eucharists,

simply because they are sensible enough to feed along the
same pastures without quarrelling over the richest tufts
of grass.

When the flesh partaken of (either actually or sym-
bolically) is not that of a divinised animal, but the flesh
of a human-formed god—as in the mysteries of Dionysus
or Osiris or Christ—then we are led to suspect (and of
course this theory is widely held and supported) that the
rites date from a very far-back period when a human
being, as representative of the tribe, was actually slain,
dismembered and partly devoured ; though as time went
on, the rite gradually became glossed over and mitigated
into a love-communion through the sharing of bread and
wine.

It is curious anyhow that the dismemberment or division
into fragments of the body of a god (as in the case of
Dionysus, Osiris, Attis, Prajápati and others) should be so
frequent a tenet of the old religions, and so commonly associated with a love-feast of reconciliation and resurrection.
It may be fairly interpreted as a symbol of Nature-dismem-
berment in Winter and resurrection in Spring ; but we must
also not forget that it may (and indeed must) have stood
as an allegory of *tribal* dismemberment and reconciliation
—the tribe, conceived of as a divinity, having thus suffered
and died through the inbreak of sin and the self-motive,
and risen again into wholeness by the redemption of love
and sacrifice. Whatever view the rank and file of the
tribe may have taken of the matter, I think it is incon-
testable that the more thoughtful regarded these rites as
full of mystic and spiritual meaning. It is of the nature,
as I have said before, of these early symbols and ceremonies
that they held so many meanings in solution ; and it is
this fact which gave them a poetic or creative quality,
and their great hold upon the public mind.

I use the word " tribe " in many places here as a matter
of convenience ; not forgetting however that in some

cases " clan " might be more appropriate, as referring to a section of a tribe ; or " people " or " folk " as referring to unions of *several* tribes. It is impossible of course to follow out all the gradations of organisation from tribal up to national life ; but it may be remembered that while animal totems prevail as a rule in the earlier stages, human-formed gods become more conspicuous in the later developments. All through, the practice of the Eucharist goes on, in varying forms adapting itself to the surrounding conditions ; and where in the later societies a religion like Mithraism or Christianity includes people of very various race, the Rite loses quite naturally its tribal significance and becomes a celebration of allegiance to a particular god—of unity within a special Church, in fact. Ultimately it may become--as for a brief moment in the history of the early Christians it seemed likely to do—a celebration of allegiance to all Humanity, irrespective of race or creed or colour of skin or of mind ; though unfortunately that day seems still far distant and remains yet unrealised. It must not be overlooked, however, that the religion of the Persian Bâb, first promulgated in 1845 to 1850--and a subject I shall deal with presently--had as a matter of fact this all embracing and universal scope.

To return to the Golden Age or Garden of Eden. Our conclusion seems to be that there really was such a period of comparative harmony in human life--to which later generations were justified in looking back, and looking back with regret. It corresponded in the psychology of human Evolution to stage One. The second stage was that of the Fall ; and so one is inevitably led to the conjecture and the hope that a third stage will redeem the earth and its inhabitants to a condition of comparative blessedness.

X

THE SAVIOUR-GOD AND THE VIRGIN-MOTHER

FROM the consideration of the world-wide belief in a past Golden Age, and the world-wide practice of the Eucharist, in the sense indicated in the last chapter, to that of the equally widespread belief in a human-divine Saviour, is a brief and easy step. Some thirty years ago, dealing with this subject,[1] I wrote as follows :—" The true Self of man consists in his organic relation with the whole body of his fellows ; and when the man abandons his true Self he abandons also his true relation to his fellows. The mass-Man must rule in each unit-man, else the unit-man will drop off and die. But when the outer man tries to separate himself from the inner, the unit-man from the mass-Man, then the reign of individuality begins—a false and impossible individuality of course, but the only means of coming to the consciousness of the true individuality." And further, " Thus this divinity in each creature, being that which constitutes it and causes it to cohere together, was conceived of as that creature's saviour, healer—healer of wounds of body and wounds of heart—the Man within the man, whom it was not only possible to know, but whom to know and be united with was the alone salvation. This, I take it, was the law of health—and of holiness—as

---

[1] See *Civilisation : its Cause and Cure*, ch. i.

accepted at some elder time of human history, and by us seen as through a glass darkly."

I think it is impossible not to see—however much in our pride of Civilisation (!) we like to jeer at the pettinesses of tribal life—that these elder people perceived as a matter of fact and direct consciousness the redeeming presence (within each unit-member of the group) of the larger life to which he belonged. This larger life was a reality— "a Presence to be felt and known"; and whether he called it by the name of a Totem-animal, or by the name of a Nature-divinity, or by the name of some gracious human-limbed God—some Hercules, Mithra, Attis, Orpheus, or what-not—or even by the great name of Humanity itself, it was still in any case the Saviour, the living incarnate Being by the realisation of whose presence the little mortal could be lifted out of exile and error and death and suffering into splendour and life eternal.

It is impossible, I think, not to see that the myriad worship of "Saviours" all over the world, from China to Peru, can only be ascribed to the natural working of some such law of human and tribal psychology—from earliest times and in all races the same—springing up quite spontaneously and independently, and (so far) unaffected by the mere contagion of local tradition. To suppose that the Devil, long before the advent of Christianity, put the idea into the heads of all these earlier folk, is really to pay *too* great a compliment both to the power and the ingenuity of his Satanic Majesty—though the ingenuity with which the early Church *did* itself suppress all information about these pre-Christian Saviours almost rivals that which it credited to Satan! And on the other hand to suppose this marvellous and universal consent of belief to have sprung by mere contagion from one accidental source would seem equally far fetched and unlikely.

But almost more remarkable than the world-encircling belief in human-divine Saviours is the equally widespread legend of their birth from Virgin-mothers.   There is hardly a god—as we have already had occasion to see—whose worship as a benefactor of mankind attained popularity in any of the four continents, Europe, Asia, Africa and America—who was not reported to have been born from a Virgin, or at least from a mother who owed the Child not to any earthly father, but to an impregnation from Heaven.   And this seems at first sight all the more astonishing because the belief in the possibility of such a thing is so entirely out of the line of our modern thought. So that while it would seem not unnatural that such a legend should have sprung up spontaneously in some odd benighted corner of the world, we find it very difficult to understand how in that case it should have spread so rapidly in every direction, or—if it did not spread—how we are to account for its *spontaneous* appearance in all these widely sundered regions.

I think here, and for the understanding of this problem, we are thrown back upon a very early age of human evolution—the age of Magic.   Before any settled science or philosophy or religion existed, there were still certain Things—and consequently also certain Words which had a tremendous influence on the human mind, which in fact affected it deeply.   Such a word, for instance, is ' Thunder ' ; to hear thunder, to imitate it, even to mention it, are sure ways of rousing superstitious attention and imagination. Such another word is ' Serpent,' another ' Tree,' and so forth.   There is no one who is insensible to the reverberation of these and other such words and images [1] ;   and among them, standing prominently out, are the two ' Mother ' and ' Virgin.'   The word Mother touches the deepest springs of human feeling.   As the earliest word

[1] Nor is it difficult to see how out of the discreet use of such words and images, combined with elementary forms like the square, the triangle and the circle, and elementary numbers like 3, 4, 5, etc., quite a science, so to speak, of Magic arose.

learnt and clung to by the child, it twines itself with the heart-strings of the man even to his latest day. Nor must we forget that in a primitive state of society (the Matriarchate) that influence was probably even greater than now; for the father of the child being (often as not) *unknown* the attachment to the mother was all the more intense and undivided. The word Mother had a magic about it which has remained even until to-day. But if that word rooted itself deep in the heart of the Child, the other word ' virgin ' had an obvious magic for the full grown and sexually mature Man—a magic which it, too, has never lost.

There is ample evidence that one of the very earliest objects of human worship was the Earth itself, conceived of as the fertile Mother of all things. Gaia or Gê (the earth) had temples and altars in almost all the cities of Greece. Rhea or Cybele, sprung from the Earth, was " mother of all the gods." Demeter (" earth mother ") was honoured far and wide as the gracious patroness of the crops and vegetation. Ceres, of course, the same. Maia in the Indian mythology and Isis in the Egyptian are forms of Nature and the Earth-spirit, represented as female; and so forth. The Earth, in these ancient cults, was the mystic source of all life, and to it, as a propitiation, life of all kinds was sacrificed. [There are strange accounts of a huge fire being made, with an altar to Cybele in the midst, and of deer and fawns and wild animals, and birds and sheep and corn and fruits being thrown pell-mell into the flames.[1]] It was, in a way, the most natural, as it seems to have been the earliest and most spontaneous of cults—the worship of the Earth-mother, the all-producing eternal source of life, and on account of her never-failing ever-renewed fertility conceived of as an immortal Virgin.

But when the Saviour legend sprang up as indeed I think it must have sprung up, in tribe after tribe and

[1] See Pausanias iv. 32. 6; and Lucian, *De Syria Dea*, 49.

people after people, independently—then, whether it
sprang from the divinisation of some actual man who
showed the way of light and deliverance to his fellows
" sitting in darkness," or whether from the personification
of the tribe itself as a god, in either case the question of
the hero's parentage was bound to arise. If the ' saviour '
was plainly a personification of the tribe, it was obviously
impossible to suppose him the son of a mortal mother.
In that case—and as the tribe was generally traced in
the legends to some primeval Animal or Mountain or thing
of Nature—it was probably easy to think of him (the
saviour) as also born out of Nature's womb, descended
perhaps from that pure Virgin of the World who *is* the
Earth and Nature, who rules the skies at night, and stands
in the changing phases of the Moon, and is worshiped
(as we have seen) in the great constellation Virgo. If,
on the other hand, he was the divinisation of some actual
man, more or less known either personally or by tradition
to his fellows, then in all probability the name of his mortal
mother would be recognised and accepted ; but as to his
father, that side of parentage being, as we have said,
generally very uncertain, it would be easy to suppose some
heavenly Annunciation, the midnight visit of a God, and
what is usually termed a Virgin-birth.

There are two elements to be remembered here, as
conspiring to this conclusion. One is the condition of
affairs in a remote matriarchal period, when descent was
reckoned always through the maternal line, and the
fatherhood in each generation was obscure or unknown
or commonly left out of account ; and the other is the
fact—so strange and difficult for us to realise—that among
some very primitive peoples, like the Australian aborigines,
the necessity for a woman to have intercourse with a male,
in order to bring about conception and child-birth, was
actually not recognised. Scientific observation had not
always got as far as that, and the matter was still under

the domain of Magic! [1] A Virgin-Mother was therefore a quite imaginable (not to say ' conceivable ') thing ; and indeed a very beautiful and fascinating thing, combining in one image the potent magic of two very wonderful words. It does not seem impossible that considerations of this kind led to the adoption of the doctrine or legend of the virgin-mother and the heavenly father among so many races and in so many localities—even without any contagion of tradition among them.

Anyhow, and as a matter of fact, the world-wide dissemination of the legend *is* most remarkable. Zeus, Father of the gods, visited Semele, it will be remembered, in the form of a thunderstorm ; and she gave birth to the great saviour and deliverer Dionysus. Zeus, again, impregnated Danae in a shower of gold ; and the child was Perseus, who slew the Gorgons (the powers of darkness) and saved Andromeda (the human soul [2]). Devaki, the radiant Virgin of the Hindu mythology, became the wife of the god Vishnu and bore Krishna, the beloved hero and prototype of Christ. With regard to Buddha St. Jerome says [3] " It is handed down among the Gymnosophists of India that Buddha, the founder of their system, was brought forth by a Virgin from her side." The Egyptian Isis, with the child Horus on her knee, was honoured centuries before the Christian era, and worshiped under the names of " Our Lady," " Queen of Heaven," " Star of the Sea," " Mother of God," and so forth. Before her, Neith, the

---

[1] Probably the long period (nine months) elapsing between cohabitation and childbirth confused early speculation on the subject. Then clearly cohabitation was *not* always followed by childbirth. And, more important still, the number of virgins of a mature age in primitive societies was so very minute that the fact of their childlessness attracted no attention—whereas in *our* societies the sterility of the whole class is patent to everyone.

[2] For this interpretation of the word *Andromeda* see *The Perfect Way* by Edward Maitland, preface to First Edition, 1881.

[3] *Contra Jovian*, Book I ; and quoted by Rhys Davids in his *Buddhism*, p. 183.

Virgin of the World, whose figure bends from the sky over the earthly plains and the children of men, was acclaimed as mother of the great god Osiris. The saviour Mithra, too, was born of a Virgin, as we have had occasion to notice before ; and on the Mithraic monuments the mother suckling her child is a not uncommon figure.[1]

The old Teutonic goddess Hertha (the Earth) was a Virgin, but was impregnated by the heavenly Spirit (the Sky) ; and her image with a child in her arms was to be seen in the sacred groves of Germany.[2] The Scandinavian Frigga, in much the same way, being caught in the embraces of Odin, the All-father, conceived and bore a son, the blessed Balder, healer and saviour of mankind. Quetzalcoatl, the (crucified) saviour of the Aztecs, was the son of Chimalman, the Virgin Queen of Heaven.[3] Even the Chinese had a mother-goddess and virgin with child in her arms[4] ; and the ancient Etruscans the same.[5]

Finally, we have the curiously large number of *black* virgin mothers who are or have been worshiped. Not only cases like Devaki the Indian goddess, or Isis the Egyptian, who would naturally appear black-skinned or dark ; but the large number of images and paintings of the same kind, yet extant—especially in the Italian churches—and passing for representations of Mary and

[1] See Doane's *Bible Myths*, p. 332, and Dupuis' *Origins of Religious Beliefs.*

[2] R. P. Knight's *Ancient Art and Mythology*, p. 21.

[3] See Kingsborough's *Mexican Antiquities*, vol. vi, p. 176, where it is said " an ambassador was sent from heaven on an embassy to a Virgin of Tulan, called Chimalman . . . announcing that it was the will of the God that she should conceive a son ; and having delivered her the message he rose and left the house ; and as soon as he had left it she conceived a son, without connexion with man, who was called Quetzalcoatle, who they say is the god of air." Further, it is explained that Quetzalcoatl sacrificed himself, drawing forth his own blood with thorns ; and that the word Quetzalcoatlo-topitzin means " our well-beloved son."

[4] Doane, p. 327.

[5] See Inman's *Pagan and Christian Symbolism*, p. 27.

the infant Jesus. Such are the well-known image in the chapel at Loretto, and images and paintings besides in the churches at Genoa, Pisa, Padua, Munich and other places. It is difficult not to regard these as very old Pagan or pre-Christian relics which lingered on into Christian times and were baptised anew—as indeed we know many relics and images actually were—into the service of the Church. " Great is Diana of the Ephesians " ; and there is I believe more than one black figure extant of this Diana, who, though of course a virgin, is represented with innumerable breasts [1]—not unlike some of the archaic statues of Artemis and Isis. At Paris, far on into Christian times there was, it is said, on the site of the present Cathedral of Notre Dame, a Temple dedicated to ' our Lady ' Isis ; and images belonging to the earlier shrine would in all probability be preserved with altered name in the later.

All this illustrates not only the wide diffusion of the doctrine of the Virgin-mother, but its extreme antiquity. The subject is obscure, and worthy of more consideration than has yet been accorded to it ; and I do not feel able to add anything to the tentative explanations given a page or two back, except perhaps to suppose that the vision of the Perfect Man hovered dimly over the mind of the human race on its first emergence from the purely animal stage ; and that a quite natural speculation with regard to such a being was that he would be born from a Perfect Woman—who according to early ideas would necessarily be the Virgin Earth itself, mother of all things. Anyhow it was a wonderful Intuition, slumbering as it would seem in the breast of early man, that the Great Earth after giving birth to all living creatures would at last bring forth a Child who should become the Saviour of the human race.

There is of course the further theory, entertained by

[1] See illustration, p. 30, in Inman's *Pagan and Christian Symbolism*.

some, that virgin-parturition—a kind of Parthenogenesis—
has as a matter of fact occasionally occurred among mortal
women, and even still does occur.   I should be the last
to deny the *possibility* of this (or of anything else in Nature),
but, seeing the immense difficulties in the way of *proof*
of any such asserted case, and the absence so far of any
thoroughly attested and verified instance, it would, I
think, be advisable to leave this theory out of account
at present.

But whether any of the *explanations* spoken of are right
or wrong, and whatever explanation we adopt, there
remains the *fact* of the universality over the world of this
legend—affording another instance of the practical solidarity and continuity of the Pagan Creeds with Christianity.

XI

RITUAL DANCING

IT is unnecessary to labour the conclusion of the last **two**
or three chapters, namely that Christianity grew out of
the former Pagan Creeds and is in its general outlook and
origins continuous and of one piece with them. I have
not attempted to bring together *all* the evidence in favour
of this contention, as such a work would be too vast, but
more illustrations of its truth will doubtless occur to readers,
or will emerge as we proceed.

I think we may take it as proved (1) that from the
earliest ages, and before History, a great body of religious
belief and ritual—first appearing among very primitive
and unformed folk, whom we should call ' savages '—has
come slowly down, broadening and differentiating itself
on the way into a great variety of forms, but embodying
always certain main ideas which became in time the
accepted doctrines of the later Churches—the Indian,
the Egyptian, the Mithraic, the Christian, and so forth.
What these ideas in their general outline have been we
can perhaps best judge from our " Apostles' Creed," **as**
it is recited every Sunday in our churches.

" I believe in God the Father Almighty, Maker of heaven
and earth : And in Jesus Christ his only Son our Lord,
who was conceived by the Holy Ghost, born of the Virgin
Mary, suffered under Pontius Pilate, was crucified, dead

and buried. He descended into Hell; the third day he
rose again from the dead, He ascended into heaven, and
sitteth on the right hand of God the Father Almighty;
from thence he shall come to judge the quick and the dead.
I believe in the Holy Ghost; the holy Catholic Church;
the communion of Saints; the Forgiveness of sins; the
Resurrection of the body, and the life everlasting.
Amen."

Here we have the All-Father and Creator, descending
from the Sky in the form of a spirit to impregnate the
earthly Virgin-mother, who thus gives birth to a Saviour-
hero. The latter is slain by the powers of Evil, is buried
and descends into the lower world, but rises again as
God into heaven and becomes the leader and judge of
mankind. We have the confirmation of the Church (or,
in earlier times, of the Tribe) by means of a Eucharist
or Communion which binds together all the members,
living or dead, and restores errant individuals through
the Sacrifice of the hero and the Forgiveness of their sins;
and we have the belief in a bodily Resurrection and continued life of the members within the fold of the Church
(or Tribe), itself regarded as eternal.

One has only, instead of the word 'Jesus,' to read
Dionysus or Krishna or Hercules or Osiris or Attis, and
instead of 'Mary' to insert Semele or Devaki or Alcmene
or Neith or Nana, and for Pontius Pilate to use the name
of any terrestrial tyrant who comes into the corresponding
story, and lo! the creed fits in all particulars into the
rites and worship of a pagan god. I need not enlarge
upon a thesis which is self-evident from all that has gone
before. I do not say, of course, that *all* the religious beliefs
of Paganism are included and summarised in our Apostles'
Creed, for—as I shall have occasion to note in the next
chapter—I think some very important religious elements
are there *omitted*; but I do think that all the beliefs which
are summarised in the said creed had already been fully

represented and elaborately expressed in the non-Christian religions and rituals of Paganism.

Further (2) I think we may safely say that there is no certain proof that the body of beliefs just mentioned sprang from any one particular centre far back and radiated thence by dissemination and mental contagion over the rest of the world ; but the evidence rather shows that these beliefs were, for the most part, the *spontaneous* outgrowths (in various localities) of the human mind at certain stages of its evolution ; that they appeared, in the different races and peoples, at different periods according to the degree of evolution, and were largely independent of intercourse and contagion, though of course, in cases, considerably influenced by it ; and that one great and all-important occasion and provocative of these beliefs was actually the *rise of self-consciousness*—that is, the coming of the mind to a more or less distinct awareness of itself and of its own operation, and the consequent development and growth of Individualism, and of the Self-centred attitude in human thought and action.

In the third place (3) I think we may see—and this is the special subject of the present chapter—that at a very early period, when humanity was hardly capable of systematic expression in what we call Philosophy or Science, it could not well rise to an ordered and literary expression of its beliefs, such as we find in the later religions and the ' Churches ' (Babylonian, Jewish, East Indian, Christian, or what-not), and yet that it *felt* these beliefs very intensely and was urged, almost compelled, to their utterance in some form or other. And so it came about that people expressed themselves in a vast mass of ritual and myth —customs, ceremonies, legends, stories—which on account of their popular and concrete form were handed down for generations, and some of which linger on still in the midst of our modern civilisation. These rituals and legends were, many of them, absurd enough, rambling and childish in character, and preposterous in conception, yet they gave the expression needed ; and some of them of course, as we have seen, were full of meaning and suggestion.

A critical and commercial Civilisation, such as ours, in which (notwithstanding much *talk* about Art) the artistic sense is greatly lacking, or at any rate but little diffused, does not as a rule understand that poetic *rites*, in the evolution of peoples, came naturally before anything like ordered poems or philosophy or systematised *views* about life and religion—such as *we* love to wallow in ! Things were *felt* before they were spoken. The loading of diseases into disease-boats, of sins onto scapegoats, the propitiation of the forces of nature by victims, human or animal, sacrifices, ceremonies of re-birth, eucharistic feasts, sexual communions, orgiastic celebrations of the common life, and a host of other things—all *said* plainly enough what was meant, but not in *words*. Partly no doubt it was that at some early time words were more difficult of command and less flexible in use than actions (and at all times are they not less expressive ?). Partly it was that mankind was in the child-stage. The Child delights in ritual, in symbol, in expression through material objects and actions :

> See, at his feet some little plan or chart,
> Some fragment from his dream of human life,
> Shaped by himself with newly-learned art ;
>   A wedding or a festival,
>   A mourning or a funeral ;
>   And this hath now his heart.

And primitive man in the child-stage felt a positive joy in ritual celebrations, and indulged in expressions which we but little understand ; for these had then his heart.

One of the most pregnant of these expressions was *Dancing*. Children dance instinctively. They dance with rage ; they dance with joy, with sheer vitality ; they dance with pain, or sometimes with savage glee at the suffering of others; they delight in mimic combats, or in animal plays and disguises. There are such things as Courting-dances, when the mature male and female go through a ritual together—not only in civilised ball-rooms and the back-parlours of inns, but in the farmyards where the rooster pays his addresses to the hen, or the yearling bull to the cow—with quite recognised formalities; there are elaborate ceremonials performed by the Australian bower-birds and many other animals. All these things— at any rate in children and animals—come before speech; and anyhow we may say that *love-rites*, even in mature and civilised man, hardly *admit* of speech. Words only vulgarise love and blunt its edge.

So Dance to the savage and the early man was not merely an amusement or a gymnastic exercise (as the books often try to make out), but it was also a serious and intimate part of life, an expression of religion and the relation of man to non-human Powers. Imagine a young dancer—and the admitted age for ritual dancing was commonly from about eighteen to thirty—coming forward on the dancing-ground or platform for the *invocation of Rain*. We have unfortunately no kinematic records, but it is not impossible or very difficult to imagine the various gestures and movements which might be considered appropriate to such a rite in different localities or among different peoples. A modern student of Dalcroze Eurhythmics would find the problem easy. After a time a certain ritual dance (for rain) would become stereotyped and generally adopted. Or imagine a young Greek leading an invocation to Apollo *to stay some plague* which was ravaging the country. He might well be accompanied by a small body of co-dancers; but he would be the leader and chief representative. Or it might be a war-dance as a more or less magical preparation for the raid or foray. We are familiar enough with accounts of war-dances among

American Indians. C. O. Müller in his *History and Antiquities of the Doric Race* [1] gives the following account of the Pyrrhic dance among the Greeks, which was danced in full armour :—" Plato says that it imitated all the attitudes of defence, by avoiding a thrust or a cast, retreating, springing up, and crouching—as also the opposite movements of attack with arrows and lances, and also of every kind of thrust. So strong was the attachment to this dance at Sparta that, long after it had in the other Greek states degenerated into a Bacchanalian revel, it was still danced by the Spartans as a warlike exercise, and boys of fifteen were instructed in it." Of the *Hunting-dance* I have already given instances. [2] It always had the character of Magic about it, by which the game or quarry might presumably be influenced ; and it can easily be understood that if the Hunt was not successful the blame might well be attributed to some neglect of the usual ritual mimes or movements—no laughing matter for the leader of the dance.

Or there were dances belonging to the ceremonies of *Initiation*— dances both by the initiators and the initiated. Jane E. Harrison in *Themis* (p. 24) says, " Instruction among savage peoples is always imparted in more or less mimetic dances. At initiation you learn certain dances which confer on you definite social status. When a man is too old to dance, he hands over his dance to another and a younger, and he then among some tribes ceases to exist socially. . . . The dances taught to boys at initiation are frequently if not always *armed* dances. These are not necessarily warlike. The accoutrement of spear and shield was in part decorative, in part a provision for making the necessary hubbub." (Here Miss Harrison

---

[1] Book IV, ch. 6, § 7.

[2] See also Winwood Reade's *Savage Africa*, ch. xviii, in which he speaks of the ' gorilla dance,' before hunting gorillas, as a " religious festival."

reproduces a photograph of an Initiation dance among
the Akikúyu of British East Africa.) The Initiation-
dances blend insensibly and naturally with the *Mystery
and Religion dances*, for indeed initiation was for the most
part an instruction in the mysteries and social rites of
the Tribe. They were the expression of things which
would be hard even for us, and which for rude folk would
be impossible, to put into definite words. Hence arose
the expression—whose meaning has been much discussed
by the learned—" to dance out (ἐξορχεῖσθαι) a mystery." [1]
Lucian, in a much-quoted passage,[2] observes: "You cannot
find a single ancient mystery in which there is not dancing
. . . and this much all men know, that most people say
of the revealers of the mysteries that they ' dance them
out.'" Andrew Lang, commenting on this passage,[3]
continues : " Clemens of Alexandria uses the same term
when speaking of his own ' appalling revelations.' So
closely connected are mysteries with dancing among savages
that when Mr. Orpen asked Qing, the Bushman hunter,
about some doctrines in which Qing was not initiated, he said :
' Only the initiated men of that dance know these things.'
To ' dance ' this or that means to be acquainted with this
or that myth, which is represented in a dance or *ballet
d'action*. So widely distributed is the practice that Acosta
in an interesting passage mentions it as familiar to the
people of Peru before and after the Spanish conquest."
[And we may say that when the ' mysteries ' are of a sexual
nature it can easily be understood that to ' dance them
out ' is the only way of explaining them !]

Thus we begin to appreciate the serious nature and the
importance of the dance among primitive folk. To dub
a youth " a good dancer " is to pay him a great compliment.

---

[1] Meaning apparently either simply to represent, or, sometimes
to *divulge*, a mystery.

[2] περὶ Ὀρχήσεως, ch. xv. 277.

[3] *Myth, Ritual and Religion*, i, 272.

Among the well-known inscriptions on the rocks in the island of Thera in the Ægean sea there are many which record in deeply graven letters the friendship and devotion to each other of Spartan warrior-comrades ; it seems strange at first to find how often such an epithet of praise occurs as Bathycles *dances well,* Eumelos is a *perfect dancer* (ἀριστος ὀρχεστας). One hardly in general expects one warrior to praise another for his dancing ! But when one realises what is really meant—namely the fitness of the loved comrade to lead in religious and magical rituals —then indeed the compliment takes on a new complexion. Religious dances, in dedication to a god, have of course been honoured in every country. Müller, in the work just cited,[1] describes a lively dance called the *hyporchema* which, accompanied by songs, was used in the worship of Apollo. " In this, besides the chorus of singers who usually danced around *the blazing altar,* several persons were appointed to accompany the action of the poem with an appropriate pantomimic display." It was probably some similar dance which is recorded in Exodus, ch. xxxii, when Aaron made the Israelites a golden Calf (image of the Egyptian Apis). There was an altar and a fire and burnt offerings for sacrifice, and the people dancing around. Whether in the Apollo ritual the dancers were naked I cannot say, but in the affair of the golden Calf they evidently were, for it will be remembered that it was just this which upset Moses' equanimity so badly— " when he *saw that the people were naked* "—and led to the breaking of the two tables of stone and the slaughter of some thousands of folk. It will be remembered also that David on a sacrificial occasion danced naked before the Lord.[2]

It may seem strange that dances in honour of a god should be held naked ; but there is abundant evidence that this

---

[1] Book II, ch. viii, § 14.
[2] 2 Sam. vi.

was frequently the case, and it leads to an interesting speculation. Many of these rituals undoubtedly owed their sanctity and solemnity to their extreme antiquity. They came down in fact from very far back times when the average man or woman—as in some of the Central African tribes to-day—wore simply nothing at all ; and like all religious ceremonies they tended to preserve their forms long after surrounding customs and conditions had altered. Consequently nakedness lingered on in sacrificial and other rites into periods when in ordinary life it had come to be abandoned or thought indecent and shameful. This comes out very clearly in both instances above-quoted from the Bible. For in Exodus xxxii. 25 it is said that " Aaron had made them (the dancers) naked *unto their shame* among their enemies (*read* opponents)," and in 2 Sam. vi. 20 we are told that Michal came out and sarcastically rebuked the " glorious king of Israel " for " shamelessly uncovering himself, like a vain fellow " (for which rebuke, I am sorry to say, David took a mean revenge on Michal). In both cases evidently custom had so far changed that to a considerable section of the population these naked exhibitions had become indecent, though as parts of an acknowledged ritual they were still retained and supported by others. The same conclusion may be derived from the commands recorded in Exodus xx. 26 and xxviii. 42, that the priests be not " uncovered " before the altar—commands which would hardly have been needed had not the practice been in vogue.

Then there were dances (partly magical or religious) performed at rustic and agricultural festivals, like the *Epilenios*, celebrated in Greece at the gathering of the grapes.[1] Of such a dance we get a glimpse in the Bible (Judges xxi. 20) when the elders advised the children of Benjamin to go out and lie in wait in the vineyards, at the time of the yearly feast ; and " when the daughters of Shiloh come out

[1] Επιλήνιοι ὕμνοι: hymns sung over the winepress (Dictionary).

to dance in the dances, then come ye out of the vineyards and catch you every man a wife from the daughters of Shiloh "—a touching example apparently of early so-called ' marriage by capture ' !   Or there were dances, also partly or originally religious, of a quite orgiastic and Bacchanalian character, like the *Bryallicha* performed in Sparta by men and women in hideous masks, or the *Deimalea* by Sileni and Satyrs waltzing in a circle ; or the *Bibasis* carried out by both men and women—a quite gymnastic exercise in which the performers took a special pride in striking their own buttocks with their heels ! or others wilder still, which it would perhaps not be convenient to describe.

We must see how important a part Dancing played in that great panorama of Ritual and Religion (spoken of in the last chapter) which, having originally been led up to by the ' Fall of Man,' has ever since the dawn of history gradually overspread the world with its strange procession of demons and deities, and its symbolic representations of human destiny.   When it is remembered that ritual dancing was the matrix out of which the *Drama* sprang, and further that the drama in its inception (as still to-day in India) was an affair of religion and was acted in, or in connexion with, the Temples, it becomes easier to understand how all this mass of ceremonial sacrifices, expiations, initiations, Sun and Nature festivals, eucharistic and orgiastic communions and celebrations, mystery-plays, dramatic representations, myths and legends, etc., which I have touched upon in the preceding chapters—together with all the emotions, the desires, the fears, the yearnings and the wonderment which they represented—have practically sprung from the same root : a root deep and necessary in the psychology of Man.   Presently I hope to show that they will all practically converge again in the end to one meaning, and prepare the way for one great Synthesis to come—an evolution also necessary and inevitable in human psychology.

In that truly inspired Ode from which I quoted a few pages back, occur those well-known words whose repetition now will, on account of their beauty, I am sure be excused :—

> Our birth is but a sleep and a forgetting :
> The Soul that rises with us, our life's Star,
> Hath had elsewhere its setting,
> And cometh from afar ;
> Not in entire forgetfulness,
> And not in utter nakedness,
> But trailing clouds of glory do we come
> From God, who is our home :
> Heaven lies about us in our infancy !
> Shades of the prison-house begin to close
> Upon the growing Boy,
> But He beholds the light and whence it flows,
> He sees it in his joy ;
> The Youth, who daily farther from the east
> Must travel, still is Nature's Priest,
> And by the vision splendid
> Is on his way attended ;
> At length the Man perceives it die away,
> And fade into the light of common day.

Wordsworth—though he had not the inestimable advantage of a nineteenth-century education and the inheritance of the Darwinian philosophy—does nevertheless put the matter of the Genius of the Child in a way which (with the alteration of a few conventional terms) we scientific moderns are quite inclined to accept. We all admit now that the Child does not come into the world with a mental *tabula rasa* of entire forgetfulness but on the contrary as the possessor of vast stores of sub-conscious memory, derived from its ancestral inheritances ; we all admit that a certain grace and intuitive insight and even prophetic quality, in the child-nature, are due to the harmonisation of these racial inheritances in the infant, even before it is born ;

and that after birth the impact of the outer world serves rather to break up and disintegrate this harmony than to confirm and strengthen it. Some psychologists indeed nowadays go so far as to maintain that the child is not only ' Father of the man,' but superior to the man,[1] and that Boyhood and Youth and Maturity are attained to not by any addition but by a process of loss and subtraction. It will be seen that the last ten lines of the above quotation rather favour this view.

But my object in making the quotation was not to insist on the truth of its application to the individual Child, but rather to point out the remarkable way in which it illustrates what I have said about the *Childhood of the Race*.   In fact, if the quotation be read over again with this interpretation (which I do not say Wordsworth intended) that the ' birth ' spoken of is the birth or evolution of the distinctively self-conscious Man from the Animals and the animal-natured, unself-conscious human beings of a preceding age, then the parable unfolds itself perfectly naturally and convincingly.   *That* birth certainly was a sleep and a forgetting ; the grace and intuition and instinctive perfection of the animals was lost.   But the forgetfulness was not entire ; the memory lingered long of an age of harmony, of an Eden-garden left behind.   And trailing clouds of this remembrance the first tribal men, on the edge of but not yet *within* the civilisation-period, appear in the dawn of History.

As I have said before, the period of the dawn of Self-consciousness was also the period of the dawn of the practical and inquiring Intellect ; it was the period of the babyhood of both ; and so we perceive among these early people (as we also do among children) that while in the main the heart and the intuitions were right, the intellect was for

---

[1] " Man in the course of his life falls away more and more from the specifically *human* type of his early years, but the Ape in the course of his short life goes very much farther along the road of degradation and premature senility " (*Man and Woman*, by Havelock Ellis, p. 24).

a long period futile and rambling to a degree. As soon as
the mind left the ancient bases of instinct and sub-conscious
racial experience it fell into a hopeless bog, out of which
it only slowly climbed by means of the painfully-gathered
stepping-stones of logic and what we call Science. " Heaven
lies about us in our infancy." Wordsworth perceived
that wonderful world of inner experience and glory out of
which the child emerges ; and some even of us may perceive
that similar world in which the untampered animals *still*
dwell, and *out* of which self-regarding Man in the history
of the race was long ago driven. But a curse went with
the exile. As the Brain grew, the Heart withered. The
inherited instincts and racially accumulated wisdom, on
which the first men thrived and by means of which they
achieved a kind of temporary Paradise, were broken up ;
delusions and disease and dissension set in. Cain turned
upon his brother and slew him ; and the shades of the
prison-house began to close. The growing Boy, however,
(by whom we may understand the early tribes of Mankind)
had yet a radiance of Light and Joy in his life ; and the
Youth—though traveling daily farther from the East—
still remained Nature's priest, and by the vision splendid
was on his way attended : but

> At length the Man perceived it die away,
> And fade into the light of common day.

What a strangely apt picture in a few words (if we like
to take it so) of the long pilgrimage of the Human Race,
its early and pathetic clinging to the tradition of the Eden-
garden, its careless and vigorous boyhood, its meditative
youth, with consciousness of sin and endless expiatory
ritual in Nature's bosom, its fleeting visions of salvation,
and finally its complete disillusionment and despair in the
world-slaughter and unbelief of the twentieth century !

Leaving Wordsworth, however, and coming back to our

main line of thought, we may point out that while early peoples were intellectually mere babies—with their endless yarns about heroes on horseback leaping over wide rivers or clouds of monks flying for hundreds of miles through the air, and their utter failure to understand the general concatenations of cause and effect—yet practically and in their instinct of life and destiny they were, as I have already said, by no means fools ; certainly not such fools as many of the arm-chair students of these things delight to represent them. For just as, a few years ago, we modern civilisees, studying outlying nations, the Chinese for instance, rejoiced (in our vanity) to pick out every quaint peculiarity and absurdity and monstrosity of a supposed topsyturveydom, and failed entirely to see the real picture of a great and eminently sensible people ; so in the case of primitive men we have been, and even still are, far too prone to catalogue their cruelties and obscenities and idiotic superstitions, and to miss the sane and balanced setting of their actual lives.

Mr. R. R. Marett, who has a good practical acquaintance with his subject, had in the *Hibbert Journal* for October 1918 an article on " The Primitive Medicine Man " in which he shows that the latter is as a rule anything but a fool and a knave—although like ' medicals ' in all ages he *hocuspocuses* his patients occasionally ! He instances the medicine-man's excellent management, in most cases, of childbirth, or of wounds and fractures, or his primeval skill in trepanning or trephining—all of which operations, he admits, may be accompanied with grotesque and superstitious ceremonies, yet show real perception and ability. We all know —though I think the article does not mention the matter— what a considerable list there is of drugs and herbs which the modern art of healing owes to the ancient medicine-man, and it may be again mentioned that one of the most up-to-date treatments—the use of a prolonged and exclusive diet of *milk* as a means of giving the organism a new start in severe cases—has really come down to us through the ages from this early source.[1] The real medicine-man, Mr. Marett says, is largely a ' faith-healer ' and ' soul-doctor '; he believes in his vocation, and undergoes much for the sake of it : " The main point is to grasp that by his special initiation and the rigid taboos which he practises—not to speak of occasional remarkable gifts, say of trance and ecstasy, which he may inherit by nature and have improved by art—he *has* access to a wonder-working power. . . . And the great need of primitive folk is for this healer of souls." Our author further insists on the enormous play and influence of Fear in the savage mind—a point we have touched on already—and gives instances of *Thanatomania,* or cases where, after a quite slight and superficial wound, the patient becomes so depressed that he, quite needlessly, persists in dying ! Such cases, obviously, can only be countered by Faith, or something (whatever it may be) which restores courage, hope and energy to the mind. Nor need I point out that the situation is exactly the same among a vast number of ' patients ' to-day. As to the value, in his degree, of the medicine-man many modern observers and students quite agree with the above.[2] Also as the present chapter is on *Ritual Dancing* it may not be out of place to call attention to the supposed healing of sick people in Ceylon and other places by *Devil-dancing*—the enormous output of energy and noise in the ritual possibly having the effect of reanimating the patient (if it does not kill him), or of expelling the disease from his organism.

With regard to the practical intelligence of primitive peoples, derived from their close contact with life and

---

[1] Milk (" fast-milk " or *vrata*) was, says Mr. Hewitt, the only diet in the Soma-sacrifice. See *Ruling Races of Prehistoric Times* (preface) The Soma itself was a fermented drink prepared with ceremony from the milky and resin like sap of certain plants, and much used in sacrificial offerings. (See Monier-Williams, *Sanskrit Dictionary.*)

[2] See Winwood Reade (*Savage Africa*), Salamon Reinach (*Cults, Myths and Religions*), and others.

nature, Bishop Colenso's experiences among the Zulus may appropriately be remembered. When expounding the Bible to these supposedly backward ' niggers ' he was met at all points by practical interrogations and arguments which he was perfectly unable to answer—especially over the recorded passage of the Red Sea by the Israelites in a single night. From the statistics given in the Sacred Book these naughty savages proved to him absolutely conclusively that the numbers of the fugitives were such that even supposing them to have marched—men, women and children—*five abreast* and in close order, they would have formed a column 100 miles long, and this not including the baggage, sheep and cattle ! Of course the feat was absolutely impossible. They could not have passed the Red Sea in a night or a week of nights.

But the sequel is still more amusing and instructive. Colenso, in his innocent sincerity, took the side of the Zulus, and feeling sure the Church at home would be quite glad to have its views with regard to the accuracy of Bible statistics corrected, wrote a book embodying the amendments needed. Modest as his criticisms were, they raised a *storm* of protest and angry denunciation, which even led to his deposition for the time being from his bishopric ! While at the same time an avalanche of books to oppose his heresy poured forth from the press. Lately I had the curiosity to look through the British Museum catalogue and found that in refutation of Colenso's *Pentateuch Examined* some 140 (a hundred and forty) volumes were at that time published ! To-day, I need hardly say, all these arm-chair critics and their works have sunk into utter obscurity, but the arguments of the Zulus and their Bishop still stand unmoved and immovable.

This is a case of searching intelligence shown by ' savages,' an intelligence founded on intimate knowledge of the needs of actual life.   I think we may say that a similarly instinctive intelligence (sub-conscious if you like) has guided the tribes

of men on the whole in their long passage through the
Red Sea of the centuries, from those first days of which I
speak even down to the present age, and has in some
strange, even if fitful, way kept them along the path
of that final emancipation towards which Humanity is
inevitably moving.

XII

THE SEX-TABOO

IN the course of the last few chapters I have spoken more than once of the solidarity and continuity of Christianity, in its essential doctrines, with the Pagan rites. There is, however, one notable exception to this statement. I refer of course to Christianity's treatment of Sex. It is certainly very remarkable that while the Pagan cults generally made a great deal of all sorts of sex-rites, laid much stress upon them, and introduced them in what we consider an unblushing and shameless way into the worship of their most honoured gods, the Christian Church on the whole took quite the opposite line—ignored sex, contemned it, and did much despite to the perfectly natural instincts connected with it. I say ' the Christian Church,' because there is nothing to show that Jesus himself (if we admit his figure as historical) adopted any such extreme or *doctrinaire* attitude ; and the quite early Christian teachers (with the chief exception of Paul) do not exhibit this bias to any great degree. In fact, as is well known, strong currents of pagan usage and belief ran through the Christian assemblies of the first three or four centuries. " The Christian art of this period remained delightfully pagan. In the catacombs we see the Saviour as a beardless youth, like a young Greek god ; sometimes represented, like Hermes the guardian of the flocks, bearing a ram or lamb round his neck ; sometimes as Orpheus tuning his lute among the wild animals " [1] The followers of Jesus were at times even accused—whether rightly or wrongly I know not— of celebrating sexual mysteries at their love-feasts. But as the Church through the centuries grew in power and scope —with its monks and their mutilations and asceticisms, and its celibate clergy, and its absolute refusal to recognise the sexual meaning of its own acclaimed symbols (like the Cross, the three fingers of Benediction, the Fleur de Lys and so forth)—it more and more consistently defined itself as anti-sexual in its outlook, and stood out in that way in marked contrast to the earlier Nature-religions.

It may be said of course that this anti-sexual tendency can be traced in others of the pre-Christian Churches, especially the later ones, like the Buddhist, the Egyptian, and so forth ; and this is perfectly true ; but it would seem that in many ways the Christian Church marked the culmination of the tendency ; and the fact that other cults participated in the taboo makes us all the more ready and anxious to inquire into its real cause.

To go into a disquisition on the Sex-rites of the various pre-Christian religions would be ' a large order '—larger than I could attempt to fill ; but the general facts in this connexion are fairly patent. We know, of course, from the Bible that the Syrians in Palestine were given to sexual worships. There were erect images (phallic) and " groves " (symbols of the female) on every high hill and under every green tree ; [2] and these same images and the rites connected with them crept into the Jewish Temple and were popular enough to maintain their footing there for a long period from King Rehoboam onwards, notwithstanding the efforts of Josiah [3] and other reformers to extirpate them. Moreover there were girls and men (*hierodouloi*) regularly attached during this period to the Jewish Temple as to the heathen

---

[1] *Angels' Wings*, by E. Carpenter, p. 104.
[2] 1 Kings xiv. 22–24.   [3] 2 Kings xxiii.

Temples, for the rendering of sexual services, which were recognised in many cases as part of the ritual. Women were persuaded that it was an honour and a privilege to be fertilised by a ' holy man ' (a priest or other man connected with the rites), and children resulting from such unions were often called " Children of God "—an appellation which no doubt sometimes led to a legend of miraculous birth ! Girls who took their place as *hierodouloi* in the Temple or Temple-precincts were expected to surrender themselves to men-worshipers in the Temple, much in the same way, probably, as Herodotus describes in the temple of the Babylonian Venus Mylitta, where every native woman, once in her life, was supposed to sit in the Temple and have intercourse with some stranger.[1]   Indeed the Syrian and Jewish rites dated largely from Babylonia. " The Hebrews entering Syria," says Richard Burton,[2] " found it religionised by Assyria and Babylonia, when the Accadian Ishtar had passed West, and had become Ashtoreth, Ashtaroth, or Ashirah, the Anaitis of Armenia, the Phoenician Astarte, and the Greek Aphrodite, the great Moongoddess who is queen of Heaven and Love."   The word translated " grove " as above, in our Bible, is in fact *Asherah*, which connects it pretty clearly with the Babylonian Queen of Heaven.

In India again, in connexion with the Hindu Temples and their rites, we have exactly the same institution of girls attached to the Temple service—the Nautch-girls—whose functions in past times were certainly sexual, and whose dances in honour of the god are, even down to the present day, decidedly amatory in character.   Then we have the very numerous *lingams* (conventional representations of the male organ) to be seen, scores and scores of them, in the arcades and cloisters of the Hindu Temples—

---

[1] See *Herodotus* i. 199 ; also a reference to this custom in the apocryphal *Baruch*, vi. 42, 43.

[2] *The Thousand Nights and a Night* (1886 edn.), vol. x, p. 229

to which women of all classes, especially those who wish
to become mothers, resort, anointing them copiously with
oil, and signalising their respect and devotion to them in
a very practical way. As to the *lingam* as representing
the male organ, in some form or other—as upright stone
or pillar or obelisk or slender round tower—it occurs all
over the world, notably in Ireland, and forms such a mem-
orial of the adoration paid by early folk to the great emblem
and instrument of human fertility, as cannot be mistaken.
The pillars set up by Solomon in front of his temple were
obviously from their names—Jachin and Boaz [1]—meant
to be emblems of this kind ; and the fact that they were
crowned with pomegranates—the universally accepted
symbol of the female—confirms and clinches this interpretation. The obelisks before the Egyptians' temples were
signs of the same character. The well-known T-shaped
cross was in use in pagan lands long before Christianity, as
a representation of the male member, and also at the same
time of the ' tree ' on which the god (Attis or Adonis or
Krishna or whoever it might be) was crucified ; and the
same symbol combined with the oval (or *yoni*) formed
the Crux Ansata ♀ of the old Egyptian ritual—a figure
which is to-day sold in Cairo as a potent charm, and con-
fessedly indicates the conjunction of the two sexes in one
design.[2] MacLennan in *The Fortnightly Review* (Oct. 1869)
quotes with approval the words of Sanchoniathon, as saying
that " men first worship plants, next the heavenly bodies,

[1] " He shall establish " and " In it is strength " are in the Bible the
marginal interpretations of these two words.
[2] The connexion between the production of fire by means of the
fire-drill and the generation of life by sex-intercourse is a very obvious
one, and lends itself to magical ideas. J. E. Hewitt in his *Ruling
Races of Prehistoric Times* (1894) says (vol. i, p. 8) that " Magha,
the mother-goddess worshipped in Asia Minor, was originally the
socket-block from which fire was generated by the fire-drill." Hence
we have, he says, the Magi of Persia, and the Maghadas of Indian
History, also the word ' Magic.'

supposed to be animals, then 'pillars' (emblems of the Procreator), and last, the anthropomorphic gods."

It is not necessary to enlarge on this subject. The facts of the connexion of sexual rites with religious services nearly everywhere in the early world are, as I say, sufficiently patent to every inquirer. But it *is* necessary to try to understand the *rationale* of this connexion. To dispatch all such cases under the mere term "religious prostitution" is no explanation. The term suggests, of course, that the plea of religion was used simply as an excuse and a cover for sexual familiarities ; but though this kind of explanation commends itself, no doubt, to the modern man—whose religion is as commercial as his sex-relationships are—and though in *cases* no doubt it was a true explanation—yet it is obvious that among people who took religion seriously, as a matter of life and death, and who did not need hypocritical excuses or covers for sex-relationships, it cannot be accepted as in general the *right* explanation. No, the real explanation is—and I will return to this presently—that sexual relationships are so deep and intimate a part of human nature that from the first it has been simply impossible to keep them *out* of religion—it being of course the object of religion to bring the whole human being into some intelligible relation with the physical, moral, and if you like supernatural order of the great world around him. Sex was felt from the first to be part, and a foundational part, of the great order of the world and of human nature ; and therefore to separate it from Religion was unthinkable and a kind of contradiction in terms.[1]

If that is true—it will be asked—how was it that that divorce *did* take place—that the taboo did arise ? How was it that the Jews, under the influence of Josiah and the Hebrew prophets, turned their faces away from sex and

[1] For further development of this subject see ch. xv (pp. 244–248) *infra.*

strenuously opposed the Syrian cults ? How was it that
this reaction extended on into Christianity and became
even more definite in the Christian Church—that monks
went by thousands into the deserts of the Thebaid, and
that the early Fathers and Christian apologists could not
find terms foul enough to hurl at Woman as the symbol
(to them) of nothing but sex-corruption and delusion ?
How was it that this contempt of the body and degradation
of sex-things went on far into the Middle Ages of Europe,
and ultimately created an organised system of hypocrisy,
and concealment and suppression of sex-instincts, which,
acting as cover to a vile commercial Prostitution and as
a breeding ground for horrible Disease, has lasted on even
to the edge of the present day ?

This is a fair question, and one which demands an answer.
There must have been a reason, and a deep-rooted one, for
this remarkable reaction and *volte-face* which has characterised Christianity, and, perhaps to a lesser degree, other
both earlier and later cults like those of the Buddhists,
the Egyptians, the Aztecs,[1] and so forth.

It may be said—and this is a fair answer on the *surface*
of the problem—that the main reason *was* something in
the nature of a reaction. The excesses and corruptions of
sex in Syria had evidently become pretty bad, and that
very fact may have led to a pendulum-swing of the Jewish
Church in the opposite direction ; and again in the same
way the general laxity of morals in the decay of the Roman
empire may have confirmed the Church of early Christendom
in its determination to keep along the great high road of
asceticism. The Christian followed on the Jewish and
Egyptian Churches, and in this way a great tradition of
sexual continence and anti-pagan morality came right down
the centuries even into modern times.

This seems so far a reasonable theory, but I think we
shall go farther and get nearer the heart of the problem if

[1] For the Aztecs, see *Acosta*, vol. ii, p. 324 (London, 1604).

we revert to the general clue which I have followed already more than once—the clue of the necessary evolution of human Consciousness. In the first or animal stage of human evolution, Sex was (as among the animals) a perfectly necessary, instinctive and unself-conscious activity. It was harmonious with itself, natural, and unproductive of evil. But when the second stage set in, in which man became preponderantly *self*-conscious, he inevitably set about deflecting sex-activities to his own private pleasure and advantage ; he employed his budding intellect in scheming the derailment of passion and desire from tribal needs and Nature's uses to the poor details of his own gratification. If the first stage of harmonious sex-instinct and activity may be held as characteristic of the Golden Age, the second stage must be taken to represent the Fall of man and his expulsion from Paradise in the Garden of Eden story. The pleasure and glory of Sex having been turned to self-purposes, Sex itself became the great Sin. A sense of guilt overspread man's thoughts on the subject. " He knew that he was naked," and he fled from the voice and face of the Lord. From that moment one of the main objects of his life (in its inner and newer activities) came to be the *denial* of Sex. Sex was conceived of as the great Antagonist, the old Serpent lying ever in wait to betray him ; and there arrived a moment in the history of every race, and of every representative religion, when the sexual rites and ceremonies of the older time lost their naïve and quasi-innocent character and became afflicted with a sense of guilt and indecency. This extraordinarily interesting and dramatic moment in human evolution was of course that in which self-consciousness grew powerful enough to penetrate to the centre of human vitality, the *sanctum* of man's inner life, his sexual instinct, and to deal it a terrific blow—a blow from which it has never yet recovered, and from which indeed it will not recover, until the very nature of man's inner life is changed.

It may be said that it was very foolish of Man to deny and to try to expel a perfectly natural and sensible thing, a necessary and indispensable part of his own nature. And that, as far as I can see, is perfectly true. But sometimes it is unavoidable, it would seem, to do foolish things—if only to convince oneself of one's own foolishness. On the other hand, this policy on the part of Man was certainly very wise—wiser than he knew—for in attempting to drive out Sex (which of course he could not do) he entered into a conflict which was bound to end in the expulsion of *something;* and that something was the domination, within himself, of self-consciousness, the very thing which makes and ever has made sex detestable. Man did not succeed in driving the snake out of the Garden, but he drove himself out, taking the real old serpent of self-greed and self-gratification with him. When some day he returns to Paradise this latter will have died in his bosom and been cast away, but he will find the good Snake there as of old, full of healing and friendliness, among the branches of the Tree of Life.

Besides it is evident from other considerations that this moment of the denial of sex *had* to come. When one thinks of the enormous power of this passion, and its age-long hold upon the human race, one realises that once liberated from the instinctive bonds of nature, and backed by a self-conscious and self-seeking human intelligence it was on the way to become a fearful curse.

A monstrous Eft was of old the Lord and Master of Earth ;
For him did his high sun flame, and his river billowing ran.

And this may have been all very well and appropriate in the carboniferous Epoch, but *we* in the end of Time have no desire to fall under any such preposterous domination or to return to the primal swamps from which organic nature has so slowly and painfully emerged.

I say it was the entry of self-consciousness into the sphere of Sex, and the consequent use of the latter for private ends, which poisoned this great race-power at its root. For above all, Sex, as representing through Childbirth the life of the Race (or of the Tribe, or, if you like, of Humanity at large) should be sacred and guarded from merely selfish aims, and therefore to use it only for such aims is indeed a desecration. And even if—as some maintain and I think rightly [1]—sex is not *merely* for child-birth and physical procreation, but for mutual vitalising and invigoration, it still subserves union and not egotism ; and to use it egotistically is to commit the sin of Separation indeed. It is to cast away and corrupt the very bond of life and fellowship. The ancient peoples at any rate threw an illumination of religious (that is, of communal and public) value over sex-acts, and to a great extent made them into matters either of Temple-ritual and the worship of the gods, or of communal and pandemic celebration, as in the Saturnalia and other similar festivals. We have certainly no right to regard these celebrations—of either kind—as insincere. They were, at any rate in their inception, genuinely religious or genuinely social and festal ; and from either point of view they were far better than the secrecy of private indulgence which characterizes our modern world in these matters. The thorough and shameless commercialism of Sex has alas ! been reserved for what is called " Christian civilisation," and with it (perhaps as a necessary consequence) Prostitution and Syphilis have grown into appalling evils, accompanied by a gigantic degradation of social standards, and upgrowth of petty Philistinism and *niaiserie*. Love, in fact, having in this modern world-movement been denied, and its natural manifestations affected with a sense of guilt and of sin, has really languished and ceased to play its natural part in life ; and a vast

[1] See Havelock Ellis, *The Objects of Marriage*, a pamphlet published by the " British Society for the Study of Sex-psychology."

number of people—both men and women, finding themselves barred or derailed from the main object of existence, have turned their energies to 'business' or 'money-making' or 'social advancement' or something equally futile, as the only poor substitute and *pis aller* open to them.

Why (again we ask) did Christianity make this apparently great mistake? And again we must reply : Perhaps the mistake was not so great as it appears to be. Perhaps this was another case of the necessity of learning by loss. Love had to be denied, in the form of sex, in order that it might thus the better learn its own true values and needs. Sex had to be rejected, or defiled with the sense of guilt and self-seeking, in order that having cast out its defilement it might return one day, transformed in the embrace of love. The whole process has had a deep and strange world-significance. It has led to an immensely long period of suppression—suppression of two great instincts—the physical instinct of sex and the emotional instinct of love. Two things which should naturally be conjoined have been separated ; and both have suffered. And we know from the Freudian teachings what suppressions in the root-instincts necessarily mean. We know that they inevitably terminate in diseases and distortions of proper action, either in the body or in the mind, or in both ; and that these evils can only be cured by the liberation of the said instincts again to their proper expression and harmonious functioning in the whole organism. No wonder then that, with this agelong suppression (necessary in a sense though it may have been) which marks the Christian dispensation, there should have been associated endless Sickness and Crime and sordid Poverty, the Crucifixion of animals in the name of Science and of human workers in the name of Wealth, and wars and horrors innumerable ! Hercules writhing in the Nessus-shirt or Prometheus nailed to the rocks are only as figures of a toy miniature compared with this vision of the great and divine Spirit of Man caught in the clutches of those dread Diseases which through the centuries have been eating into his very heart and vitals.

It would not be fair to pile on the Christian Church the blame for all this. It had, no doubt, its part to play in the whole great scheme, namely, to accentuate the self-motive ; and it played the part very thoroughly and successfully. For it must be remembered (what I have again and again insisted on) that in the pagan cults it was always the salvation of the *clan*, the *tribe*, the *people* that was the main consideration ; the advantage of the individual took only a very secondary part. But in Christendom—after the communal enthusiasms of apostolic days and of the medieval and monastic brotherhoods and sisterhoods had died down—religion occupied itself more and more with each man or woman's *individual* salvation, regardless of what might happen to the community ; till, with the rise of Protestantism and Puritanism, this tendency reached such an extreme that, as some one has said, each man was absorbed in polishing up his own little soul in a corner to himself, in entire disregard to the damnation which might come to his neighbor. Religion, and Morality too, under the commercial régime became, as was natural, perfectly selfish. It was always : " Am *I* saved ? Am *I* doing the right thing ? Am *I* winning the favour of God and man ? Will *my* claims to salvation be allowed ? Did *I* make a good bargain in allowing Jesus to be crucified for me ? " The poison of a diseased self-consciousness entered into the whole human system.

As I say, one must not blame the Christians too much for all this—partly because, *after* the communal periods which I have just mentioned, Christianity was evidently deeply influenced by the rise of *Commercialism*, to which during the last two centuries it has so carefully and piously adapted itself ; and partly because—if our view is anywhere

near right—this microbial injection of self-consciousness
was just the necessary work which (in conjunction with
commercialism) it *had* to perform. But though one does
not blame Christianity one cannot blind oneself to its defects
—the defects necessarily arising from the part it had to
play. When one compares a healthy Pagan ritual—say
of Apollo or Dionysus—including its rude and crude sacrifices
if you like, but also including its whole-hearted spontaneity
and dedication to the common life and welfare—with the
morbid self-introspection of the Christian and the eternally
recurring question " What shall I do to be saved ? "—the
comparison is not favourable to the latter. There is (at
any rate in modern days) a mawkish milk-and-wateriness
about the Christian attitude, and also a painful self-consciousness, which is not pleasant ; and though Nietzsche's
blonde beast is a sufficiently disagreeable animal, one almost
thinks that it were better to be *that* than to go about with
one's head meekly hanging on one side, and talking always
of altruism and self-sacrifice, while in reality one's heart was
entirely occupied with the question of one's own salvation.
There is besides a lamentable want of grit and substance
about the Christian doctrines and ceremonials. Somehow
under the sex-taboo they became spiritualised and etherialised out of all human use. Study the initiation-rites of
any savage tribe—with their strict discipline of the young
braves in fortitude, and the overcoming of pain and fear ;
with their very detailed lessons in the arts of war and life
and the duties of the grown man to his tribe ; and with
their quite practical instruction in matters of Sex ; and
then read our poor little Baptismal and Confirmation services,
which ought to correspond thereto. How thin and attenuated and weak the latter appear ! Or compare the Holy
Communion, as celebrated in the sentimental atmosphere
of a Protestant Church, with an ancient Eucharistic feast
of real jollity and community of life under the acknowledged
presence of the god ; or the Roman Catholic service of the

Mass, including its genuflexions and mock oblations and droning ritual sing-song, with the actual sacrifice in early days of an animal-god-victim on a blazing altar ; and I think my meaning will be clear.   We do not want, of course, to return to all the crudities and barbarities of the past ; but also we do not want to become attenuated and spiritualised out of all mundane sense and recognition, and to live in an otherworld Paradise void of application to earthly affairs.

The sex-taboo in Christianity was apparently, as I have said, an effort of the human soul to wrest itself free from the entanglement of physical lust—which lust, though normal and appropriate and in a way gracious among the animals, had through the domination of self-consciousness become diseased and morbid or monstrous in Man.   The work thus done has probably been of the greatest value to the human race ; but, just as in other cases it has sometimes happened that the effort to do a certain work has resulted in the end in an unbalanced exaggeration, so here.   We are beginning to see now the harmful side of the repression of sex, and are tentatively finding our way back again to a more pagan attitude.   And as this return-movement is taking place at a time when, from many obvious signs, the self-conscious, grasping, commercial conception of life is preparing to go on the wane, and the sense of solidarity to re-establish itself, there is really good hope that our return-journey may prove in some degree successful.

Man progresses generally, not both legs at once like a sparrow, but by putting one leg forward first, and then the other.   There was this advantage in the Christian taboo of sex that by discouraging the physical and sensual side of love it did for the time being allow the spiritual side to come forward.   But, as I have just now indicated, there is a limit to that process.   We cannot always keep one leg first in walking, and we do not want, in life, always to put the spiritual first, nor always the material and sensual. The two sides in the long run have to keep pace with each other.

And it may be that a great number of the very curious and seemingly senseless taboos that we find among the primitive peoples can be partly explained in this way : that is, that by ruling out certain directions of activity they enabled people to concentrate more effectually, for the time being, on other directions. To primitive folk the great world, whose ways are puzzling enough in all conscience to *us*, must have been simply bewildering in its dangers and complications. It was an amazement of Fear and Ignorance. Thunderbolts might come at any moment out of the blue sky, or a demon out of an old tree trunk, or a devastating plague out of a bad smell—or apparently even out of nothing at all ! Under those circumstances it was perhaps wise, wherever there was the smallest *suspicion* of danger or ill-luck, to create a hard and fast *taboo*—just as we tell our children *on no account* to walk under a ladder (thereby creating a superstition in their minds), partly because it would take too long to explain all about the real dangers of paint-pots and other things, and partly because for the children themselves it seems simpler to have a fixed and inviolable law than to argue over every case that occurs The priests and elders among early folk no doubt took the line of *forbiddal* of activities, as safer and simpler, even if carried sometimes too far, than the opposite, of easy permission and encouragement. Taboos multiplied—many of them quite senseless—but perhaps in this perilous maze of the world, of which I have spoken, it really *was* simpler to cut out a large part of the labyrinth, as forbidden ground, thus rendering it easier for the people to find their way in those portions of the labyrinth which remained. If you read in Deuteronomy (ch. xiv) the list of birds and beasts and fishes permitted for food among the Israelites, or tabooed, you will find the list on the whole reasonable, but you will be struck by some curious exceptions (according

to our ideas), which are probably to be explained by the
necessity of making the rules simple enough to be compre-
hended by everybody—even if they included the forbiddal
of some quite eatable animals.

At some early period, in Babylonia or Assyria, a very
stringent taboo on the Sabbath arose, which, taken up in
turn by the Jewish and Christian Churches, has ruled the
Western World for three thousand years or more, and still
survives in a quite senseless form among some of our rural
populations, who will see their corn rot in the fields rather
than save it on a Sunday.[1]   It is quite likely that this taboo
in its first beginning was due not to any need of a weekly
rest-day (a need which could never be felt among nomad
savages, but would only occur in some kind of industrial
and stationary civilisation), but to some superstitious fear,
connected with such things as the changes of the Moon,
and the probable *ill-luck* of any enterprise undertaken on
the seventh day, or any day of Moon-change.   It is probable,
however, that as time went on and Society became more
complex, the advantages of a weekly *rest-day* (or market-
day) became more obvious and that the priests and legis-
lators deliberately turned the taboo to a social use.[2]
The learned modern Ethnologists, however, will generally
have none of this latter idea.   As a rule they delight in
representing early peoples as totally destitute of common
sense (which is supposed to be a monopoly of us moderns !) ;
and if the Sabbath-arrangement has had any value or use
they insist on ascribing this to pure accident, and not to
the application of any sane argument or reason.

It is true indeed that a taboo—in order to be a proper
taboo—must not rest in the general mind on argument or
reason.   It may have had good sense in the past or even

[1] For other absurd Sunday taboos see Westermarck on *The Moral
Ideas*, vol. ii, p. 289.
[2] For a tracing of this taboo from useless superstition to practical
utility see Hastings's *Encycl. Religion and Ethics*, art. "The Sabbath."

an underlying good sense in the present, but its foundation must rest on something beyond. It must be an absolute *fiat*—something of the nature of a Mystery [1] or of Religion or Magic—and not to be disputed. This gives it its blood-curdling quality. The rustic does not know what would happen to him if he garnered his corn on Sunday, nor does the diner-out in polite society know what would happen if he spooned up his food with his knife—but they both are stricken with a sort of paralysis at the very suggestion of infringing these taboos.

Marriage-customs have always been a fertile field for the generation of taboos. It seems doubtful whether anything like absolute promiscuity ever prevailed among the human race, but there is much to show that wide choice and intercourse were common among primitive folk and that the tendency of later marriage custom has been on the whole to *limit* this range of choice. At some early period the forbiddal of marriage between those who bore the same totem-name took place. Thus in Australia " no man of the Emu stock might marry an Emu woman ; no Blacksnake might marry a Blacksnake woman, and so forth " [2] Among the Kamilaroi and the Arunta of S. Australia the tribe was divided into classes or clans, sometimes four, sometimes eight, and a man of one particular clan was only marriageable with a woman of another particular clan—say (1) with (3) or (2) with (4), and so on.[3] Customs with a similar tendency, but different in detail, seem to have prevailed among native tribes in Central Africa and N. America. And the regulations in all this matter have been so (apparently) entirely arbitrary in the various cases that it would almost appear as if the bar of kinship through the Totem had been the *excuse*, originating perhaps in some superstition, but that the real and more abiding object was simply limita-

[1] See Westermarck, *Ibid.*, ii. 586.
[2] *Myth, Ritual and Religion*, i, p. 66.
[3] See Spencer and Gillen, *Native Tribes of Australia*.

tion. And this perhaps was a wise line to take. A taboo on promiscuity had to be created, and for this purpose any current prejudice could be made use of.[1]

With us moderns the whole matter has taken a different complexion. When we consider the enormous amount of suffering and disease, both of mind and body, arising from the sex-suppression of which I have just spoken, especially among women, we see that mere unreasoning taboos— which possibly had their place and use in the past—can be tolerated no longer. We are bound to turn the search-light of reason and science on a number of superstitions which still linger in the dark and musty places of the Churches and the Law courts. Modern inquiry has shown conclusively not only the foundational importance of sex in the evolution of each human being, but also the very great *variety* of its spontaneous manifestations in different individuals and the vital necessity that these should be recognised, if society is ever to expand into a rational human form. It is not my object here to sketch the future of marriage and sex-relations generally—a subject which is now being dealt with very effectively from many sides ; but only to insist on our using our good sense in the whole matter, and refusing any longer to be bound by senseless pre-judgments.

Something of the same kind may be said with regard to Nakedness, which in modern Civilisation has become the object of a very serious and indeed harmful taboo, both of speech and act. As someone has said, it became in the end of the nineteenth century almost a crime to mention by name any portion of the human body within a radius of about twenty inches from its centre (!) and as a matter of fact a few dress-reformers of that period were actually brought into court and treated as criminals for going about with legs bare up to the knees, and shoulders and chest

[1] The author of *The Mystic Rose* seems to take this view. See p. 214 of that book.

uncovered! Public follies such as these have been responsible for much of the bodily and mental disease and suppression just mentioned, and the sooner they are sent to limbo the better. No sensible person would advocate promiscuous nakedness any more than promiscuous sex-relationship; nor is it likely that aged and deformed people would at any time wish to expose themselves. But surely there is enough good sense and appreciation of grace and fitness in the average human mind for it to be able to liberate the body from senseless concealment, and give it its due expression. The Greeks of old, having on the whole clean bodies, treated them with respect and distinction. The young men appeared quite naked in the *palaestra*, and even the girls of Sparta ran races publicly in the same condition; [1] and some day when our bodies (and minds too) have become clean we shall return to similar institutions. But that will not be just yet. As long as the defilement of this commercial civilisation is on us we shall prefer our dirt and concealment. The powers that be will protest against change. Heinrich Scham, in his charming little pamphlet *Nackende Menschen*,[2] describes the consternation of the commercial people at such ideas:

" ' What will become of us,' cried the tailors, ' if you go naked ? '

" And all the lot of them, hat, cravat, shirt, and shoe-makers joined in the chorus.

" '*And where shall I carry my money ?* ' cried one who had just been made a director."

[1] See Theocritus, Idyll xviii.
[2] Published at Leipzig about 1893.

XIII

THE GENESIS OF CHRISTIANITY

REFERRING back to the existence of something resembling
a great World-religion which has come down the centuries,
continually expanding and branching in the process, we
have now to consider the genesis of that special brand or
branch of it which we call Christianity. Each religion or
cult, pagan or Christian, has had, as we have seen, a vast
amount in common with the general World-religion ; yet
each has had its own special characteristics. What have
been the main characteristics of the Christian branch, as
differentiating it from the other branches ?

We saw in the last chapter that a certain ascetic attitude
towards Sex was one of the most salient marks of the
Christian Church : and that whereas most of the pagan
cults (though occasionally favouring frightful austerities
and cruel sacrifices) did on the whole rejoice in pleasure
and the world of the senses, Christianity—following largely
on Judaism—displayed a tendency towards renunciation
of the world and the flesh, and a withdrawal into the inner
and more spiritual regions of the mind. The same tendency
may be traced in the Egyptian and Phrygian cults of that
period. It will be remembered how Juvenal (Sat. VI,
510–40) chaffs the priests of Cybele at Rome for making
themselves " eunuchs for the kingdom of heaven's sake,"
or the rich Roman lady for plunging in the wintry Tiber

for a propitiation to Isis. No doubt among the later pagans
" the long intolerable tyranny of the senses over the soul "
had become a very serious matter. But Christianity
represented perhaps the most powerful reaction against
this ; and this reaction had, as indicated in the last chapter,
the enormously valuable result that (for the time) it disentangled love from sex and established Love, pure and
undefiled, as ruler of the world. " God of Love." But, as
also indicated, the divorce between the two elements of
human nature, carried to an extreme, led in time to a
crippling of both elements and the development of a certain
morbidity and self-consciousness which, it cannot be denied,
is painfully marked among some sections of Christians—
especially those of the altruistic and ' philanthropic ' type.

Another characteristic of Christianity which is also very
fine in its way but has its limits of utility, has been its
insistence on " morality." Some modern writers indeed
have gone so far—forgetting, I suppose, the Stoics—
as to claim that Christianity's chief mark is its high
morality, and that the pagans generally were quite
wanting in the moral sense ! This, of course, is a
profound mistake. I should say that, in the true sense
of the word, the early and tribal peoples have been much
more ' moral ' as a rule—that is, ready as individuals to
pay respect to the needs of the community—than the later
and more civilised societies. But the mistake arises from
the different interpretations of the word ; for whereas
all the pagan religions insisted very strongly on the just-
mentioned kind of morality, which we should call *civic
duty to one's neighbor*, the Christians made morality to consist more especially in a man's *duty to God*. It became
with them a private affair between a man's self and God,
rather than a public affair ; and thus led in the end to a
very obnoxious and quite pharisaic kind of morality, whose
chief inspiration was not the helping of one's fellow-man
but the saving of one's own soul.

There may perhaps be other salient points of differentiation between Christianity and the preceding pagan religions ; but for the present we may recognise these two—(a) the tendency towards a renunciation of the world, and the consequent cultivation of a purely spiritual love and (b) the insistence on a morality whose inspiration was a private sense of duty to God rather than a public sense of duty to one's neighbor and to society generally.   It may be interesting to trace the causes which led to this differentiation.

Three centuries before our era the conquests of Alexander had had the effect of spreading the Greek thought and culture over most of the known world.   A vast number of small bodies of worshipers of local deities, with their various rituals and religious customs, had thus been broken up, or at least brought into contact with each other and partially modified and hellenised.   The orbit of a more general conception of life and religion was already being traced.   By the time of the founding of the first Christian Church the immense conquests of Rome had greatly extended and established the process.   The Mediterranean had become a great Roman lake.   Merchant ships and routes of traffic crossed it in all directions ; tourists visited its shores.   The known world had become one.   The numberless peoples, tribes, nations, societies within the girdle of the Empire, with their various languages, creeds, customs, religions, philosophies, were profoundly influencing each other.[1]   A great fusion was taking place ; and it was becoming inevitable that the next great religious movement would have a world-wide character.

It was probable that this new religion would combine many elements from the preceding rituals in one cult.   In

---

[1] For an enlargement on this theme see Glover's *Conflict of Religions in the early Roman Empire* ; also S. J. Case, *Evolution of Early Christianity* (University of Chicago, 1914).   The Adonis worship, for instance, (a resurrection-cult) " was still thriving in Syria and Cyprus when Paul preached there," and the worship of Isis and Serapis had already reached Athens, Rome and Naples.

connexion with the fine temples and elaborate services of
Isis and Cybele and Mithra there was growing up a powerful
priesthood ; Franz Cumont [1] speaks of " the learned priests
of the Asiatic cults " as building up, on the foundations
of old fetichism and superstition, a complete religious
philosophy—just as the Brahmins had built the monism
of the Vedanta on the " monstrous idolatries of Hinduism."
And it was likely that a similar process would evolve the
new religion expected.   Toutain again calls attention to
the patronage accorded to all these cults by the Roman
Emperors, as favouring a new combination and synthesis :
—" Hadrien, Commode, Septime Sévère, Julia Domna,
Elagabal, Alexandre Sévère, en particulier ont contribué
personnellement à la popularité et au succès des cultes
qui se celebraient en l'honneur de Serapis et d'Isis, des
divinités syriennes et de Mithra." [2]

It was also probable that this new Religion would show
(as indicated in the last chapter) a reaction against mere
sex-indulgence ; and, as regards its standard of Morality
generally, that, among so many conflicting peoples with
their various civic and local customs, it could not well
identify itself with any *one* of these but would evolve an
inner inspiration of its own which in its best form would
be love of the neighbor, regardless of the race, creed or
customs of the neighbor, and whose sanction would not
reside in any of the external authorities thus conflicting
with each other, but in the sense of the soul's direct responsibility to God.

So much for what we might expect *a priori* as to the
influence of the surroundings on the general form of the
new Religion.   And what about the kind of creed or creeds
which that religion would favour ?   Here again we must
see that the influence of the surroundings compelled a

[1] See Cumont, *Religions Orientales dans le Paganisme Romain*
(Paris, 1906), p. 253.

[2] *Cultes païens dans l'Empire Romain* (2 vols., 1911), vol. ii, p. 263.

certain result. Those doctrines which we have described in the preceding chapters—doctrines of Sin and Sacrifice, a Saviour, the Eucharist, the Trinity, the Virgin-birth, and so forth—were in their various forms seething, so to speak, all around. It was impossible for any new religious synthesis to escape them; all it could do would be to appropriate them, and to give them perhaps a colour of its own. Thus it is into the midst of this germinating mass that we must imagine the various pagan cults, like fertilising streams, descending. To trace all these streams would of course be an impossible task; but it may be of use, as an example of the process, to take the case of some particular belief. Let us take the belief in the coming of a Saviour-god; and this will be the more suitable as it is a belief which has in the past been commonly held to be distinctive of Christianity. Of course we know now that it is not in any sense distinctive, but that the long tradition of the Saviour comes down from the remotest times, and perhaps from every country of the world.[1] The Messianic prophecies of the Jews and the fifty-third chapter of Isaiah emptied themselves into the Christian teachings, and infected them to some degree with a Judaic tinge. The " Messiah " means of course the Anointed One. The Hebrew word occurs some 40 times in the Old Testament; and each time in the Septuagint or Greek translation (made mainly in the third century *before* our era) the word is translated χριστός, or Christos, which again means Anointed. Thus we see that the idea or the word " The Christ " was in vogue in Alexandria as far back certainly as 280 B.C., or nearly three centuries before Jesus. And what the word " The Anointed " strictly speaking means, and from what the expression is probably derived, will appear later. In *The Book of Enoch*, written not later than B.C. 170,[2] the Christ is spoken of as already existing in heaven,

---

[1] Even to-day the Arabian lands are always vibrating with prophecies of a coming Mahdi.

[2] See Edition by R. H. Charles (1893).

and about to come as Judge of all men, and is definitely
called " the Son of Man." The Book of Revelations is
full of passages from *Enoch* ; so are the Epistles of Paul ;
so too the Gospels. The Book of Enoch believes in a Golden
Age that is to come ; it has Dantesque visions of Heaven
and Hell, and of Angels good and evil, and it speaks of a
" garden of Righteousness " with the " Tree of Wisdom "
in its midst. Everywhere, says Prof. Drews, in the first
century B.C., there was the longing for a coming Saviour.

But the Saviour-god, as we also know, was a familiar
figure in Egypt. The great Osiris was the Saviour of the
world, both in his life and death : in his life through the
noble works he wrought for the benefit of mankind, and in
his death through his betrayal by the powers of darkness
and his resurrection from the tomb and ascent into heaven.[1]
The Egyptian doctrines descended through Alexandria
into Christianity—and though they did not influence the
latter deeply until about 300 A.D., yet they then succeeded
in reaching the Christian Churches, giving a colour to their
teachings with regard to the Saviour, and persuading them
to accept and honour the Egyptian worship of Isis in the
Christian form of the Virgin Mary.

Again, another great stream of influence descended from
Persia in the form of the cult of Mithra. Mithra, as we
have seen,[2] stood as a great Mediator between God and man.
With his baptisms and eucharists, and his twelve disciples,
and his birth in a cave, and so forth, he seemed to the
early Fathers an invention of the devil and a most dangerous
mockery on Christianity—and all the more so because his
worship was becoming so exceedingly popular. The cult
seems to have reached Rome about B.C. 70. It spread
far and wide through the Empire. It extended to Great
Britain, and numerous remains of Mithraic monuments
and sculptures in this country—at York, Chester and other
places—testify to its wide acceptance even here. At

[1] See ch. ii, *supra.*   [2] *Supra*, ch. ii.

Rome the vogue of Mithraism became so great that in the third century A.D., it was quite doubtful [1] whether it *or* Christianity would triumph; the Emperor Aurelian in 273 founded a cult of the Invincible Sun in connexion with Mithraism; [2] and as St. Jerome tells us in his letters,[3] the latter cult had at a later time to be suppressed in Rome and Alexandria by *physical force*, so powerful was it.

Nor was force the only method employed. *Imitation* is not only the sincerest flattery, but it is often the most subtle and effective way of defeating a rival. The priests of the rising Christian Church were, like the priests of *all* religions, not wanting in craft; and at this moment when the question of a World-religion was in the balance, it was an obvious policy for them to throw into their own scale as many elements as possible of the popular Pagan cults. Mithraism had been flourishing for 600 years; and it is, to say the least, *curious* that the Mithraic doctrines and legends which I have just mentioned should all have been adopted (quite unintentionally of course!) into Christianity; and still more so that some others from the same source, like the legend of the Shepherds at the Nativity and the doctrine of the Resurrection and Ascension, which are *not* mentioned at all in the original draft of the earliest Gospel (St. Mark), should have made their appearance in the Christian writings at a later time, when Mithraism was making great forward strides. History shows that as a Church progresses and expands it generally feels

---

[1] See Cumont, *op. cit.*, who says, p. 171 :—" Jamais, pas même à l'epoque des invasions mussulmanes, l'Europe ne sembla plus près de devenir asiatique qu'au moment où Dioclétien reconnaissait officiellement en Mithra le protecteur de l'empire reconstitué." See also Cumont's *Mystères de Mithra*, preface. The Roman Army, in fact, stuck to Mithra throughout, as against Christianity; and so did the Roman nobility. (See S. Augustine's *Confessions*, Book VIII, ch. 2.)

[2] Cumont indeed says that the identification of Mithra with the Sun (the emblem of imperial power) formed one reason why Mithraism was *not* persecuted at that time.

[3] Epist. cvii, *ad Laetam*. See Robertson's *Pagan Christs*, p. 350.

compelled to enlarge and fortify its own foundations by inserting material which was not there at first. I shall shortly give another illustration of this ; at present I will merely point out that the Christian writers, as time went on, not only introduced new doctrines, legends, miracles and so forth—most of which we can trace to antecedent pagan sources—but that they took especial pains to destroy the pagan records and so obliterate the evidence of their own dishonesty. We learn from Porphyry [1] that there were several elaborate treatises setting forth the religion of Mithra ; and J. M. Robertson adds (*Pagan Christs*, p. 325) : " everyone of these has been destroyed by the care of the Church, and it is remarkable that even the treatise of Firmicus is mutilated at a passage (v.) where he seems to be accusing Christians of following Mithraic usages." While again Professor Murray says, " The polemic literature of Christianity is loud and triumphant ; the books of the Pagans have been *destroyed*." [2]

Returning to the doctrine of the Saviour, I have already in preceding chapters given so many instances of belief in such a deity among the pagans—whether he be called Krishna or Mithra or Osiris or Horus or Apollo or Hercules —that it is not necessary to dwell on the subject any further in order to persuade the reader that the doctrine was ' in the air ' at the time of the advent of Christianity. Even Dionysus, then a prominent figure in the ' Mysteries,' was called Eleutherios, *The Deliverer*. But it may be of interest to trace the same doctrine among the *pre-Christian* sects of Gnostics. The Gnostics, says Professor Murray,[3] " are still commonly thought of as a body of *Christian* heretics. In reality there were Gnostic sects scattered over

---

[1] *De Abstinentia*, ii. 56 ; iv. 16.

[2] *Four Stages*, p. 180. We have probably an instance of this destruction in the total disappearance of Celsus' lively attack on Christianity (180 A.D.), of which, however, portions have been fortunately preserved in Origen's rather prolix refutation of the same.

[3] *Four Stages*, p. 143.

the Hellenistic world *before* Christianity as well as after. They must have been established in Antioch and probably in Tarsus well before the days of Paul or Apollos. Their Saviour, like the Jewish Messiah, was established in men's minds before the Saviour of the Christians. ' If we look close,' says Professor Bousset, ' the result emerges with great clearness that the figure of the Redeemer as such did not wait for Christianity to force its way into the religion of Gnôsis, but was already present there under various forms.' "

This Gnostic Redeemer, continues Professor Murray, " is descended by a fairly clear genealogy from the ' Tritos Sôtêr ' (' third Saviour ')[1] of early Greece, contaminated with similar figures, like Attis and Adonis from Asia Minor, Osiris from Egypt, and the special Jewish conception of the Messiah of the Chosen people. He has various names, which the name of Jesus or ' Christos,' ' the Anointed,' tends gradually to supersede. Above all, he is in some sense Man, or ' the second Man ' or ' the Son of Man ' . . . He is the real, the ultimate, the perfect and eternal Man, of whom all bodily men are feeble copies." [2]

This passage brings vividly before the mind the process of which I have spoken, namely, the fusion and mutual interchange of ideas on the subject of the Saviour during the period anterior to our era. Also it exemplifies to us through what an abstract sphere of Gnostic religious speculation the doctrine had to travel before reaching its expression in Christianity.[3] This exalted and high philosophical

[1] There seems to be some doubt about the exact meaning of this expression. Even Zeus himself was sometimes called ' Soter,' and at feasts, it is said, the *third* goblet was always drunk in his honour.

[2] See also *The Gnostic Story of Jesus Christ*, by Gilbert T. Sadler (C. W. Daniel, 1919).

[3] When traveling in India I found that the Gñanis or Wise Men there quite commonly maintained that Jesus (judging from his teaching) must have been initiated at some time in the esoteric doctrines of the Vedanta.

conception passed on and came out again to some degree
in the Fourth Gospel and the Pauline Epistles (especially
I Cor. xv) ; but I need hardly say it was not maintained.
The enthusiasm of the little scattered Christian bodies—
with their communism of practice with regard to *this*
world and their intensity of faith with regard to the next
—began to wane in the second and third centuries A.D.
As the Church (with capital initial) grew, so was it less
and less occupied with real religious feeling, and more and
more with its battles against persecution from outside,
and its quarrels and dissensions concerning heresies within
its own borders. And when at the Council of Nicæa (325
A.D.) it endeavoured to establish an official creed, the
strife and bitterness only increased. " There is no wild
beast," said the Emperor Julian, " like an angry theologian."
Where the fourth Evangelist had preached the gospel of
Love, and Paul had announced redemption by an inner and
spiritual identification with Christ, " As in Adam all die,
so in Christ shall all be made alive " ; and whereas some
at any rate of the Pagan cults had taught a glorious salvation by the new birth of a divine being within each man :
" *Be of good cheer, O initiates in the mystery of the liberated
god ; For to you too out of all your labours and sorrows shall
come Liberation* "—the Nicene creed had nothing to pro-
pound except some extremely futile speculations about
the relation to each other of the Father and the Son, and
the relation of *both* to the Holy Ghost, and of all *three* to
the Virgin Mary—speculations which only served for the
renewal of shameful strife and animosities—riots and bloodshed and murder—within the Church, and the mockery of
the heathen without. And as far as it dealt with the crucifixion, death and resurrection of the Lord it did not differ
from the score of preceding pagan creeds, except in the
thorough materialism and lack of poetry in statement
which it exhibits. After the Council of Nicæa, in fact,
the Judaic tinge in the doctrines of the Church becomes

more apparent, and more and more its Scheme of Salvation through Christ takes the character of a rather sordid and huckstering bargain by which Man gets the better of God by persuading the latter to sacrifice his own Son for the redemption of the world! With the exception of a few episodes like the formation during the Middle Ages of the noble brotherhoods and sisterhoods of Friars and Nuns, dedicated to the help and healing of suffering humanity, and the appearance of a few real lovers of mankind (and the animals) like St. Francis—(and these manifestations can hardly be claimed by the Church, which pretty consistently opposed them)—it may be said that after about the fourth century the real spirit and light of early Christian enthusiasm died away. The incursions of barbarian tribes from the North and East, and later of Moors and Arabs from the South, familiarised the European peoples with the ideas of bloodshed and violence ; gross and material conceptions of life were in the ascendant ; and a romantic and aspiring Christianity gave place to a worldly and vulgar Churchianity.

I have in these two or three pages dealt only—and that very briefly—with the entry of the pagan doctrine of the Saviour into the Christian field, showing its transformation there and how Christianity could not well escape having a doctrine of a Saviour, or avoid giving a colour of its own to that doctrine. To follow out the same course with other doctrines, like those which I have mentioned above, would obviously be an endless task—which must be left to each student or reader to pursue according to his opportunity and capacity. It is clear anyhow, that all these elements of the pagan religions—pouring down into the vast reservoir, or rather whirlpool, of the Roman Empire, and mixing among all these numerous brotherhoods, societies, *collegia*, mystery-clubs, and groups which were at that time looking out intently for some new revelation or inspiration—did more or less automatically act and react upon each other, and by the general conditions prevailing were modified, till they ultimately combined and took united shape in the movement which we call Christianity, but which only—as I have said—narrowly escaped being called Mithraism—so nearly related and closely allied were these cults with each other.

At this point it will naturally be asked : " And where in this scheme of the Genesis of Christianity is the chief figure and accredited leader of the movement—namely Jesus Christ himself—for to all appearance in the account here given of the matter he is practically non-existent or a negligible quantity ? " And the question is a very pertinent one, and very difficult to answer. " Where is the founder of the Religion ? "—or to put it in another form : " Is it necessary to suppose a human and visible Founder at all ? " A few years ago such a mere question would have been accounted rank blasphemy, and would only—if passed over—have been ignored on account of its supposed absurdity. To-day, however, owing to the enormous amount of work which has been done of late on the subject of Christian origins, the question takes on quite a different complexion. And from Strauss onwards a growingly influential and learned body of critics is inclined to regard the whole story of the Gospels as *legendary*. Arthur Drews, for instance, a professor at Karlsruhe, in his cele- brated book *The Christ-Myth*,[1] places David F. Strauss as first in the myth field—though he allows that Dupuis in *L'origine de tous les cultes* (1795) had given the clue to the whole idea. He then mentions Bruno Bauer (1877) as contending that Jesus was a pure invention of Mark's, and John M. Robertson as having in his *Christianity and My- thology* (1900) given the first thoroughly reasoned exposition of the legendary theory ; also Emilio Bossi in Italy, who

---

[1] *Die Christus-mythe* : verbesserte und erweitezte Ausgabe, Jena, 1910.

wrote *Jesu Christo non e mai esistito*, and similar authors
in Holland, Poland, and other countries, including W.
Benjamin Smith, the American author of *The Pre-christian
Jesus* (1906), and P. Jensen in *Das Gilgamesch Epos in den
Welt-literatur* (1906), who makes the Jesus-story a variant of
the Babylonian epic, 2000 B.C. A pretty strong list ! [1] " But,"
continues Drews, " ordinary historians still ignore all this."
Finally, he dismisses Jesus as " a figure swimming obscurely
in the mists of tradition." Nevertheless I need hardly
remark that, large and learned as the body of opinion here
represented is, a still larger (but less learned) body fights
desperately for the actual *historicity* of Jesus, and some
even still for the old view of him as a quite unique and
miraculous revelation of Godhood on earth.

At first, no doubt, the *legendary* theory seems a little
too far-fetched. There is a fashion in all these things,
and it *may* be that there is a fashion even here. But when
you reflect how rapidly legends grow up even in these days
of exact Science and an omniscient Press ; how the figure
of Shakespeare, dead only 300 years, is almost completely
lost in the mist of Time, and even the authenticity of his
works has become a subject of controversy ; when you
find that William Tell, supposed to have lived some 300
years again before Shakespeare, and whose deeds in minutest
detail have been recited and honoured all over Europe,
is almost certainly a pure invention, and never existed ;
when you remember—as mentioned earlier in this book [2]—
that it was more than five hundred years after the supposed
birth of Jesus before any serious effort was made to establish
the date of that birth—and that then a purely mythical
date was chosen : the 25th December, the day of the *Sun's*
new birth after the winter solstice, and the time of the
supposed birth of Apollo, Bacchus, and the other Sungods ;

[1] To which we may also add Schweitzer's *Quest o the historical
Jesus* (1910).
[2] Ch. II, *supra*.

when, moreover, you think for a moment what the state of historical criticism must have been, and the general standard of credibility, 1,900 years ago, in a country like Syria, and among an ignorant population, where any story circulating from lip to lip was assured of credence if sufficiently marvelous or imaginative ;—why, then the legendary theory does not seem so improbable. There is no doubt that after the destruction of Jerusalem (in A.D. 70), little groups of believers in a redeeming ' Christ ' were formed there and in other places, just as there had certainly existed, in the first century B.C., groups of Gnostics, Therapeutæ, Essenes and others whose teachings were very *similar* to the Christian, and there was now a demand from many of those groups for ' writings ' and ' histories ' which should hearten and confirm the young and growing Churches. The Gospels and Epistles, of which there are still extant a great abundance, both apocryphal and canonical, met this demand ; but how far their records of the person of Jesus of Nazareth are reliable history, or how far they are merely imaginative pictures of the kind of man the Saviour might be expected to be,[1] is a question which, as I have already said, is a difficult one for skilled critics to answer, and one on which I certainly have no intention of giving a positive verdict. Personally I must say I think the ' legendary ' solution quite likely, and in some ways more satisfactory than the opposite one—for the simple reason that it seems much more encouraging to suppose that the story of Jesus, (gracious and beautiful as it is) is a myth which gradually formed itself in the conscience of mankind, and thus points the way of humanity's future evolution, than to suppose it to be the mere record of an unique and miraculous interposition of Providence, which depended entirely on the powers above, and could hardly be expected to occur again

[1] One of Celsus' accusations against the Christians was that their Gospels had been written " several times over " (see Origen, *Contra Celsum*, ii. 26, 27).

However, the question is not what we desire, but what we can prove to be the actual fact. And certainly the difficulties in the way of regarding the Gospel story (or stories, for there is not one consistent story) as *true* are enormous. If anyone will read, for instance, in the four Gospels, the events of the night preceding the crucifixion and reckon the time which they would necessarily have taken to enact— the Last Supper, the agony in the Garden, the betrayal by Judas, the haling before Caiaphas and the Sanhedrin, and then before Pilate in the Hall of Judgment (though courts for the trial of malefactors do not *generally* sit in the middle of the night) ; then—in Luke—the interposed visit to Herod, and the *return* to Pilate ; Pilate's speeches and washing of hands before the crowd ; then the scourging and the mocking and the arraying of Jesus in purple robe as a king ; then the preparation of a Cross and the long and painful journey to Golgotha ; and finally the Crucifixion at sunrise ;—he will see—as has often been pointed out— that the whole story is physically impossible. As a record of actual events the story is impossible ; but as a record or series of notes derived from the witnessing of a " mystery-play "—and such plays with *very similar* incidents were common enough in antiquity in connexion with cults of a dying Saviour, it very likely *is* true (one can see the very dramatic character of the incidents : the washing of hands, the threefold denial by Peter, the purple robe and crown of thorns, and so forth) ; and as such it is now accepted by many well-qualified authorities.[1]

[1] Dr. Frazer in *The Golden Bough* (vol. ix, " The Scapegoat,' p. 400) speaks of the frequency in antiquity of a Mystery-play relating to a God-man who gives his life and blood for the people ; and he puts forward tentatively and by no means dogmatically the following note :—" Such a drama, if we are right, was the original story of Esther and Mordecai, or (to give their older names) Ishtar and Marduk. It was played in Babylonia, and from Babylonia the returning Captives brought it to Judæa, where it was acted, rather as an historical than a mythical piece, by players who, having to die in grim earnest on a cross or gallows, were naturally drawn from the gaol

There are many other difficulties. The raising of Lazarus, already dead three days, the turning of water into wine (a miracle attributed to Bacchus, of old), the feeding of the five thousand, and others of the marvels are, to say the least, not easy of digestion. The " Sermon on the Mount " which, with the " Lord's Prayer " embedded in it, forms the great and accepted repository of ' Christian ' teaching and piety, is well known to be a collection of sayings from pre-christian writings, including the Psalms, Isaiah, Ecclesiasticus, the *Secrets of Enoch*, the *Shemoneh-esreh* (a book of Hebrew prayers), and others ; and the fact that this collection was really made *after* the time of Jesus, and could not have originated from him, is clear from the stress which it lays on " persecutions " and " false prophets " —things which were certainly not a source of trouble at the time Jesus is supposed to be speaking, though they were at a later time—as well as from the occurrence of the word " Gentiles," which being here used apparently in contradistinction to " Christians " could not well be appropriate at a time when no recognised Christian bodies as yet existed.

But the most remarkable point in this connexion is the absolute silence of the Gospel of Mark on the subject of the Resurrection and Ascension—that is, of the *original* Gospel, for it is now allowed on all hands that the twelve verses Mark xvi. 9 to the end, are a later insertion. Considering the nature of this event, astounding indeed, if physically true, and unique in the history of the world, it is strange that this Gospel—the earliest written of the four Gospels, and nearest in time to the actual evidence—

rather than the green-room. A chain of causes, which because we cannot follow them might—in the loose language of common life be called an accident, determined that the part of the dying god in this annual play should be thrust upon Jesus of Nazareth, whom the enemies he had made in high places by his outspoken strictures were resolved to put out of the way." See also vol. iv, " The Dying God," in the same book.

makes no mention of it. The next Gospel in point of time
—that of Matthew—mentions the matter rather briefly
and timidly, and reports the story that the body had been
stolen from the sepulchre. Luke enlarges considerably
and gives a whole long chapter to the resurrection and
ascension ; while the Fourth Gospel, written fully twenty
years later still—say about A.D. 120—gives two chapters
and a *great variety of details !*

This increase of detail, however, as one gets farther
and farther from the actual event is just what one always
finds, as I have said before, in legendary traditions. A
very interesting example of this has lately come to light
in the case of the traditions concerning the life and death
of the Persian Bâb. The Bâb, as most of my readers will
know, was the Founder of a great religious movement
which now numbers (or numbered before the Great War)
some millions of adherents, chiefly Mahommedans, Christians, Jews and Parsees. The period of his missionary
activity was from 1845 to 1850. His Gospel was singularly
like that of Jesus—a gospel of love to mankind—only (as
might be expected from the difference of date) with an
even wider and more deliberate inclusion of *all* classes,
creeds and races, sinners and saints ; and the incidents
and *entourage* of his ministry were also singularly similar.
He was born at Shiraz in 1820, and growing up a promising
boy and youth, fell at the age of 21 under the influence
of a certain Seyyid Kazim, leader of a heterodox sect, and
a kind of fore-runner or John the Baptist to the Bâb. The
result was a period of mental trouble (like the " temptation in the wilderness "), after which the youth returned
to Shiraz and at the age of twenty-five began his own mission.
His real name was Mirza Ali Muhammad, but he called
himself thenceforth *The Bâb*, i.e. the Gate (" I am the
Way ") ; and gradually there gathered round him disciples,
drawn by the fascination of his personality and the devotion of his character. But with the rapid increase of his

following great jealousy and hatred were excited among the Mullahs, the upholders of a fanatical and narrow-minded Mahommedanism and quite corresponding to the Scribes and Pharisees of the New Testament. By them he was denounced to the Turkish Government. He was arrested on a charge of causing political disturbance, and was condemned to death. Among his disciples was one favourite,[1] who was absolutely devoted to his Master and refused to leave him at the last. So together they were suspended over the city wall (at Tabriz) and simultaneously shot. This was on the 8th July, 1850.

In November 1850—or between that date and October 1851, a book appeared, written by one of the Bâb's earliest and most enthusiastic disciples—a merchant of Kashan—and giving in quite simple and unpretending form a record of the above events. There is in it no account of miracles or of great pretensions to godhood and the like. It is just a plain history of the life and death of a beloved teacher. It was cordially received and circulated far and wide; and we have no reason for doubting its essential veracity. And 'even if proved now to be inaccurate in one or two details, this would not invalidate the moral of the rest of the story—which is as follows:

After the death of the Bâb a great persecution took place (in 1852); there were many Bâbi martyrs, and for some years the general followers were scattered. But in time they gathered themselves together again; successors to the original prophet were appointed—though not without dissensions—and a Bâbi church, chiefly at Acca or Acre in Syria, began to be formed. It was during this period that a great number of legends grew up—legends of miraculous babyhood and boyhood, legends of miracles performed by the mature Bâb, and so forth; and when the newly-forming Church came to look into the matter it concluded

[1] Mirza Muhammad Ali; and one should note the similarity of the two names.

(quite naturally!) that such a simple history as I have
outlined above would never do for the foundation of its
plans, now grown somewhat ambitious. So a new Gospel
was framed, called the *Tarikh-i-Jadid* (" The new History "
or " The new Way "), embodying and including a lot of
legendary matter, and issued with the authority of " the
Church." This was in 1881-2 ; and comparing this with
the original record (called *The point of Kaf*) we get a
luminous view of the growth of fable in those thirty brief
years which had elapsed since the Bâb's death. Meanwhile
it became very necessary of course to withdraw from circu-
lation as far as possible all copies of the original record,
lest they should give the lie to the later ' Gospel ' ; and
this apparently was done very effectively—so effectively
indeed that Professor Edward Browne (to whom the world
owes so much on account of his labours in connexion with
Bâbism), after arduous search, came at one time to the
conclusion that the original was no longer extant. Most
fortunately, however, the well-known Comte de Gobineau
had in the course of his studies on Eastern Religions acquired
a copy of *The point of Kaf;* and this, after his death,
was found among his literary treasures and identified (as
was most fitting) by Professor Browne himself.

Such in brief is the history of the early Bâbi Church [1]
—a Church which has grown up and expanded greatly
within the memory of many yet living. Much might be
written about it, but the chief point at present is for us
to note the well-verified and interesting example it gives
of the rapid growth in Syria of a religious legend and the
reasons which contributed to this growth—and to be warned
how much more rapidly similar legends probably grew up
in the same land in the middle of the First Century, A.D.

[1] For literature, see Edward G. Browne's *Traveller's Narrative
on the Episode of the Bâb* (1891), and his *New History of the Bâb* translated from the Persian of the *Tarikh-i-Jadid* (Cambridge, 1893). Also
Sermons and Essays by Herbert Rix (Williams and Norgate, 1907),
pp. 295-325, " The Persian Bâb."

The story of the Bâb is also interesting to us because, while
this mass of legend was formed around it, there is no possible
doubt about the actual existence of a historical nucleus
in the person of Mirza Ali Muhammad.

On the whole, one is sometimes inclined to doubt whether
any great movement ever makes itself felt in the world,
without dating first from some powerful personality or
group of personalities, *round* which the idealising and myth-
making genius of mankind tends to crystallize. But one
must not even here be too certain. Something of the
Apostle Paul we know, and something of ' John ' the
Evangelist and writer of the Epistle 1 John ; and that
the ' Christian ' doctrines dated largely from the preaching
and teaching of these two we cannot doubt ; but Paul
never saw Jesus (except " in the Spirit "), nor does he ever
mention the man personally, or any incident of his actual
life (the " crucified Christ " being always an ideal figure) ;
and ' John ' who wrote the Gospel was certainly not the
same as the disciple who " lay in Jesus' bosom "—though
an intercalated verse, the last but one in the Gospel, asserts
the identity.[1]

There may have been a historic Jesus—and if so, to get
a reliable outline of his life would indeed be a treasure ;
but at present it would seem there is no sign of that. If
the historicity of Jesus, in any degree, could be proved,
it would give us reason for supposing—what I have personally always been inclined to believe—that there was also
a historical nucleus for such personages as Osiris, Mithra,
Krishna, Hercules, Apollo and the rest. The question,
in fact, narrows itself down to this, Have there been in
the course of human evolution certain, so to speak, *nodal*
points or periods at which the psychologic currents ran
together and condensed themselves for a new start ; and

[1] It is obvious, in fact, that the *whole* of the last chapter of St.
John is a later insertion, and again that the two last verses of that
chapter are later than the chapter itself !

has each such node or point of condensation been marked
by the appearance of an actual and heroic man (or woman)
who supplied a necessary impetus for the new departure,
and gave his name to the resulting movement ? *or* is it
sufficient to suppose the automatic formation of such nodes
or starting-points without the intervention of any special
hero or genius, and to imagine that in each case the myth-
making tendency of mankind *created* a legendary and
inspiring figure and worshiped the same for a long period
afterwards as a god ?

As I have said before, this is a question which, interesting
as it is, is not really very important.   The main thing being
that the prophetic and creative spirit of mankind *has* from
time to time evolved those figures as idealisations of its
" heart's desire " and placed a halo round their heads.
The long procession of them becomes a *real* piece of History
—the history of the evolution of the human heart, and of
human consciousness.   But with the psychology of the
whole subject I shall deal in the next chapter.

I may here, however, dwell for a moment on two other
points which belong properly to this chapter. I have
already mentioned the great reliance placed by the advocates
of a unique ' revelation ' on the high morality taught in the
Gospels and the New Testament generally.   There is no
need of course to challenge that morality or to depreciate
it unduly ; but the argument assumes that it is so greatly
superior to anything of the kind that had been taught
before that we are compelled to suppose something like a
revelation to explain its appearance—whereas of course
anyone familiar with the writings of antiquity, among the
Greeks or Romans or Egyptians or Hindus or later Jews,
knows perfectly well that the reported sayings of Jesus
and the Apostles may be paralleled abundantly from these
sources.   I have illustrated this already from the Sermon
on the Mount.   If anyone will glance at the *Testament of*

the Twelve Patriarchs—a Jewish book composed about
120 B.C.—he will see that it is full of moral precepts, and
especially precepts of love and forgiveness, so ardent and
so noble that it hardly suffers in any way when compared
with the New Testament teaching, and that consequently
no special miracle is required to explain the appearance
of the latter.

The twelve Patriarchs in question are the twelve sons
of Jacob, and the book consists of their supposed death-
bed scenes, in which each patriarch in turn recites his own
(more or less imaginary) life and deeds and gives pious
counsel to his children and successors. It is composed in
a fine and poetic style, and is full of lofty thought, remindful in scores of passages of the Gospels—words and all—
the coincidences being too striking to be accidental. It
evidently had a deep influence on the authors of the Gospels,
as well as on St. Paul. It affirms a belief in the coming of
a Messiah, and in salvation for the Gentiles. The following
are some quotations from it : [1] Testament of Zebulun
(p. 116) : " My children, I bid you keep the commands of
the Lord, and show mercy to your neighbours, and have
compassion towards all, not towards men only, but also
towards beasts." Dan (p. 127) : " Love the Lord through
all your life, and one another with a true heart." Joseph
(p. 173) : " I was sick, and the Lord visited me ; in prison,
and my God showed favor unto me." Benjamin (p. 209) :
" For as the sun is not defiled by shining on dung and mire,
but rather drieth up both and driveth away the evil
smell, so also the pure mind, encompassed by the defile-
ments of earth, rather cleanseth them and is not itself
defiled."

I think these quotations are sufficient to prove the high
standard of this book, which was written in the Second
Century B.C., and *from* which the New Testament authors
copiously borrowed.

[1] The references being to the Edition by R. H. Charles (1907).

The other point has to do with my statement at the beginning of this chapter that two of the main ' characteristics ' of Christianity were its insistence on (a) a tendency towards renunciation of the world, and a consequent cultivation of a purely spiritual love, and (b) on a morality whose inspiration was a private sense of duty to God rather than a public sense of duty to one's neighbour and to society generally. I think, however, that the last-mentioned characteristic ought to be viewed in relation to a third, namely, (c) the extraordinarily *democratic* tendency of the new Religion.[1] Celsus (A.D. 200) jeered at the early Christians for their extreme democracy : " It is only the simpletons, the ignoble, the senseless—slaves and womenfolk and children—whom they wish to persuade [to join their churches] or *can* persuade "—" wool-dressers and cobblers and fullers, the most uneducated and vulgar persons," and " whosoever is a sinner, or unintelligent or a fool, in a word, whoever is god-forsaken (κακοδαίμων), him the Kingdom of God will receive."[2] Thus Celsus, the accomplished, clever, philosophic and withal humorous critic, laughed at the new religionists, and prophesied their speedy extinction. Nevertheless he was mistaken. There is little doubt that just the inclusion of women and weaklings and outcasts did contribute *largely* to the spread of Christianity (and Mithraism). It brought hope and a sense of human dignity to the despised and rejected of the earth. Of the immense numbers of lesser officials who carried on the vast organisation of the Roman Empire, most perhaps, were taken from the ranks of the freedmen and *quondam* slaves, drawn from a great variety of races and already

[1] It is important to note, however, that this same democratic tendency was very marked in Mithraism. " Il est certain," says Cumont, " qu'il a fait ses premières conquêtes dans les classes inférieures de la société, et c'est l'a un fait considérable ; le mithracisme est resté longtemps la réligion des humbles." *Mystères de Mithra*, p. 68.

[2] See Glover's *Conflict of Religions in the early Roman Empire*, ch. viii.

familiar with pagan cults of all kinds—Egyptian, Syrian, Chaldean, Iranian, and so forth.[1] This fact helped to give to Christianity—under the fine tolerance of the Empire— its democratic character and also its willingness to accept all. The rude and menial masses, who had hitherto been almost beneath the notice of Greek and Roman culture, flocked in ; and though this was doubtless, as time went on, a source of weakness to the Church, and a cause of dissension and superstition, yet it was in the inevitable line of human evolution, and had a psychological basis which I must now endeavour to explain.

[1] See Toutain, *Cultes païens*, vol. ii, conclusion.

XIV

THE MEANING OF IT ALL

THE general drift and meaning of the present book must now, I think, from many hints scattered in the course of it, be growing clear. But it will be well perhaps in this chapter, at the risk of some repetition, to bring the whole argument together. And the argument is that since the dawn of humanity on the earth—many hundreds of thousands or perhaps a million years ago—there has been a slow psychologic evolution, a gradual development or refinement of Consciousness, which at a certain stage has spontaneously given birth in the human race to the phenomena of religious belief and religious ritual—these phenomena (whether in the race at large or in any branch of it) always following, step by step, a certain order depending on the degrees of psychologic evolution concerned ; and that it is this general fact which accounts for the strange similarities of belief and ritual which have been observed all over the world and in places far remote from each other, and which have been briefly noted in the preceding chapters.

And the main stages of this psychologic evolution— those at any rate with which we are here concerned—are Three : the stage of Simple Consciousness, the stage of Self-consciousness, and a third Stage which for want of a better word we may term the stage of Universal Consciousness. Of course these three stages may at some future

time be analysed into lesser degrees, with useful result—
but at present I only desire to draw attention to them in
the rough, so to speak, to show that it is from them and
from their passage one into another that there has flowed
by a perfectly natural logic and concatenation the strange
panorama of humanity's religious evolution—its superstitions and magic and sacrifices and dancings and ritual
generally, and later its incantations and prophecies, and
services of speech and verse, and paintings and forms of
art, and figures of the gods.   A wonderful Panorama indeed,
or poem of the Centuries, or, if you like, World-symphony
with three great leading motives !

   And first we have the stage of Simple Consciousness.
For hundreds of centuries (we cannot doubt) Man possessed
a degree of consciousness not radically different from that
of the higher Animals, though probably more quick and
varied. He saw, he heard, he felt, he noted. He acted
or reacted, quickly or slowly, in response to these impressions.
But the consciousness of him*self*, as a being separate from
his impressions, as separate from his surroundings, had
not yet arisen or taken hold on him.   He was an instinctive
part of Nature.   And in this respect he was very near to
the Animals. Self-consciousness in the animals, in a
germinal form is there, no doubt, but *embedded*, so to speak,
in the general world consciousness.   It is on this account
that the animals have such a marvellously acute perception
and instinct, being embedded in Nature. And primitive
Man had the same. Also we must, as I have said before,
allow that man in that stage must have had the same sort
of grace and perfection of form and movement as we admire
in the (wild) animals now.   It would be quite unreasonable
to suppose that he, the crown in some sense of creation,
was from the beginning a lame and ill-made abortion. For
a long long period the tribes of men, like the tribes of the
higher animals, must have been (on the whole, and allowing

for occasional privations and sufferings and conflicts)
well adapted to their surroundings and harmonious with
the earth and with each other. There must have been
a period resembling a Golden Age—some condition at any
rate which, compared with subsequent miseries, merited
the epithet ' golden.'

It was during this period apparently that the system
of Totems arose. The tribes felt their relationship to their
winged and fourfooted mates (including also other objects
of nature) so deeply and intensely that they adopted the
latter as their emblems. The pre-civilisation Man fairly
worshiped the animals and was proud to be called after
them. Of course we moderns find this strange. We,
whose conceptions of these beautiful creatures are mostly
derived from a broken-down cab-horse, or a melancholy
milk-rummaged cow in a sooty field, or a diseased and
despondent lion or eagle at the Zoo, have never even seen
or loved them and have only wondered with our true commercial instinct what profit we could extract from them.
But they, the primitives, loved and admired the animals ;
they domesticated many of them by the force of a natural
friendship,[1] and accorded them a kind of divinity. This
was the age of tribal solidarity and of a latent sense of
solidarity with Nature. And the point of it all is (with
regard to the subject we have in hand) that this was also
the age from which by a natural evolution the sense of
Religion came to mankind. If Religion in man *is* the sense
of ties binding his inner self to the powers of the universe
around him, then it is evident I think that primitive man
as I have described him possessed the *reality* of this sense
—though so far buried and subconscious that he was hardly
aware of it. It was only later, and with the coming of

---

[1] See ch. iv, *supra.* Tylor in his *Primitive Culture* (vol. i, p. 469,
edn. 1903) says : " The sense of an absolute psychical distinction
between man and beast, so prevalent in the civilised world, is hardly
to be found among the lower races."

the *Second Stage*, that this sense began to rise distinctly into consciousness.

Let us pass then to the Second Stage.   There is a moment in the evolution of a child—somewhere perhaps about the age of three [1]—when the simple almost animal-like consciousness of the babe is troubled by a new element—*self-*consciousness.   The change is so marked, so definite, that (in the depth of the infant's eyes) you can almost *see* it take place.   So in the evolution of the human race there has been a period—also marked and definite, though extending intermittent over a vast interval of time—when on men in general there dawned the consciousness of *themselves*, of their own thoughts and actions.   The old simple acceptance of sensations and experiences gave place to *reflection*. The question arose : " How do these sensations and experiences affect *me* ?   What can *I* do to modify them, to encourage the pleasurable, to avoid or inhibit the painful, and so on ? "   From that moment a new motive was added to life.   The mind revolved round a new centre.   It began to spin like a little eddy round its own axis.   It studied *itself* first and became deeply concerned about its own pleasures and pains, losing touch the while with the larger life which once dominated it—the life of Nature, the life of the Tribe.   The old unity of the spirit, the old solidarity, were broken up.

I have touched on this subject before, but it is so important that the reader must excuse repetition.   There came an inevitable severance, an inevitable period of strife.   The magic mirror of the soul, reflecting nature as heretofore in calm and simple grace, was suddenly cracked across. The new self-conscious man (not all at once but gradually) became alienated from his tribe.   He lapsed into strife with his fellows.   Ambition, vanity, greed, the love of

[1] See Bucke's *Cosmic Consciousness* (Philadelphia, 1901), pp. 11 and 39 ; also W. McDougall's *Social Psychology* (1908), p. 146— where the same age is tentatively suggested.

domination, the desire for property and possessions, set
in.   The influences of fellowship and solidarity grew feebler.
He became alienated from his great Mother.   His instincts
were less and less sure—and that in proportion as brain-
activity and self-regarding calculation took their place.
Love and mutual help were less compelling in proportion as
the demands of self-interest grew louder and more insistent.
Ultimately the crisis came.   Cain murdered his brother
and became an outcast.   The Garden of Eden and the
Golden Age closed their gates behind him.   He entered
upon a period of suffering—a period of labour and toil
and sorrow such as he had never before known, and such
as the animals certainly have never known.   And in that
distressful state, in that doleful valley of his long pilgrimage,
he still remains to-day

Thus has the canker of self-consciousness done its work.
It would be foolish and useless to rail against the process,
or to blame any one for it.   It had to be.   Through this
dismal vale of self-seeking mankind had to pass—if only
in order at last to find the True Self which was (and still
remains) its goal.   The pilgrimage will not last for ever.
Indeed there are signs that the recent Great War and the
following Events mark the lowest point of descent and the
beginning of the human soul's return to sanity and ascent
towards the heavenly Kingdom.   No doubt Man *will*
arrive again *some* day at the grace, composure and leisurely
beauty of life which the animals realised long ago, though
he seems a precious long time about it ; and when all this
nightmare of Greed and Vanity and Self-conceit and Cruelty
will come again to its Golden Age and to that Paradise of
and Lust of oppression and domination, which marks the
present period, is past—and it *will* pass—then Humanity
redemption and peace which has for so long been prophesied.

But we are dealing with the origins of Religion ; and
what I want the reader to see is that it was just this breaking
up of the old psychologic unity and continuity of man with

his surroundings which led to the whole panorama of the rituals and creeds. Man, centering round himself, necessarily became an exile from the great Whole. He committed the sin (if it was a sin) of Separation. Anyhow Nemesis was swift. The sense of loneliness and the sense of guilt came on him. The realisation of himself as a separate conscious being necessarily led to his attributing a similar consciousness of some kind to the great Life around him. Action and reaction are equal and opposite. Whatever he may have felt before, it became clear to him now that beings more or less like himself—though doubtless vaster and more powerful—moved behind the veil of the visible world. From that moment the belief in Magic and Demons and Gods arose or slowly developed itself ; and in the midst of this turmoil of perilous and conflicting powers, he perceived himself an alien and an exile, stricken with Fear, stricken with the sense of Sin. If before, he had experienced fear—in the kind of automatic way of self-preservation in which the animals feel it—he now, with fevered self-regard and excited imagination, experienced it in double or treble degree. And if, before, he had been aware that fortune and chance were not always friendly and propitious to his designs, he now perceived or thought he perceived in every adverse happening the deliberate persecution of the powers, and an accusation of guilt directed against him for some neglect or deficiency in his relation to them. Hence by a perfectly logical and natural sequence there arose the belief in other-world or supernatural powers, whether purely fortuitous and magical or more distinctly rational and personal ; there arose the sense of Sin, or of offence against these powers ; there arose a complex ritual of Expiation—whether by personal sacrifice and suffering or by the sacrifice of victims. There arose too a whole catalogue of ceremonies—ceremonies of Initiation, by which the novice should learn to keep within the good grace of the Powers, and under the blessing of his Tribe

and the protection of its Totem ; ceremonies of Eucharistic
meals which should restore the lost sanctity of the common
life and remove the sense of guilt and isolation ; ceremonies
of Marriage and rules and rites of sex-connexion, fitted to
curb the terrific and demonic violence of passions which
else indeed might easily rend the community asunder.
And so on. It is easy to see that granted an early stage
of simple unreflecting nature-consciousness, and granting
this broken into and, after a time, shattered by the arrival
of *self*-consciousness there would necessarily follow in
spontaneous yet logical order a whole series of religious
institutions and beliefs, which phantasmal and unreal
as they may appear to us, were by no means unreal to our
ancestors. It is easy also to see that as the psychological
process was necessarily of similar general character in every
branch of the human race and all over the world, so the
religious evolutions—the creeds and rituals—took on much
the same complexion everywhere ; and, though they differed
in details according to climate and other influences, ran
on such remarkably parallel lines as we have noted.

Finally, to make the whole matter clear, let me repeat
that this event, the inbreak of Self-consciousness, took
place, or *began* to take place, an enormous time ago, perhaps
in the beginning of the Neolithic Age.   I dwell on the word
" began " because I think it is probable that in its beginnings,
and for a long period after, this newborn consciousness
had an infantile and very innocent character, quite different
from its later and more aggressive forms—just as we see
self-consciousness in a little child has a charm and a grace
which it loses later in a boastful or grasping boyhood and
manhood. So we may understand that though self-
consciousness may have begun to appear in the human
race at this very early time (and more or less contempor-
aneously with the invention of very rude tools and unformed
language), there probably did elapse a very long period—
perhaps the whole of the Neolithic Age—before the evils

of this second stage of human evolution came to a head. Max Müller has pointed out that among the words which are *common* to the various branches of Aryan language, and which therefore belong to the very early period before the separation of these branches, there are *not* found the words denoting war and conflict and the weapons and instruments of strife—a fact which suggests a long continuance of peaceful habit among mankind *after* the first formation and use of language.

That the birth of language and the birth of self-consciousness were *approximately* simultaneous is a probable theory, and one favoured by many thinkers ; [1] but the slow beginnings of both must have been so very protracted that it is perhaps useless to attempt any very exact determination. Late researches seem to show that language began in what might be called *tribal* expressions of mood and feeling (*holophrases* like " go-hunting-kill-bear ") without reference to individual personalities and relationships ; and that it was only at a later stage that words like " I " and " Thou " came into use, and the holophrases broke up into "parts of speech" and took on a definite grammatical structure.[2] If true, these facts point clearly to a long foreground of rude communal language, something like though greatly superior to that of the animals, preceding or preparing the evolution of Self-consciousness proper, in the forms of " I " and " Thou " and the grammar of personal actions and relations. " They show that the plural and all other forms of number in grammar arise not by multiplication of an original ' I,' but by selection and

---

[1] Dr. Bucke (*Cosmic Consciousness*) insists on their simultaneity, but places both events excessively far back, as we should think, i.e. 200,000 or 300,000 years ago. Possibly he does not differentiate sufficiently between the rude language of the holophrase and the much later growth of formed and grammatical speech.

[2] See A. E. Crawley's *Idea of the Soul*, ch. ii ; Jane Harrison's *Themis*, pp. 473–5 ; and E. J. Payne's *History of the New World called America*, vol. ii, pp. 115 *sq.*, where the beginning of self-consciousness is associated with the break-up of the holophrase.

gradual *exclusion* from an original collective ' we.' "[1]   According to this view the birth of self-consciousness in the human family, or in any particular race or section of the human family, must have been equally slow and hesitating ; and it would be easy to imagine, as just said, that there may have been a very long and ' golden ' period at its beginning, before the new consciousness took on its maturer and harsher forms.

All estimates of the Time involved in these evolutions of early man are notoriously most divergent and most difficult to be sure of ; but if we take 500,000 years ago for the first appearance of veritable Man (*homo primigenius*),[2] and (following Professor W. J. Sollas)[3] 30,000 or 40,000 years ago for the first tool-using men (*homo sapiens*) of the Chellean Age (palaeolithic), 15,000 for the rock-paintings and inscriptions of the Aurignacian and Magdalenian peoples, and 5,000 years ago for the first actual historical records that have come down to us, we may perhaps get something like a proportion between the different periods.   That is to say, half a million years for the purely animal man in his different forms and grades of evolution. Then somewhere towards the end of palaeolithic or commencement of neolithic times Self-consciousness dimly beginning and, after some 10,000 years of slow germination and pre-historic culture, culminating in the actual historic period and the dawn of civilisation 40 or 50 centuries ago, and to-day (we hope), reaching the climax which precedes or foretells its abatement and transformation.

No doubt many geologists and anthropologists would favour periods greatly *longer* than those here mentioned ; but possibly there would be some agreement as to the *ratio*

[1] *Themis*, p. 471.

[2] Though Dr. Arthur Keith, *Ancient Types of Man* (1911), pp. 93 and 102, puts the figure at more like a million.

[3] See *Ancient Hunters* (1915) ; also Hastings's *Encycl.* art. " Ethnology " ; and Havelock Ellis, " The Origin of War," in *The Philosophy of Conflict and other Essays*.

to each other of the times concerned : that is, the said
authorities would probably allow for a *very long* animal-
man [1] period corresponding to the first stage ; for a much
shorter aggressively 'self-conscious' period, corresponding
to the Second Stage—perhaps lasting only one thirtieth
or fiftieth of the time of the first period ; and then—if
they looked forward at all to a third stage—would be inclined
for obvious reasons to attribute to that again a very extended
duration.

However, all this is very speculative. To return to the
difficulty about Language and the consideration of those
early times when words adequate to the expression of
religious or magical ideas simply did not exist, it is clear
that the only available, or at any rate the *chief* means of
expression, in those times, must have consisted in gestures,
in attitudes, in ceremonial *actions*—in a more or less elaborate
ritual, in fact.[2] Such ideas as Adoration, Thanksgiving,
confession of Guilt, placation of Wrath, Expiation, Sacrifice,
Celebration of Community, sacramental Atonement, and
a score of others could at that time be expressed by appropriate rites—and as a matter of fact are often so expressed
even now—*more* readily and directly than by language.
'Dancing'—when that word came to be invented—did
not mean a mere flinging about of the limbs in recreation,
but any expressive movements of the body which might be
used to convey the feelings of the dancer or of the audience
whom he represented.   And so the 'religious dance' became
a most important part of ritual.

So much for the second stage of Consciousness.   Let us
now pass on to the Third Stage.   It is evident that the
process of disruption and dissolution—disruption both of

---

[1] I use the phrase 'animal-man' here, not with any flavour of
contempt or reprobation, as the dear Victorians would have used
it, but with a sense of genuine respect and admiration such as one
feels towards the animals themselves.

[2] See *supra*, ch. ix, pp. 147, 148 and xi, pp. 165, 166.

the human mind, and of society round about it, due to the action of the Second Stage—could not go on indefinitely. There are hundreds of thousands of people at the present moment who are dying of mental or bodily disease—their nervous systems broken down by troubles connected with excessive self-consciousness—selfish fears and worries and restlessness. Society at large is perishing both in industry and in warfare through the domination in its organism of the self-motives of greed and vanity and ambition. This cannot go on for ever. Things must either continue in the same strain, in which case it is evident that we are approaching a crisis of utter dissolution, *or* a new element must enter in, a new inspiration of life, and we (as individuals) and the society of which we form a part, must make a fresh start. What is that new and necessary element of regeneration ?

It is evident that it must be a new birth—the entry into a further stage of consciousness which must supersede the present one. Through some such crisis as we have spoken of, through the extreme of suffering, the mind of Man, *as at present constituted,* has to die.[1] Self-consciousness has to die, and be buried, and rise again in a new form. Probably nothing but the extreme of suffering can bring this about.[2] And what is this new form in which consciousness has to rearise ? Obviously, since the miseries of the world during countless centuries have dated from that fatal attempt to make the little personal *self* the centre of effort and activity, and since that attempt has inevitably led to disunity and discord and death, both within the mind itself and within the body of society, there is nothing left but the return to a Consciousness which shall have Unity as its foundation-principle, and which shall proceed from the

[1] " The mind must be restrained in the heart till it comes to an end," says the Maitráyana-Brahmana-Upanishad.

[2] One may remember in this connexion the *tapas* of the Hindu yogi, or the ordeals of initiates into the pagan Mysteries generally.

direct *sense and perception* of such an unity throughout
creation. The simple mind of Early Man and the Animals
was of that character—a consciousness, so to speak, continuous through nature, and though running to points of
illumination and foci of special activity in individuals, yet
at no point essentially broken or imprisoned in separate
compartments. (And it is this *continuity* of the primitive
mind which enables us, .as I have already explained, to
understand the mysterious workings of instinct and intuition.) To some such unity-consciousness we have to
return ; but clearly it will not be—it is not—of the simple
inchoate character of the First Stage, for it has been en-
riched, deepened, and greatly extended by the experience
of the Second Stage. It is in fact, a new order of mentality
—the consciousness of the Third Stage.

In order to understand the operation and qualities of
this Third Consciousness, it may be of assistance just now
to consider in what more or less rudimentary way or ways
it figured in the pagan rituals and in Christianity. We
have seen the rude Siberyaks in North-Eastern Asia or
the ' Grizzly ' tribes of North American Indians in the
neighborhood of Mount Shasta paying their respects and
adoration to a captive bear—at once the food-animal,
and the divinity of the Tribe. A tribesman had slain a
bear—and, be it said, had slain it not in a public hunt
with all due ceremonies observed, but privately for his
own satisfaction. He had committed, therefore, a sin
theoretically unpardonable ; for had he not—to gratify
his personal desire for food—levelled a blow at the guardian
spirit of the Tribe ? Had he not alienated himself from
his fellows by destroying its very symbol ? There was
only one way by which he could regain the fellowship of
his companions. He must make amends by some public
sacrifice, and instead of retaining the flesh of the animal
for himself he must share it with the whole tribe (or clan)

in a common feast, while at the same time, tensest prayers and thanks are offered to the animal for the gift of his body for food. The Magic formula demanded nothing less than this—else dread disaster would fall upon the man who sinned, and upon the whole brotherhood. Here, and in a hundred similar rites, we see the three phases of tribal psychology—the first, in which the individual member simply remains within the compass of the tribal mind, and only acts in harmony with it ; the second, in which the individual steps outside and to gratify his personal *self* performs an action which alienates him from his fellows ; and the third, in which, to make amends and to prove his sincerity, he submits to some sacrifice, and by a common feast or some such ceremony is received back again into the unity of the fellowship. The body of the animal-divinity is consumed, and the latter becomes, both in the spirit and in the flesh, the Saviour of the tribe.

In course of time, when the Totem or Guardian-spirit is no longer merely an Animal, or animal-headed Genius, but a quite human-formed Divinity, still the same general outline of ideas is preserved—only with gathered intensity owing to the specially human interest of the drama. The Divinity who gives his life for his flock is no longer just an ordinary Bull or Lamb, but Adonis or Osiris or Dionysus or Jesus. He is betrayed by one of his own followers, and suffers death, but rises again redeeming all with himself in the one fellowship ; and the corn and the wine and the wild flesh which were his body, and which he gave for the sustenance of mankind, are consumed in a holy supper of reconciliation. It is always the return to unity which is the ritual of Salvation, and of which the symbol is the Eucharist—the second birth, the formation of " a new creature when old things are passed away." For " Except a man be born again, he cannot see the Kingdom of God " ; and " the first man is of the earth, earthy, but the second man is the Lord from heaven." Like a strange refrain, and from centuries before our era, comes down this belief in a god who is imprisoned in each man, and whose liberation is a new birth and the beginning of a new creature : " Rejoice, ye initiates in the mystery of the liberated god " —rejoice in the thought of the hero who died as a mortal in the coffin, but rises again as Lord of all !

Who then was this " Christos " for whom the world was waiting three centuries before our era (and indeed centuries before that) ? Who was this " thrice Saviour " whom the Greek Gnostics acclaimed ? What was the meaning of that "coming of the Son of Man " whom Daniel beheld in vision among the clouds of heaven ? or of the " perfect man " who, Paul declared, should deliver us from the bondage of corruption into the glorious liberty of the children of God ? What was this salvation which time after time and times again the pagan deities promised to their devotees, and which the Eleusinian and other Mysteries represented in their religious dramas with such convincing enthusiasm that even Pindar could say " Happy is he who has seen them (the Mysteries) before he goes beneath the hollow earth : that man knows the true end of life and its source divine " ; and concerning which Sophocles and Aeschylus were equally enthusiastic ? [1]

Can we doubt, in the light of all that we have already said, what the answer to these questions is ? As with the first blossoming of self-consciousness in the human mind came the dawn of an immense cycle of experience— a cycle indeed of exile from Eden, of suffering and toil and blind wanderings in the wilderness, yet a cycle absolutely necessary and unavoidable—so now the redemption, the return, the restoration has to come through another forward step, in the same domain. Abandoning the quest and the glorification of the separate isolated self we have to return to the cosmic universal life. It is the blossoming indeed

[1] See Farnell's *Cults of the Greek States*, vol. iii, p. 194 ; also *The Mysteries, Pagan and Christian,* by S. Cheetham, D.D. (London, 1897).

of this ' new ' life in the deeps of our minds which *is* salvation,
and which all the expressions which I have just cited have
indicated. It is this presence which all down the ages
has been hailed as Saviour and Liberator: the daybreak of a
consciousness so much vaster, so much more glorious, than
all that has gone before that the little candle of the local self
is swallowed up in its rays. It is the return home, the
return into direct touch with Nature and Man—the liberation from the long exile of separation, from the painful
sense of isolation and the odious nightmare of guilt and
' sin.' Can we doubt that this new birth—this third stage
of consciousness, if we like to call it so—has to come, that
it is indeed not merely a pious hope or a tentative theory,
but a *fact* testified to already by a cloud of witnesses in
the past—witnesses shining in their own easily recognisable
and authentic light, yet for the most part isolated from
each other among the arid and unfruitful wastes of Civilisation, like glow-worms in the dry grass of a summer night ?

Since the first dim evolution of human self-consciousness
an immense period, as we have said—perhaps 30,000 years,
perhaps even more—has elapsed. Now, in the present
day this period is reaching its culmination, and though
it will not terminate immediately, its end is, so to speak,
in sight. Meanwhile, during all the historical age behind
us—say for the last 4,000 or 5,000 years—evidence has been
coming in (partly in the religious rites recorded, partly
in oracles, poems and prophetic literature) of the onset
of this further illumination—" the light which never was
on sea or land "—and the cloud of witnesses, scattered
at first, has in these later centuries become so evident and
so notable that we are tempted to believe in or to anticipate
a great and general new birth, as now not so very far off.[1]
[We should, however, do well to remember, in this con-

---

[1] For an amplification of all this theme, see Dr. Bucke's remarkable and epoch-making book, *Cosmic Consciousness* (first published
at Philadelphia, 1901).

nexion, that many a time already in history the Millennium has been prophesied, and yet not arrived punctual to date, and to take to ourselves the words of ' Peter,' who somewhat grievously disappointed at the long-delayed second coming of the Lord Jesus in the clouds of heaven, wrote in his second Epistle : " There shall come in the last days scoffers, walking after their own lusts, and saying, Where is the promise of his coming ? for since the fathers fell asleep, all things continue as they were from the beginning of the creation." [1]]

I say that all through the historical age behind us there has been evidence—even though scattered—of salvation and the return of the Cosmic life. Man has never been so completely submerged in the bitter sea of self-centredness but what he has occasionally been able to dash the spray from his eyes and glimpse the sun and the glorious light of heaven. From how far back we cannot say, but from an immense antiquity come the beautiful myths which indicate this.

Cinderella, the cinder-maiden, sits unbeknown in her earthly
    hutch ;
Gibed and jeered at she bewails her lonely fate ;
Nevertheless youngest-born she surpasses her sisters and endues
    a garment of the sun and stars ;
From a tiny spark she ascends and irradiates the universe,
    and is wedded to the prince of heaven.

How lovely this vision of the little maiden sitting un-beknown close to the Hearth-fire of the universe—herself indeed just a little spark from it ; despised and rejected ; rejected by the world, despised by her two elder sisters (the body and the intellect) ; yet she, the soul, though latest-born, by far the most beautiful of the three. And of the Prince of Love who redeems and sets her free ; and of her

<hr>

[1] 2 Peter iii. 4 ; written probably about A.D. 150.

238 PAGAN AND CHRISTIAN CREEDS

wedding-garment the glory and beauty of all nature and of the heavens! The parables of Jesus are charming in their way, but they hardly reach this height of inspiration.

Or the world-old myth of Eros and Psyche. How strange that here again there are three sisters (the three stages of human evolution), and the latest-born the most beautiful of the three, and the jealousies and persecutions heaped on the youngest by the others, and especially by Aphrodite the goddess of mere sensual charm. And again the coming of the unknown, the unseen Lover, on whom it is not permitted for mortals to look; and the long, long tests and sufferings and trials which Psyche has to undergo before Eros may really take her to his arms and translate her to the heights of heaven. Can we not imagine how when these things were represented in the Mysteries the world flocked to see them, and the poets indeed said, " Happy are they that see and seeing can understand ? " Can we not understand how it was that the Amphictyonic decree of the second century B.C. spoke of these same Mysteries as enforcing the lesson that " the greatest of human blessings is fellowship and mutual trust " ?

XV

THE ANCIENT MYSTERIES

THUS we come to a thing which we must not pass over, because it throws great light on the meaning and interpretation of all these rites and ceremonies of the great World-religion. I mean the subject of the Ancient Mysteries. And to this I will give a few pages.

These Mysteries were probably survivals of the oldest religious rites of the Greek races, and in their earlier forms consisted not so much in worship of the gods of Heaven as of the divinities of Earth, and of Nature and Death. Crude, no doubt, at first, they gradually became (especially in their Eleusinian form) more refined and philosophical ; the rites were gradually thrown open, on certain conditions, not only to men generally, but also to women, and even to slaves ; and in the end they influenced Christianity deeply.[1]

There were apparently three forms of teaching made use of in these rites : these were λεγόμενα, things *said ;* δεικνύμενα, things *shown ;* and δρώμενα, things *performed* or *acted.*[2] I have given already some instances of things said—texts whispered for consolation in the neophyte's ear, and so forth ; of the *third* group, things enacted, we have a fair amount of evidence. There were

---

[1] See Edwin Hatch, D.D., *The Influence of Greek Ideas and Usages on the Christian Church* (London, 1890), pp. 283–5.

[2] Cheetham, *op. cit.,* pp. 49–61 *sq.*

ritual dramas or passion-plays, of which an important one dealt with the descent of Koré or Proserpine into the underworld, as in the Eleusinian representations,[1] and her redemption and restoration to the upper world in Spring ; another with the sufferings of Psyche and her rescue by Eros, as described by Apuleius [2]—himself an initiate in the cult of Isis. There is a parody by Lucian, which tells of the birth of Apollo, the marriage of Coronis, and the coming of Aesculapius as Saviour ; there was the dying and rising again of Dionysus (chief divinity of the Orphic cult) ; and sometimes the mystery of the birth of Dionysus as a holy child.[3] There was, every year at Eleusis, a solemn and lengthy procession or pilgrimage made, symbolic of the long pilgrimage of the human soul, its sufferings and deliverance.

"Almost always," says Dr. Cheetham, "the suffering of a god—suffering followed by triumph—seems to have been the subject of the sacred drama." Then occasionally to the Neophytes, after taking part in the pilgrimage, and when their minds had been prepared by an ordeal of darkness and fatigue and terrors, was accorded a revelation of Paradise, and even a vision of Transfiguration—the form of the Hierophant himself, or teacher of the Mysteries, being seen half-lost in a blaze of light.[4] Finally, there was the eating of food and drinking of barley-drink from the sacred chest [5]—a kind of Communion or Eucharist.

---

[1] See Farnell, *op. cit.*, iii. 158 *sq.*
[2] See *The Golden Ass.*
[3] Farnell, iii. 177.   [4] *Ibid.*, 179 *sq.*
[5] *Ibid.*, 186. Sacred chests, in which holy things were kept, figure frequently in early rites and legends—as in the case of the ark of the Jewish tabernacle, the ark or box carried in celebrations of the mysteries of Bacchus (Theocritus, Idyll xxvi), the legend of Pandora's box which contained the seeds of all good and evil, the ark of Noah which saved all living creatures from the flood, the Argo of the argonauts, the moonshaped boat in which Isis floating over the waters gathered together the severed limbs of Osiris, and so brought about his resurrection, and the many chests or coffins out

Apuleius in *The Golden Ass* gives an interesting account
of his induction into the mysteries of Isis : how, bidding
farewell one evening to the general congregation outside,
and clothed in a new linen garment, he was handed by
the priest into the inner recesses of the temple itself ; how
he " approached the confines of death, and having trod
on the threshold of Proserpine (the Underworld), returned
therefrom, being borne through all the elements. At
midnight I saw the sun shining with its brilliant light :
and I approached the presence of the Gods beneath and
the Gods above, and stood near and worshipped them."
During the night things happened which must not be
disclosed ; but in the morning he came forth " consecrated
by being dressed in twelve stoles painted with the figures
of animals."[1]   He ascended a pulpit in the midst of the
Temple, carrying in his right hand a burning torch, while
a chaplet encircled his head, from which palm-leaves projected like rays of light. " Thus arrayed like the *Sun*,
and placed so as to resemble a statue, on a sudden, the
curtains being drawn aside, I was exposed to the gaze of
the multitude. After this I celebrated the most joyful
day of my initiation, as my natal day [day of the New
Birth] and there was a joyous banquet and mirthful conversation."

One can hardly refuse to recognise in this account the
description of some kind of ceremony which was supposed
to seal the illumination of a man and his new birth into
divinity—the animal origin, the circling of all experience,
the terrors of death, and the resurrection in the form of

of which the various gods (Adonis, Attis, Osiris, Jesus), having been
laid there in death, rose again for the redemption of the world.   They
all evidently refer to the mystic womb of Nature and of Woman,
and are symbols of salvation and redemption.   (For a full discussion
of this subject, see *The Great Law of religious origins*, by W. Williamson,
 chi ivi)

[1] An allusion no doubt to the twelve signs of the Zodiac, the path-
way of the Sun, as well as to the practice of the ancient priests of
wearing the skins of totem-animals in sign of their divinity.

the Sun, the symbol of all light and life. The very word
" illumination " carries the ideas of light and a new birth
with it. Reitzenstein in his very interesting book on the
Greek Mysteries [1] speaks over and over again of the illumination (φωτισμός) which was held to attend Initiation
and Salvation. The doctrine of Salvation indeed (σωτηρία)
was, as we have already seen, rife and widely current in
the Second Century B.C. It represented a real experience,
and the man who shared this experience became a θεῖος
ἄνθρωπος or divine man.[2] In the Orphic Tablets the
phrase " I am a child of earth and the starry heaven, but
my race is of heaven (alone) " occurs more than once.
In one of the longest of them the dead man is instructed
" after he has passed the waters (of Lethe) where the white
Cypress and the House of Hades are " to address these
very words to the guardians of the Lake of Memory while
he asks for a drink of cold water from that Lake. In
another the dead person himself is thus addressed : " Hail,
thou who hast endured the Suffering, such as indeed thou
hadst never suffered before ; *thou hast become god from
man !* " [3] Ecstasy was the acme of the religious life ; and,
what is especially interesting to us, Salvation or the divine
nature was open to all men—to all, that is, who should go
through the necessary stages of preparation for it.[4]

Reitzenstein contends (p. 26) that in the Mysteries,
transfiguration (μεταμορφώσις), salvation (σωτηρία), and
new birth (παλιγγενεσία) were often conjoined. He says

---

[1] *Die hellenistischen Mysterien-Religionen*, by R. Reitzenstein,
Leipzig, 1910.

[2] Reitzenstein, p. 12.

[3] These Tablets (so-called) are instructions to the dead as to their
passage into the other world, and have been found in the tombs,
in Italy and elsewhere inscribed on very thin gold plates and buried
with the departed. See *Manual of Greek Antiquities* by Percy Gardner
and F. B. Jevons (1895) ; also *Prolegomena to Greek Religion* by Jane
E. Harrison (1903).

[4] Reitzenstein pp. 15 and 18 ; also S. J. Case, *Evolution of Early
Christianity*, p. 301.

(p. 31), that in the Egyptian Osiris-cult, the Initiate acquires a nature "equal to God" (ἰσόθεος), the very same expression as that used of Christ Jesus in Philippians ii. 6 ; he mentions Apollonius of Tyana and Sergius Paulus as instances of men who by their contemporaries were considered to have attained this nature ; and he quotes Akhnaton (Pharaoh of Egypt in 1375 B.C.) as having said, "Thou art in my heart ; none other knows Thee, save thy son Akhnaton ; Thou hast initiated him into thy wisdom and into thy power." He also quotes the words of Hermes (Trismegistus)—"Come unto Me, even as children to their mother's bosom : Thou art I, and I am Thou ; what is thine is mine, and what is mine is thine ; for indeed I am thine image (εἴδωλον)," and refers to the dialogue between Hermes and Tat, in which they speak of the great and mystic New Birth and Union with the All—with all Elements, Plants and Animals, Time and Space.

"The Mysteries," says Dr. Cheetham very candidly, "influenced Christianity considerably and modified it in some important respects" ; and Dr. Hatch, as we have seen, not only supports this general view, but follows it out in detail.[1] He points out that the membership of the Mystery-societies was very numerous in the earliest times, A.D. ; that their general aims were good, including a sense of true religion, decent life, and brotherhood ; that cleanness from crime and confession were demanded from the neophyte ; that confession was followed by baptism (κάθαρσις) and that by sacrifice ; that the term φωτισμός (illumination) was adopted by the Christian Church as the name for the new birth of baptism ; that the Christian usage of placing a seal on the forehead came from the same source ; that baptism itself after a time was called a mystery (μυστήριον) ; that the sacred cakes and barley-drink of the Mysteries became the milk and honey and bread and wine of the first Christian Eucharists, and that the occasional

[1] See Hatch, *op. cit.*, pp. 290 *sq.*

sacrifice of a lamb on the Christian altar ("whose mention is often suppressed") probably originated in the same way. Indeed, the conception of the communion-table *as* an altar and many other points of ritual gradually established themselves from these sources as time went on.[1] It is hardly necessary to say more in proof of the extent to which in these ancient representations "things said" and "scenes enacted" forestalled the doctrines and ceremonials of Christianity.

But what of the second group above-mentioned, the "things *shown*"? It is not so easy naturally to get exact information concerning these, but they seem to have been specially holy objects, probably things connected with very ancient rituals in the past—such as sacred stones, old and rude images of the gods, magic nature-symbols, like that half-disclosed ear of corn above-mentioned (Ch. V, *supra*). "In the Temple of Isis at Philae," says Dr. Cheetham, "the dead body of Osiris is represented with stalks of corn springing from it, which a priest waters from a vessel. An inscription says: 'This is the form of him whom we may not name, Osiris of the Mysteries who sprang from the returning waters' [the Nile]." Above all, no doubt, there were images of the *phallus* and the *vulva*, the great symbols of human fertility. We have seen (Ch. XII) that the *lingam* and the *yoni* are, even down to to-day, commonly retained and honoured as holy objects in the S. Indian Temples, and anointed with oil (some of them) for a very practical reason. Sir J. G. Frazer, in his lately published volumes on *The Folk-lore of the Old Testament*, has a chapter (in vol. ii) on the very numerous sacred stones of various shapes and sizes found or spoken of in Palestine and other parts of the world. Though uncertain as to the meaning of these stones he mentions that they are "fre-

[1] See Dionysius Areop. (end of fifth century), who describes the Christian rites generally in Mystery language (Hatch, 296).

quently, though not always, *upright.*" Anointing them with
oil, he assures us, " is a widespread practice, sometimes by
women who wish to obtain children." And he concludes
the chapter by saying : " The holy stone at Bethel was
probably one of those massive standing stones or rough
pillars which the Hebrews called *masseboth,* and which,
as we have seen, were regular adjuncts of Canaanite and
early Israelitish sanctuaries." We have already mentioned
the pillars Jachin and Boaz which stood before the Temple
of Solomon, and which had an acknowledged sexual significance ; and so it seems probable that a great number of
these holy stones had a similar meaning.[1] Following this
clue it would appear likely that the *lingam* thus anointed
and worshiped in the Temples of India and elsewhere *is*
the original χρίστος,[2] adored by the human race from the
very beginning, and that at a later time, when the
Priest and the King, as objects of worship, took the place
of the Lingam, *they* also were anointed with the chrism of
fertility. That the exhibition of these emblems should
be part of the original ' Mystery '-rituals was perfectly
natural—especially because, as we have explained already,[3]
old customs often continued on in a quite naïve fashion
in the rituals, when they had come to be thought indecent
or improper by a later public opinion ; and (we may say)
was perfectly in order, because there is plenty of evidence to
show that in *savage* initiations, of which the Mysteries were
the linear descendants, all these things *were* explained to

---

[1] F. Nork, *Der Mystagog,* mentions that the Roman *Penates*
were commonly anointed with oil. J. Stuart Hay, in his *Life of
Elagabalus* (1911), says that " Elagabal was worshipped under the
symbol of a great black stone or meteorite, in the shape of a Phallus,
which having fallen from the heavens represented a true portion of
the Godhead, much after the style of those black stone images popu-
larly venerated in Norway and other parts of Europe.

[2] J. E. Hewitt, in his *Ruling Races of Pre-historic Times* (p. 64),
gives a long list of pre-historic races who worshiped the *lingam.*

[3] See Ch. XI, p. 171.

the novices, and their use actually taught.[1] No doubt also
there were some representations or dramatic incidents of
a fairly coarse character, as deriving from these ancient
sources.[2] It is, however, quaint to observe how the mere
mention of such things has caused an almost hysterical
commotion among the critics of the Mysteries—from the
day of the early Christians who (in order to belaud their
own religion) were never tired of abusing the Pagans, onward to the present day when modern scholars either on
the one hand follow the early Christians in representing
the Mysteries as sinks of iniquity or on the other (knowing
this charge could not be substantiated except in the period
of their final decadence) take the line of ignoring the sexual
interest attaching to them as non-existent or at any rate
unworthy of attention. The good Archdeacon Cheetham,
for instance, while writing an interesting book on the Mysteries, passes by this side of the subject *almost* as if it did
not exist ; while the learned Dr. Farnell, overcome apparently by the weight of his learning, and unable to confront
the alarming obstacle presented by these sexual rites and
aspects, hides himself behind the rather non-committal
remark (speaking of the Eleusinian rites) " we have no
right to imagine any part of this solemn ceremony as coarse
or obscene."[3] As Nature, however, has been known (quite

[1] See Ernest Crawley's *Mystic Rose*, ch. xiii, pp. 310 and 313 :
" In certain tribes of Central Africa both boys and girls after initiation
must as soon as possible have intercourse." Initiation being not
merely preliminary to, but often *actually* marriage. The same among
Kaffirs, Congo tribes, Senegalese, etc. Also among the Arunta of
Australia.

[2] Professor Diederichs has said that " in much ancient ritual it
was thought that mystic communion with the deity could be obtained
through the semblance of sex-intercourse—as in the Attis-Cybele
worship, and the Isis-ritual." (Farnell.) Reitzenstein says (*op. cit.*,
p. 20) that the Initiates, like some of the Christian Nuns at a later
time, believed in union with God through receiving the seed.

[3] Farnell, *op. cit.*, iii. 176. Messrs. Gardner and Jevons, in their
Manual of Greek Antiquities, above-quoted, compare the Eleusinian
Mysteries favorably with some of the others, like the Arcadian, the

frequently) to be coarse or obscene, and as the initiators
of the Mysteries were probably neither ' good ' nor ' learned,'
but were simply anxious to interpret Nature as best they
could, we cannot find fault with the latter for the way
they handled the problem, nor indeed well see how they
could have handled it better.

After all it is pretty clear that the early peoples saw
in Sex the great cohesive force which kept (we will not say
Humanity but at any rate) the Tribe together, and sus-
tained the race.   In the stage of simple Consciousness this
must have been one of the first things that the budding
intellect perceived.   Sex became one of the earliest divinities,
and there is abundant evidence that its organs and processes
generally were invested with a religious sense of awe and
sanctity.   It was in fact the symbol (or rather the actuality)
of the permanent undying life of the race, and as such was
sacred to the uses of the race.   Whatever taboos may have,
among different peoples, guarded its operations, it was not
essentially a thing to be concealed, or ashamed of.   Rather
the contrary.   For instance the early Christian writer,
Hippolytus, Bishop of Pontus (A.D. 200), in his *Refutation
of all Heresies*, Book V, says that the Samothracian Mysteries, just mentioned, celebrate Adam as the primal or
archetypal Man eternal in the heavens ; and he then continues : " Habitually there stand in the temple of the
Samothracians two images of naked men having both hands
stretched aloft towards heaven, and their *pudenda* turned
upwards, as is also the case with the statue of Mercury
on Mt. Cyllene.   And the aforesaid images are figures of
the primal man, and of that spiritual one that is born again,
in every respect of the same substance with that [first]
man."

Trophonian, the Æginæan, and the very primitive Samothracian ;
saying (p. 278) that of the last-mentioned " we know little, but safely
conjecture that in them the ideas of sex and procreation dominated
even more than in those of Eleusis."

This extract from Hippolytus occurs in the long discourse in which he ' exposes ' the heresy of the so-called *Naassene* doctrines and mysteries.   But the whole discourse should be read by those who wish to understand the Gnostic philosophy of the period contemporary with and anterior to the birth of Christianity.   A translation of the discourse, carefully analysed and annotated, is given in G. R. S. Mead's *Thrice-greatest Hermes* [1] (vol. i) ; and Mead himself, speaking of it, says (p. 141) : " The claim of these Gnostics was practically that *the good news of the Christ* [the Christos] was the consummation of the inner doctrine of the Mystery-institutions of all the nations ; the end of them all being the revelation of the Mystery of Man."   Further, he explains that the Soul, in these doctrines, was regarded as synonymous with the Cause of All ; and that its loves were twain—of Aphrodite (or Life), and of Persephone (or Death and the other world).   Also that Attis, abandoning his sex in the worship of the Mother-Goddess (*Dea Syria*), ascends to Heaven—a new man, Male-female, and the origin of all things : the hidden Mystery being the Phallus itself, erected as Hermes in all roads and boundaries and temples, the *Conductor and Reconductor of Souls.*

All this may sound strange, but one may fairly say that it represented in its degree, and in that first ' unfallen ' stage of human thought and psychology, a true conception of the cosmic Life, and indeed a conception quite sensible and admirable, until, of course, the Second Stage brought corruption.   No sooner was this great force of the cosmic life diverted from its true uses of Generation and Regeneration,[2] and appropriated by the individual to his own private pleasure—no sooner was its religious character as a tribal

---

[1] Reitzenstein, *op. cit.*, quotes the discourse largely.   The *Thrice-greatest Hermes* may also be consulted for a translation of Plutarch's *Isis and Osiris.*

[2] For the special meaning of these two terms, see *The Drama of Love and Death*, by E. Carpenter, pp. 59–61.

service [1] (often rendered within the Temple precincts) lost sight of or degraded into a commercial transaction—than every kind of evil fell upon mankind. *Corruptio optimi pessima.* It must be remembered too that simultaneous with this sexual disruption occurred the disruption of other human relations ; and we cease to be surprised that disease and selfish passions, greed, jealousy, slander, cruelty, and wholesale murder, raged—and have raged ever since.

But for the human soul—whatever its fate, and whatever the dangers and disasters that threaten it—there is always redemption waiting. As we saw in the last chapter, this corruption of Sex led (quite naturally) to its denial and rejection ; and its denial led to the differentiation from it of Love. Humanity gained by the enthronement and deification of Love, pure and undefiled, and (for the time being) exalted beyond this mortal world, and free from all earthly contacts. But again in the end, the divorce thus introduced between the physical and the spiritual led to the crippling of both. Love relegated, so to speak, to heaven, as a purely philanthropical, pious and ' spiritual ' affair, became exceedingly *dull ;* and sex, remaining on earth, but deserted by the redeeming presence, fell into mere " carnal curiosity and wretchlessness of unclean living." Obviously for the human race there remains nothing, in the final event, but the reconciliation of the physical and the spiritual, and after many sufferings, the reunion of Eros and Psyche.

There is still, however, much to be said about the Third State of Consciousness. Let us examine into it a little

---

[1] Ernest Crawley in *The Mystic Rose* challenges this identification of Religion with tribal interests ; yet his arguments are not very convincing. On p. 5 he admits that " there is a religious meaning inherent in the primitive conception and practice of *all* human relations " ; and a large part of his ch. xii is taken up in showing that even such institutions as the Saturnalia were religious in confirming the sense of social union and leading to ' extended identity.'

more closely. Clearly, since it is a new state, and not merely an extension of a former one, one cannot arrive at it by argument derived from the Second state, for all conscious Thought such as we habitually use simply keeps us *in* the Second state. No animal or quite primitive man could possibly understand what we mean by Self-consciousness till he had experienced it. Mere argument would not enlighten him. And so no one in the Second state can quite realise the Third state till he has experienced it. Still, explanations may help us to perceive in what direction to look, and to recognise in some of our experiences an approach to the condition sought.

Evidently it is a mental condition in some respects more similar to the first than to the second stage. The second stage of human psychologic evolution is an aberration, a divorce, a parenthesis. With its culmination and dismissal the mind passes back into the simple state of union with the Whole. (The state of *Ekágratá* in the Hindu philosophy : one-pointedness, singleness of mind.) And the consciousness of the Whole, and of things past and things to come and things far around—which consciousness had been shut out by the concentration on the local self—begins to return again. This is not to say, of course, that the *excursus* in the second stage has been a loss and a defect. On the contrary, it means that the Return is a bringing of all that has been gained during the period of exile (all sorts of mental and technical knowledge and skill, emotional developments, finesse and adaptability of mind) *back* into harmony with the Whole. It means ultimately a great gain. The Man, perfected, comes back to a vastly extended harmony. He enters again into a real understanding and confidential relationship with his physical body and with the body of the society in which he dwells —from both of which he has been sadly divorced ; and he takes up again the broken thread of the Cosmic Life.

Everyone has noticed the extraordinary consent sometimes

observable among the members of an animal community—how a flock of 500 birds (e.g. starlings) will suddenly change its direction of flight—the light on the wings shifting *instantaneously*, as if the impulse to veer came to all at the same identical moment ; or how bees will swarm or otherwise act with one accord, or migrating creatures (lemmings, deer, gossamer spiders, winged ants) the same. Whatever explanation of these facts we favour—whether the possession of swifter and finer means of external communication than we can perceive, or whether a common and inner sensitivity to the genius of the Tribe (the " Spirit of the Hive ") or to the promptings of great Nature around—in any case these facts of animal life appear to throw light on the possibilities of an accord and consent among the members of emancipated humanity, such as we little dream of now, and seem to bid us have good hope for the future.

It is here, perhaps, that the ancient worship of the *Lingam* comes in. The word itself is apparently connected with our word ' link,' and has originally the same meaning.[1] It is the link between the generations. Beginning with the worship of the physical Race-life, the course of psychologic evolution has been first to the worship of the Tribe (or of the Totem which represents the tribe) ; then to the worship of the human-formed *God* of the tribe—the God who dies and rises again eternally, as the tribe passes on eternal—though its members perpetually perish ; then to the conception of an undying Saviour, and the realization and distinct experience of some kind of Super-consciousness which does certainly reside, more or less hidden, in the deeps of the mind, and has been waiting through the ages for its disclosure and recognition. Then again to the recognition that in the sacrifices, the Slayer and the Slain are one—the strange and profoundly mystic perception that the God and the Victim are in essence the same—the dedication of ' Himself to Himself ' ;[2] and simultaneously

[1] See Sanskrit Dictionary.   [2] See Ch. VIII, *supra*.

with this the interpretation of the Eucharist as meaning, even for the individual, the participation in Eternal Life— the continuing life of the Tribe, or ultimately of Humanity.[1] The Tribal order rises to Humanity ; love ascends from the *lingam* to *yogam*, from physical union alone to the union with the Whole—which of course includes physical and all other kinds of union. No wonder that the good St. Paul, witnessing that extraordinary whirlpool of beliefs and practices, new and old, there in the first century A.D.—the unabashed adoration of sex side by side with the transcendental devotions of the Vedic sages and the Gnostics—became somewhat confused himself and even a little violent, scolding his disciples (1 Cor. x. 21) for their undiscriminating acceptance, as it seemed to him, of things utterly alien and antagonistic. "Ye cannot drink the cup of the Lord and the cup of devils : ye cannot be partakers of the Lord's table and the table of devils."

Every careful reader has noticed the confusedness of Paul's mind and arguments. Even taking only those Epistles (Galatians, Romans and Corinthians) which the critics assign to his pen, the thing is observable—and some learned Germans even speak of *two* Pauls.[2] But also the thing is quite natural. There can be little doubt that Paul of Tarsus, a Jew brought up in the strictest sect of the Pharisees, did at some time fall deeply under the influence of Greek thought, and quite possibly became an initiate

[1] There are many indications in literature—in prophetic or poetic form—of this awareness and distinct conviction of an eternal life, reached through love and an inner sense of union with others and with humanity at large ; indications which bear the mark of absolute genuineness and sincerity of feeling. See, for instance, Whitman's poem, " To the Garden the World " (*Leaves of Grass*, complete edition, p. 79). But an eternal life of the third order ; not, thank heaven ! an eternity of the meddling and muddling self-conscious Intellect !

[2] " Die Mysterien-anschauungen, die bei Paulus im Hintergrunde stehen, drängen sich in dem sogenannten Deuteropaulinismus mächtig vor " (Reitzenstein).

in the Mysteries. It would be difficult otherwise to account
for his constant use of the Mystery-language. Reitzenstein
says (p. 59) : " The hellenistic religious literature *must* have
been read by him ; he uses its terms, and is saturated with
its thoughts (see Rom. vi. 1–14)." And this conjoined with
his Jewish experience gave him creative power. " A great
deal in his sentiment and thought may have *remained*
Jewish, but to his Hellenism he was indebted for his love
of freedom and his firm belief in his apostleship." He
adopts terms (like σαρκικός, ψυχικός and πνευματικός) [1]
which were in use among the hellenistic sects of the time ;
and he writes, as in Romans vi. 4, 5, about being " *buried* "
with Christ or " *planted* " in the likeness of his death, in
words which might well have been used (with change of
the name) by a follower of Attis or Osiris after witnessing
the corresponding ' mysteries ' ; certainly the allusion to
these ancient deities would have been understood by every
religionist of that day. These few points are sufficient
to accentuate the two elements in Paul, the Jewish and
the Greek, and to explain (so far) the seeming confusion
in his utterances. Further it is interesting to note—as
showing the pagan influences in the N.T. writings—the
degree to which the Epistle to Philemon (ascribed to Paul)
is *full*—short as it is—of expressions like *prisoner* of the
Lord, *fellow soldier, captive* or *bondman*,[2] which were so
common at the time as to be almost a *cant* in Mithraism and
the allied cults. In 1 Peter ii. 2 3 we have the verse " As
newborn babes, desire ye the sincere *milk* of the word,
that ye may grow thereby." And again we may say that
no one in that day could mistake the reference herein
contained to old initiation ceremonies and the new birth
(as described in Chapter VIII above), for indeed milk was

[1] Reminiful of our Three Stages : the Animal, the Self-conscious,
and the Cosmic.

[2] δέσμιος, στρατιώτης, δοῦλος.

3 See also 1 Cor. iii. 2.

the well-known diet of the novice in the Isis mysteries, as well as (in some savage tribes) of the Medicine-man when practising his calling.

And here too Democracy comes in—strangely foreboded from the first in all this matter.[1] Not only does the Third Stage bring illumination, intuitive understanding of processes in Nature and Humanity, sympathy with the animals, artistic capacity, and so forth, but it necessarily brings a new Order of Society. A preposterous—one may almost say a hideous—social Age is surely drawing to its end. The *débâcle* we are witnessing to-day all over Europe (including the British Islands), the break-up of old institutions, the generally materialistic outlook on life, the coming to the surface of huge masses of diseased and fatuous populations, the scum and dregs created by the past order, all point to the End of a Dispensation. Protestantism and Commercialism, in the two fields of religion and daily life have, as I have indicated before, been occupied in concentrating the mind of each man solely on his *own* welfare, the salvation of his *own* soul or body. These two forces have therefore been disruptive to the last degree ; they mark the culmination of the Self-conscious Age—a culmination in War, Greed, Materialism, and the general principle of *Devil-take-the-hindmost*—and the clearing of the ground for the new order which is to come. So there is hope for the human race. Its evolution is not all a mere formless craze and jumble. There is an inner necessity by which Humanity unfolds from one degree or plane of consciousness to another. And if there has been a great ' Fall ' or Lapse into conflict and disease and ' sin ' and misery, occupying the major part of the Historical period hitherto, we see that this period is only brief, so to speak, in comparison with the whole curve of growth and expansion. We see also that, as I have said before, the belief in a state of salva-

[1] See the germs of Democracy in the *yoga* teaching of the Hindus and in the Upanishads, the Bhagavat Gita, and other books.

tion or deliverance has in the past ages never left itself
quite without a witness in the creeds and rituals and poems
and prophecies of mankind. Art, in some form or other,
as an activity or inspiration dating not from the conscious
Intellect, but from deeper regions of sub-conscious feeling
and intuition, has continually come to us as a message
from and an evidence of the Third stage or state, and as
a promise of its more complete realisation under other
conditions.

> Through the long night-time where the Nations wander
>   From Eden past to Paradise to be,
> Art's sacred flowers, like fair stars shining yonder,
>   Alone illumine Life's obscurity.
>
> O gracious Artists, out of your deep hearts
>   'Tis some great Sun, I doubt, by men unguessed,
> Whose rays come struggling thus, in slender darts,
>   To shadow what Is, till Time shall manifest.

With the Cosmic stage comes also necessarily the rehabilitation of the *whole* of Society in one fellowship (the
true Democracy). Not the rule or domination of one
class or caste—as of the Intellectual, the Pious, the Commercial or the Military—but the fusion or at least consen-
taneous organisation of *all* (as in the corresponding functions
of the human Body). Class rule has been the mark of that
second period of human evolution, and has inevitably
given birth during that period to wars and self-aggrandise-
ments of classes and sections, and their consequent greeds
and tyrannies over other classes and sections. It is not
found in the primitive human tribes and societies, and
will not be found in the final forms of human association.
The liberated and emancipated Man passes unconstrained
and unconstraining through all grades and planes of human
fellowship, equal and undisturbed, and never leaving his
true home and abiding place in the heart of all. Equally
necessarily with the rehabilitation of Society as an entirety

will follow the rehabilitation of the entire physical body *in* each member of Society. We have spoken already of Nakedness : its meaning and likely extent of adoption (Ch. XII, pp. 196–7). The idea that the head and the hands are the only seemly and presentable members of the organism, and that the other members are unworthy and indecent, is obviously as onesided and lopsided as that which honours certain classes in the commonwealth and despises others. Why should the head brag of its ascendancy and domination, and the heart be smothered up and hidden ? It will only be a life far more in the open air than that which we lead at present, which will restore the balance and ultimately bring us back to sanity and health.

XVI

THE EXODUS OF CHRISTIANITY

WE have dealt with the Genesis of Christianity; we now come to its Exodus. For that Christianity can *continue* to hold the field of Religion in the Western World is neither probable nor desirable. It is true, as I have remarked already, that there is a certain trouble about defining what we mean by " Christianity " similar to that about the word " Civilisation." If we select out of the great mass of doctrines and rites favoured by the various Christian Churches just those which commend themselves to the most modern and humane and rational human mind and choose to call that resulting (but rather small) body of belief and practice ' Christianity ' we are, of course, entitled to do so, and to hope (as we do hope) that this residuum will survive and go forward into the future. But this sort of proceeding is hardly fair and certainly not logical. It enables Christianity to pose as an angel of light while at the same time keeping discreetly out of sight all its own abominations and deeds of darkness. The Church—which began its career by destroying, distorting and denying the pagan sources from which it sprang ; whose bishops and other ecclesiastics assassinated each other in their theological rancour " of wild beasts," which encouraged the wicked folly of the Crusades especially the Children's Crusades—and the shameful murders of the Manicheans, the Albigenses, and the Huguenots ; which

burned at the stake thousands and thousands of poor
' witches ' and ' heretics ' ; which has hardly ever spoken
a generous word in favour or defence of the animals ; which
in modern times has supported vivisection as against the
latter, Capitalism and Commercialism as against the poorer
classes of mankind ; and whose priests in the forms of its
various sects, Greek or Catholic, Lutheran or Protestant,
have in these last days rushed forth to urge the nations to
slaughter each other with every diabolical device of Science,
and to glorify the war-cry of Patriotism in defiance of the
principle of universal Brotherhood—such a Church can
hardly claim to have established the angelic character
of its mission among mankind ! And if it be said—as it
often *is* said : " Oh ! but you must go back to the genuine
article, and the Church's real origin and one foundation
in the person and teaching of Jesus Christ," then indeed
you come back to the point which this book, as above,
enforces : namely, that as to the person of Jesus, there is
no *certainty* at all that he ever existed ; and as to the teaching
credited to him, it *is* certain that that comes down from a
period long anterior to ' Christianity ' and is part of what
may justly be called a very ancient World-religion. So, as
in the case of ' Civilisation,' we are compelled to see that
it is useless to apply the word to some ideal state of affairs
or doctrine (an ideal by no means the same in all people's
minds, or in all localities and times), but that the only
reasonable thing to do is to apply it in each case to a *historical
period*. In the case of Christianity the historical period
has lasted nearly 2,000 years, and, as I say, we can hardly
expect or wish that it should last much longer.

The very thorough and careful investigation of religious
origins which has been made during late years by a great
number of students and observers undoubtedly tends to show
that there has been something like a great World-religion
coming down the centuries from the remotest times and
gradually expanding and branching as it has come—that

is to say that the similarity (in *essence* though not always in external detail) between the creeds and rituals of widely sundered tribes and peoples is so great as to justify the view —advanced in the present volume—that these creeds and rituals are the necessary outgrowths of human psychology, slowly evolving, and that consequently they have a common origin and in their various forms a common expression. Of this great World-religion, so coming down, Christianity is undoubtedly a branch, and an important branch. But there have been important branches before ; and while it may be true that Christianity emphasizes some points which may have been overlooked or neglected in the Vedic teachings or in Buddhism, or in the Persian and Egyptian and Syrian cults, or in Mahommedanism, and so forth, it is also equally true that Christianity has itself overlooked or neglected valuable points in these religions. It has, in fact, the defects of its qualities. If the World-religion is like a great tree, one cannot expect or desire that all its branches should be directed towards the same point of the compass.

Reinach, whose studies of religious origins are always interesting and characterised by a certain Gallic grace and *netteté*, though with a somewhat Jewish non-perception of the mystic element in life, defines Religion as a combination of *animism* and *scruples*. This is good in a way, because it gives the two aspects of the subject : the inner, animism, consisting of the sense of contact with more or less intelligent beings moving in Nature ; and the outer, consisting in scruples or *taboos*. The one aspect shows the feeling which *inspires* religion, the other, the checks and limitations which *define* it and give birth to ritual. But like most anthropologists he (Reinach) is a little *too* patronising towards the " poor Indian with untutored mind." He is sorry for people so foolish as to be animistic in their outlook, and he is always careful to point out that the scruples and taboos were quite senseless in their origin, though occasionally (by accident) they turned out useful. Yet—as I have said before—Animism is a perfectly sensible, logical and *necessary* attitude of the human mind. It is a necessary attribute of man's psychical nature, by which he projects into the great World around him the image of his own mind. When that mind is in a very primitive, inchoate, and fragmentary condition, the images so projected are those of fragmentary intelligences ('spirits,' gnomes, etc.—the age of magic); when the mind rises to distinct consciousness of itself the reflexions of it are anthropomorphic 'gods'; when finally it reaches the universal or cosmic state it perceives the presence of a universal Being behind all phenomena—which Being is indeed itself—"Himself to Himself." If you like you may call the whole process by the name of Animism. It is perfectly sensible throughout. The only proviso is that you should also be sensible, and distinguish the different stages in the process.

Jane Harrison makes considerable efforts to show that Religion is primarily a reflection of the *social* Conscience (see *Themis*, pp. 482–92)—that is, that the sense in Man of a " Power that makes for righteousness " outside (and also inside) him is derived from his feeling of continuity with the Tribe and his instinctive obedience to its behests, confirmed by ages of collective habit and experience. He cannot in fact sever the navel-string which connects him with his tribal Mother, even though he desires to do so. And no doubt this view of the origin of Religion is perfectly correct. But it must be pointed out that it does not by any means exclude the view that religion derives also from an Animism by which man recognises in general Nature his foster-mother and feels himself in closest touch with *her*. Which may have come first, the Social affiliation or the Nature affiliation, I leave to the professors to determine. The term Animism may, as far as I can see, be quite well applied to the social

affiliation, for the latter is evidently only a case in which
the individual projects his own degree of consciousness
into the human group around him instead of into the
animals or the trees, but it is a case of which the justice
is so obvious that the modern man can intellectually seize
and understand it, and consequently he does not tar it
with the ' animistic ' brush.

And Miss Harrison, it must be noticed, does, in other
passages of the same book (see *Themis*, pp. 68, 69), admit
that Religion has its origin not only from unity with the
Tribe but from the sense of affiliation to Nature—the
sense of " a world of unseen power lying behind the visible
universe, a world which is the sphere, as will be seen, of
magical activity and the medium of mysticism. The
mystical element, the oneness and continuousness comes
out very clearly in the notion of *Wakonda* among the Sioux
Indians. . . . The Omahas regarded all animate and inanimate forms, all phenomena, as pervaded by a common
life, which was continuous and similar to the will-power
they were conscious of in themselves. This mysterious
power in all things they called Wakonda, and through
it all things were related to man, and to each other. In
the idea of the continuity of life, a relation was maintained
between the seen and the unseen, the dead and the living,
and also between the fragment of anything and its entirety."
Thus our general position is confirmed, that Religion in
its origin has been *inspired* by a deep instinctive conviction
or actual sense of continuity with a being or beings in the
world around, while it has derived its *form* and ritual by
slow degrees from a vast number of taboos, generated in
the first instance chiefly by superstitious fears, but gradually
with the growth of reason and observation becoming
simplified and rationalized into forms of use. On the one
side there has been the positive impulse—of mere animal
Desire and the animal urge of self-expression ; on the
other there has been the negative force of Fear based

on ignorance—the latter continually carving, moulding and shaping the former. According to this an organised study and classification of taboos might yield some interesting results ; because indeed it would throw light on the earliest forms of both religion and science. It would be seen that some taboos, like those of *contact* (say with a menstruous woman, or a mother-in-law, or a lightning-struck tree) had an obvious basis of observation, justifiable but very crude ; while others, like the taboo against harming an enemy who had contracted blood-friendship with one of your own tribe, or against giving decent burial to a murderer, were equally rough and rude expressions or indications of the growing moral sentiment of mankind. All the same there would be left, in any case, a large residuum of taboos which could only be judged as senseless, and the mere rubbish of the savage mind.

So much for the first origins of the World-religion ; and I think enough has been said in the various chapters of this book to show that the same general process has obtained throughout. Man, like the animals, began with this deep, subconscious sense of unity with surrounding Nature. When this became (in Man) fairly conscious, it led to Magic and Totemism. More conscious, and it branched, on the one hand, into figures of Gods and definite forms of Creeds, on the other into elaborate Scientific Theories—the latter based on a strong *intellectual* belief in Unity, but fervently denying any ' anthropomorphic ' or ' animistic ' *sense* of that unity. Finally, it seems that we are now on the edge of a further stage when the theories and the creeds, scientific and religious, are on the verge of collapsing, but in such a way as to leave the sense and the perception of Unity—the real content of the whole process—not only undestroyed, but immensely heightened and illuminated. Meanwhile the taboos—of which there remain some still, both religious and scientific—have been gradually breaking up and merging themselves into a reasonable and humane order of life and philosophy.

I have said that out of this World-religion Christianity really sprang. It is evident now that the time has arrived when it must either acknowledge its source and frankly endeavour to affiliate itself to the same, or failing that must perish. In the first case it will probably have to change its name ; in the second the question of its name ' will interest it no more.'

With regard to the first of these alternatives, I might venture—though with due diffidence—to make a few suggestions. Why should we not have—instead of a Holy Roman Church—a Holy *Human* Church, rehabilitating the ancient symbols and rituals, a Christianity (if you still desire to call it so) frankly and gladly acknowledging its own sources ? This seems a reasonable and even feasible proposition. If such a church wished to celebrate a Mass or Communion or Eucharist it would have a great variety of rites and customs of that kind to select from ; those that were not appropriate for use in our times or were connected with the worship of strange gods need not be rejected or condemned, but could still be commented on and explained as approaches to the same idea—the idea of dedication to the Common Life, and of reinvigoration in the partaking of it. If the Church wished to celebrate the Crucifixion or betrayal of its Founder, a hundred instances of such celebrations would be to hand, and still the thought that has underlain such celebrations since the beginning of the world could easily be disentangled and presented in concrete form anew. In the light of such teaching expressions like " I know that my Redeemer liveth " would be traced to their origin, and men would understand that notwithstanding the mass of rubbish, cant and humbug which has collected round them they really do mean something and represent the age-long instinct of Humanity feeling its way towards a more extended revelation, a new order of being, a third stage of consciousness and illumination. In such a Church or religious organisation *every* quality of human nature would have to be represented, every practice and custom allowed for and its place accorded—the magical and astronomical meanings, the rites connected with sun-worship, or with sex, or with the worship of animals ; the consecration of corn and wine and other products of the ground, initiations, sacrifices, and so forth—all (if indeed it claimed to be a World-religion) would have to be represented and recognised. For they all have their long human origin and descent in and through the pagan creeds, and they al have penetrated into and become embodied to some degree in Christianity. Christianity therefore, as I say, must either now come frankly forward and, acknowledging its parentage from the great Order of the past, seek to re-habilitate *that* and carry mankind one step forward in the path of evolution—or else it must perish. There is no other alternative.[1]

Let me give an instance of how a fragment of ancient ritual which has survived from the far Past and is still celebrated, but with little intelligence or understanding, in the Catholic Church of to-day, might be adopted in such a Church as I have spoken of, interpreted, and made eloquent of meaning to modern humanity. When I was in Ceylon nearly 30 years ago I was fortunate enough to witness a night-festival in a Hindu Temple—the great festival of Taipusam, which takes place every year in January. Of course, it was full moon, and great was the blowing up of trumpets in the huge courtyard of the Temple. The moon shone down above from among the fronds of tall coco-palms, on a dense crowd of native worshipers—men and a few women—the men for the most part clad in little

[1] Comte in founding his philosophy of Positivism seems to have had in view some such Holy Human Church, but he succeeded in making it all so profoundly dull that it never flourished. The seed of Life was not in it.

more than a loin-cloth, the women picturesque in their coloured *saris* and jewelled ear and nose rings. The images of Siva and two other gods were carried in procession round and round the temple—three or four times ; nautch girls danced before the images, musicians, blowing horns and huge shells, or piping on flageolets or beating tom-toms, accompanied them. The crowd carrying torches or high crates with flaming coco-nuts, walked or rather danced along on each side, elated and excited with the sense of the present divinity, yet pleasantly free from any abject awe. The whole thing indeed reminded one of some bas-relief of a Bacchanalian procession carved on a Greek sarcophagus —and especially so in its hilarity and suggestion of friendly intimacy with the god. There were singing of hymns and the floating of the chief actors on a raft round a sacred lake. And then came the final Act. Siva, or his image, very weighty and borne on the shoulders of strong men, was carried into the first chamber or hall of the Temple and placed on an altar with a curtain hanging in front. The crowd followed with a rush ; and then there was more music, recital of hymns, and reading from sacred books. From where we stood we could see the rite which was performed behind the curtain. Two five-branched candlesticks were lighted ; and the manner of their lighting was as follows. Each branch ended in a little cup, and in the cups five pieces of camphor were placed, all approximately equal in size. After offerings had been made, of fruit, flowers and sandalwood, the five camphors in each candlestick were lighted. As the camphor flames burned out the music became more wild and exciting, and then at the moment of their extinction the curtains were drawn aside and the congregation outside suddenly beheld the god revealed and in a blaze of light This burning of camphor was, like other things in the service, emblematic. The five lights represent the five senses. Just as camphor consumes itself and leaves no residue behind, so should the five senses, being offered to the god, consume themselves and disappear. When this is done, that happens in the soul which was now figured in the ritual—the God is revealed in the inner light.[1]

We are familiar with this parting or rending of the veil. We hear of it in the Jewish Temple, and in the Greek and Egyptian Mysteries. It had a mystically religious, and also obviously sexual, signification. It occurs here and there in the Roman Catholic ritual. In Spain, some ancient Catholic ceremonials are kept up with a brilliance and splendour hardly found elsewhere in Europe. In the Cathedral at Seville the service of the Passion, carried out on Good Friday with great solemnity and accompanied with fine music, culminates on the Saturday morning— i.e. in the interval between the Crucifixion and the Resurrection—in a spectacle similar to that described in Ceylon. A rich velvet-black curtain hangs before the High Altar. At the appropriate moment and as the very emotional strains of voices and instruments reach their climax in the " Gloria in Excelsis," the curtain with a sudden burst of sound (thunder and the ringing of all the bells) is rent asunder, and the crucified Jesus is seen hanging there revealed in a halo of glory.

There is also held at Seville Cathedral and before the High Altar every year, the very curious *Dance of the Seises* (sixes), performed now by 16 instead of (as of old) by 12 boys, quaintly dressed. It seems to be a survival of some very ancient ritual, probably astronomical, in which the two sets of six represent the signs of the Zodiac, and is celebrated during the festivals of *Corpus Christi*, the *Immaculate Conception*, and the *Carnival*.

Numerous instances might of course be adduced of how a Church aspiring to be a real Church of Humanity might adopt and re-create the rituals of the past in the light of

[1] For a more detailed account of this Temple-festival, see *Adam's Peak to Elephanta* by E. Carpenter, ch. vii.

THE EXODUS OF CHRISTIANITY 267

a modern inspiration. Indeed the difficulty would be to limit the process, for *every* ancient ritual, we can now see, has had a meaning and a message, and it would be a real joy to disentangle these and to expose the profound solidarity of human thought and aspiration from the very dawn of civilisation down to the present day. Nor would it be necessary to imagine any Act of Uniformity or dead level of ceremonial in the matter. Different groups might concentrate on different phases of religious thought and practice. The only necessity would be that they should approach the subject with a real love of Humanity in their hearts and a real desire to come into touch with the deep inner life and mystic growing-pains of the souls of men and women in all ages. In this direction M. Loisy has done noble and excellent work ; but the dead weight and selfish blinkerdom of the Catholic organisation has hampered him to that degree that he has been unable to get justice done to his liberalising designs—or, perhaps, even to reveal the full extent of them. And the same difficulty will remain. On the one hand no spiritual movement which does not take up the attitude of a World-religion has now in this age, any chance of success ; on the other, all the existing Churches—whether Roman Catholic, or Greek, or Protestant or Secularist—whether Christian or Jewish or Persian or Hindu—will in all probability adopt the same blind and blinkered and selfish attitude as that described above, and so disqualify themselves for the great rôle of world-wide emancipation, which some religion at some time will certainly have to play. It is the same difficulty which is looming large in modern World-politics, where the local selfishnesses and vainglorious " patriotisms " of the Nations are sadly impeding and obstructing the development of that sense of Internationalism and Brotherhood which is the clearly indicated form of the future, and which alone can give each nation deliverance from fear, and a promise of growth, and the confident assurance of power.

I say that Christianity must either frankly adopt this generous attitude and confess itself a branch of the great World-religion, anxious only to do honour to its source— or else it must perish and pass away. There is no other alternative. The hour of its Exodus has come. It may be, of course, that neither the Christian Church nor any branch of it, nor any other religious organisation, will step into the gap. It may be—but I do not think this is likely —that the time of rites and ceremonies and formal creeds is *past*, and churches of any kind will be no more needed in the world : not likely, I say, because of the still far backwardness of the human masses, and their considerable dependence yet on laws and forms and rituals. Still, if it should prove that that age of dependence *is* really approaching its end, that would surely be a matter for congratulation. It would mean that mankind was moving into a knowledge of the *reality* which has underlain these outer shows—that it was coming into the Third stage of its Consciousness. Having found this there would be no need for it to dwell any longer in the land of superstitions and formulæ. It would have come to the place of which these latter are only the outlying indications.

It may, therefore, happen—and this quite independently of the growth of a World-cult such as I have described, though by no means in antagonism to it—that a religious philosophy or Theosophy might develop and spread, similar to the Gñánam of the Hindus or the Gnōsis of the pre-Christian sects, which would become, first among individuals and afterwards among large bodies over the world, the religion of—or perhaps one should say the religious approach to the Third State. Books like the Upanishads of the Vedic seers, and the Bhágavat Gita, though garbled and obscured by priestly interferences and mystifications, do undoubtedly represent and give expression to the highest utterance of religious experience to be found anywhere in the world. They are indeed the manuals of human

THE EXODUS OF CHRISTIANITY   269

entrance into the cosmic state.   But as I say, and as has
happened in the case of other sacred books, a vast deal
of rubbish has accreted round their essential teachings,
and has to be cleared away.   To go into a serious explication
of the meaning of these books would be far too large an
affair, and would be foreign to the purpose of the present
volume ; but I have in the Appendix below inserted two
papers, (on " Rest " and " The Nature of the Self ") con-
taining the substance of lectures given on the above books.
These papers or lectures are couched in the very simplest
language, free from Sanskrit terms and the usual ' jargon
of the Schools,' and may, I hope, even on that account
be of use in familiarising readers who are not specially
students with the ideas and mental attitudes of the cosmic
state.   Non-differentiation (Advaita [1]) is the root attitude
of the mind inculcated.

We have seen that there has been an age of non-differentiation in the *Past*—non-differentiation from other members
of the Tribe, from the Animals, from Nature and the Spirit
or Spirits of nature ; why should there not arise a similar
sense of non-differentiation in the *Future*—similar but more
extended, more intelligent ?   Certainly this *will* arrive, in
its own appointed time.   There will be a surpassing of the
bounds of separation and division.   There will be a surpassing
of all Taboos.   We have seen the use and function of Taboos
in the early stages of Evolution and how progress and growth
have been very much a matter of their gradual extinction
and assimilation into the general body of rational thought
and feeling.   Unreasoning and idiotic taboos still linger, but
they grow weaker.   A new Morality will come which will
shake itself free from them.   The sense of kinship with
the animals (as in the old rituals)[2] will be restored ; the sense

[1] The word means " not-two-ness." Here we see a great subtlety
of definition. It is not to be " one " with others that is urged, but
to be " not two."

[2] The record of the Roman Catholic Church has been sadly callous
and inhuman in this matter of the animals.

of kinship with all the races of mankind will grow and become consolidated ; the sense of the defilement and impurity of the human body will (with the adoption of a generally clean and wholesome life) pass away ; and the body itself will come to be regarded more as a collection of shrines in which the gods may be worshiped and less as a mere organ of trivial self-gratifications ; [1] there will be no form of Nature, or of human life or of the lesser creatures, which will be barred from the approach of Man or from the intimate and penetrating invasion of his spirit ; and as in certain ceremonies and after honorable toils and labours a citizen is sometimes received into the community of his own city, so the emancipated human being on the completion of his long long pilgrimage on Earth will be presented with the Freedom of the Universe.

[1] See *The Art of Création*, by E. Carpenter.

XVII

CONCLUSION

In conclusion there does not seem much to say, except to accentuate certain points which may still appear doubtful or capable of being misunderstood.

The fact that the main argument of this volume is along the lines of psychological evolution will no doubt commend it to some, while on the other hand it will discredit the book to others whose eyes, being fixed on purely *material* causes, can see no impetus in History except through these. But it must be remembered that there is not the least reason for *separating* the two factors. The fact that psychologically man has evolved from simple consciousness to self-consciousness, and is now in process of evolution towards another and more extended kind of consciousness, does not in the least bar the simultaneous appearance and influence of material evolution. It is clear indeed that the two must largely go together, acting and reacting on each other. Whatever the physical conditions of the animal brain may be which connect themselves with simple (unreflected and unreflecting) consciousness, it is evident that these conditions—in animals and primitive man— lasted for an enormous period, before the distinct consciousness of the individual and separate *self* arose. This second order of consciousness seems to have germinated at or about the same period as the discovery of the use

271

of Tools (tools of stone, copper, bronze, &c.), the adoption
of picture-writing and the use of reflective words (like
" I " and " Thou ") ; and it led on to the appreciation of
gold and of iron with their ornamental and practical values,
the accumulation of Property, the establishment of slavery
of various kinds, the subjection of Women, the encouragement of luxury and self-indulgence, the growth of crowded
cities and the endless conflicts and wars so resulting. We
can see plainly that the incoming of the self-motive exercised
a direct stimulus on the pursuit of these material objects
and adaptations ; and that the material adaptations in their
turn did largely accentuate the self-motive ; but to insist
that the real explanation of the whole process is only to
be found along one channel—the material *or* the psychical
—is clearly quite unnecessary. Those who understand
that all matter is conscious in some degree, and that all
consciousness has a material form of some kind, will be the
first to admit this.

The same remarks apply to the Third Stage. We can
see that in modern times the huge and unlimited powers
of production by machinery, united with a growing tendency
towards intelligent Birth-control, are preparing the way
for an age of Communism and communal Plenty which
will inevitably be associated (partly as cause and partly
as effect) with a new general phase of consciousness, in-
volving the mitigation of the struggle for existence, the
growth of intuitional and psychical perception, the spread
of amity and solidarity, the disappearance of War, and
the realisation (in degree) of the Cosmic life.

Perhaps the greatest difficulty or stumbling-block to
the general acceptance of the belief in a third (or ' Golden-
Age ') phase of human evolution is the obstinate and obdurate
pre-judgment that the passing of Humanity out of the
Second stage can only mean the entire *abandonment of
self-consciousness ;* and this, people say—and quite rightly
—is both impossible and undesirable. Throughout the

preceding chapters I have striven, wherever feasible, to counter this misunderstanding—but I have little hope of success ! The *determination* of the world to misunderstand or misinterpret anything a little new or unfamiliar is a thing which perhaps only an author can duly appreciate. But while it is clear that self-consciousness originally came into being through a process of alienation and exile and fear which marked it with the Cain-like brand of loneliness and apartness, it is equally clear that to think of that apartness as an absolute and permanent separation is an illusion, since no being can really continue to live divorced from the source of its life. For a period in evolution the *self* took on this illusive form in consciousness, as of an *ignis fatuus*—the form of a being sundered from all other beings, atomic, lonely, without refuge, surrounded by dangers and struggling for itself alone and for its own salvation in the midst of a hostile environment. Perhaps some such terrible imagination was necessary at first, as it were to start Humanity on its new path. But it had its compensation, for the sufferings and tortures, mental and bodily, the privations, persecutions, accusations, hatreds, the wars and conflicts—so endured by millions of individuals and whole races—have at length stamped upon the human mind a sense of individual responsibility which otherwise perhaps would never have emerged, and whose mark can never now be effaced ; ultimately, too, these things have searched our inner nature to its very depths and exposed its bed-rock foundation. They have convinced us that this idea of ultimate separation is an illusion, and that in truth we are all indefeasible and indestructible parts of one great Unity in which " we live and move and have our being." That being so, it is clear that there remains in the end a self-consciousness which need by no means be abandoned, which indeed only comes to its true fruition and understanding when it recognises its affiliation with the Whole, and glories in an individuality which is an expression both of itself *and* of the whole. The human child at its mother's knee probably comes first to know it *has* a 'self' on some fateful day when having wandered afar it goes lost among alien houses and streets or in the trackless fields. That appalling experience—the sense of danger, of fear, of loneliness—is never forgotten ; it stamps some new sense of Being upon the childish mind, but that sense, instead of being destroyed, becomes all the prouder and more radiant in the hour of return to the mother's arms. The return, the salvation, for which humanity looks, is the return of the little individual self to harmony and union with the great Self of the universe, but by no means its extinction or abandonment—rather the finding of its own true nature as never before.

There is another thing which may be said here : namely, that the disentanglement, as above, of three main stages of psychological evolution as great formative influences in the history of mankind, does not by any means preclude the establishment of lesser stages within the boundaries of these. In all probability subdivisions of all the three will come in time to be recognised and allowed for. To take the Second stage only, it *may* appear that Self-consciousness in its first development is characterised by an accentuation of Timidity ; in its second development by a more deliberate pursuit of sensual Pleasure (lust, food, drink, &c.) ; in its third by the pursuit of mental gratifications (vanities, ambitions, enslavement of others) ; in its fourth by the pursuit of Property, as a means of attaining these objects ; in its fifth by the access of enmities, jealousies, wars and so forth, consequent on all these things ; and so on. I have no intention at present of following out this line of thought, but only wish to suggest its feasibility and the degree to which it may throw light on the social evolutions of the Past.[1]

[1] For an analysis of the nature of Self-consciousness see vol. iii, p. 375 sq. of the three ponderous tomes by Wilhelm Wundt—*Grund-*

As a kind of rude general philosophy we may say that there are only two main factors in life, namely, *Love* and *Ignorance*. And of these we may also say that the two are not in the same plane : one is positive and substantial, the other is negative and merely illusory. It may be thought at first that Fear and Hatred and Cruelty, and the like, are very positive things, but in the end we see that they are due merely to *absence* of perception, to dulness of understanding. Or we may put the statement in a rather less crude form, and say that there are only two factors in life : (1) the sense of Unity with others (and with Nature) —which covers Love, Faith, Courage, Truth, and so forth, and (2) Non-perception of the same—which covers Enmity, Fear, Hatred, Self-pity, Cruelty, Jealousy, Meanness and an endless similar list. The present world which we see around us, with its idiotic wars, its senseless jealousies of nations and classes, its fears and greeds and vanities and its futile endeavours—as of people struggling in a swamp —to find one's own salvation by treading others underfoot, is a negative phenomenon. Ignorance, *non*-perception, are at the root of it. But it is the blessed virtue of Ignorance and of non-perception that they inevitably—if only slowly and painfully—*destroy themselves*. All experience serves to dissipate them. The world, as it is, carries the doom of its own transformation in its bosom ; and in proportion as that which is negative disappears the positive element must establish itself more and more.

So we come back to that with which we began,[1] to Fear bred by Ignorance. From that source has sprung the long catalogue of follies, cruelties and sufferings which mark the records of the human race since the dawn of history ; and to the overcoming of this Fear we perforce must look

---

eiga der Physiologischen Psychologie—in which amid an enormous mass of verbiage occasional gleams of useful suggestion are to be found.

[1] See Introduction, Ch. I, *supra*.

for our future deliverance, and for the discovery, even in the midst of this world, of our true Home. The time is coming when the positive constructive element must dominate. It is inevitable that Man must ever build a state of society around him after the pattern and image of his own interior state. The whole futile and idiotic structure of commerce and industry in which we are now imprisoned springs from that falsehood of individualistic self-seeking which marks the second stage of human evolution. That stage is already tottering to its fall, destroyed by the very flood of egotistic passions and interests, of vanities, greeds, and cruelties, all warring with each other, which are the sure outcome and culmination of its operation. With the restoration of the sentiment of the Common Life, and the gradual growth of a mental attitude corresponding, there will emerge from the flood something like a solid earth— something on which it will be possible to build with good hope for the future. Schemes of reconstruction are well enough in their way, but if there is no ground of *real human solidarity* beneath, of what avail are they?

An industrial system which is no real industrial order, but only (on the part of the employers) a devil's device for securing private profit under the guise of public utility, and (on the part of the employed) a dismal and poor-spirited renunciation—for the sake of a bare living—of all real interest in life and work : such a ' system ' must infallibly pass away. It cannot in the nature of things be permanent. The first condition of social happiness and prosperity must be the sense of the Common Life. This sense, which instinctively underlay the whole Tribal order of the far past— which first came to consciousness in the worship of a thousand pagan divinities, and in the rituals of countless sacrifices, initiations, redemptions, love-feasts and communions, which inspired the dreams of the Golden Age, and flashed out for a time in the Communism of the early Christians and in their adorations of the risen Saviour—must in the end be the creative condition of a new order : it must provide the material of which the Golden City waits to be built. The long travail of the World-religion will not have been in vain, which assures this consummation. What the signs and conditions of any general advance into this new order of life and consciousness will be, we know not. It may be that as to individuals the revelation of a new vision often comes quite suddenly, and *generally* perhaps after a period of great suffering, so to society at large a similar revelation will arrive—like " the lightning which cometh out of the East and shineth even unto the West "—with unexpected swiftness. On the other hand it would perhaps be wise not to count too much on any such sudden transformation. When we look abroad (and at home) in this year of grace and hoped-for peace, 1919, and see the spirits of rancour and revenge, the fears, the selfish blindness and the ignorance, which still hold in their paralysing grasp huge classes and coteries in every country in the world, we see that the second stage of human development is by no means yet at its full term, and that, as in some vast chrysalis, for the liberation of the creature within still more and more terrible struggles *may* be necessary. We can only pray that such may not be the case. Anyhow, if we have followed the argument of this book we can hardly doubt that the destruction (which is going on everywhere) of the outer form of the present society marks the first stage of man's final liberation ; and that, sooner or later, and in its own good time, that further ' divine event ' will surely be realised.

Nor need we fear that Humanity, when it has once entered into the great Deliverance, will be again overpowered by evil. From Knowledge back to Ignorance there is no complete return. The nations that have come to enlightenment need entertain no dread of those others (however hostile they appear) who are still plunging darkly

in the troubled waters of self-greed. The dastardly Fears
which inspire all brutishness and cruelty of warfare—
whether of White against White or it may be of White
against Yellow or Black—may be dismissed for good and
all by that blest race which once shall have gained the shore
—since from the very nature of the case those who are on
dry land can fear nothing and need fear nothing from the
unfortunates who are yet tossing in the welter and turmoil
of the waves.

Dr. Frazer, in the conclusion of his great work *The Golden
Bough*,[1] bids farewell to his readers with the following
words : " The laws of Nature are merely hypotheses
devised to explain that ever-shifting phantasmagoria of
thought which we dignify with the high-sounding names
of the World and the Universe. In the last analysis magic,
religion and science are nothing but theories [of thought] ;
and as Science has supplanted its predecessors so it may
hereafter itself be superseded by some more perfect hypo-
thesis, perhaps by some perfectly different way of looking
at phenomena—of registering the shadows on the screen—
of which we in this generation can form no idea."   I imagine
Dr. Frazer is right in thinking that " a way of looking
at phenomena " different from the way of Science, may
some day prevail. But I think this change will come, not
so much by the growth of Science itself or the extension
of its ' hypotheses,' as by a growth and expansion of the
human *heart* and a change in its psychology and powers
of perception. Perhaps some of the preceding chapters
will help to show how much the outlook of humanity on
the world has been guided through the centuries by the
slow evolution of its inner consciousness. Gradually, out
of an infinite mass of folly and delusion, the human soul
has in this way disentangled itself, and will in the future
disentangle itself, to emerge at length in the light of true
Freedom. All the taboos, the insane terrors, the fatuous

[1] See " Balder," vol. ii, pp. 306, 307. (" Farewell to Nemi.")

forbiddals of this and that (with their consequent heart-searchings and distress) may perhaps have been in their way necessary, in order to rivet and define the meaning and the understanding of that word. To-day these taboos and terrors still linger, many of them, in the form of conventions of morality, uneasy strivings of conscience, doubts and desperations of religion ; but ultimately Man will emerge from all these things, *free*—familiar, that is, with them all, making use of all, allowing generously for the values of all, but hampered and bound by *none*. He will realise the inner meaning of the creeds and rituals of the ancient religions, and will hail with joy the fulfilment of their far prophecy down the ages—finding after all the long-expected Saviour of the world within his own breast, and Paradise in the disclosure there of the everlasting peace of the soul.

APPENDIX

THE TEACHING OF THE UPANISHADS

BEING THE SUBSTANCE OF TWO LECTURES TO POPULAR AUDIENCES

    I. REST

    II. THE NATURE OF THE SELF

I

REST

To some, in the present whirlpool of life and affairs it may seem almost an absurdity to talk about Rest. For long enough now rest has seemed a thing far off and unattainable. With the posts knocking at our doors ten or twelve times a day, with telegrams arriving every hour, and the telephone bell constantly ringing; with motors rushing wildly about the streets, and aeroplanes whizzing overhead, with work speeded up in every direction, and the drive in the workshops becoming more intolerable every day; with the pace of the walkers and the pace of the talkers from hour to hour insanely increasing—what room, it may well be asked, is there for Rest? And now the issues of war, redoubling the urgency of all questions, are on us.

The problem is obviously a serious one. So urgent is it that I think one may safely say the amount of insanity due to the pressure of daily life is increasing; nursing-homes have sprung up for the special purpose of treating such cases; and doctors are starting special courses of tuition in the art—now becoming very important—of systematically doing nothing! And yet it is difficult to see the outcome of it all. The clock of what is called Progress is not easily turned backward. We should not very readily agree nowadays to the abolition of telegrams or to a regulation compelling express trains to stop at every station! We can't *all* go to Nursing Homes, or afford to enjoy a winter's rest-cure in Egypt. And, if not, is the speeding-up process to go on indefinitely, incapable of being checked, and destined ultimately to land civilisation in the mad-house?

It is, I say, a serious and an urgent problem. And it is, I think, forcing a certain answer on us—which I will now endeavour to explain.

If we cannot turn back and reverse this fatal onrush of modern life (and it is evident that we cannot do so in any very brief time—though of course ultimately we might succeed) then I think there are clearly only two alternatives left—either to go forward to general dislocation and madness, or—to learn to rest even in the very midst of the hurry and the scurry.

To explain what I mean, let me use an illustration. The typhoons and cyclones of the China Seas are some of the most formidable storms that ships can encounter. Their paths in the past have been strewn with wrecks and disaster. But now with increased knowledge much of their danger has been averted. It is known that they are *circular* in character, and that though the wind on their outskirts often reaches a speed of 100 miles an hour, in the centre of the storm there is a space of complete calm—not a calm of the *sea* certainly, but a complete absence of wind. The skilled navigator, if he cannot escape the storm, steers right into the heart of it, and rests there. Even in the midst of the clatter he finds a place of quiet where he can trim his sails and adjust his future course. He knows too from his position in what direction at every point around him the wind is moving and where it will strike him when at last his ship emerges from the charmed circle.

Is it not possible, we may ask, that in the very midst of the cyclone of daily life we may find a similar resting-place ? If we can, our case is by no means hopeless. If we cannot, then indeed there is danger.

Looking back in History we seem to see that in old times people took life much more leisurely than they do now. The elder generations gave more scope in their customs and their religions for contentment and peace of mind. We associate a certain quietism and passivity with the thought of the Eastern peoples. But as civilisation traveled Westward external activity and the pace of life increased—less and less time was left for meditation and repose—till with the rise of Western Europe and America, the dominant note of life seems to have simply become one of feverish and ceaseless activity—of activity merely for the sake of activity, without any clear idea of its own purpose or object.

Such a prospect does not at first seem very hopeful ; but on second thoughts we see that we are not forced to draw any very pessimistic conclusion from it. The direction of human evolution need not remain always the same. The movement, in fact, of civilisation from East to West has now clearly completed itself. The globe has been circled, and we cannot go any *farther* to the West without coming round to the East again. It is a commonplace to say that our psychology, our philosophy and our religious sense are already taking on an Eastern colour ; nor is it difficult to imagine that with the end of the present dispensation a new era may perfectly naturally arrive in which the St. Vitus' dance of money-making and ambition will cease to be the chief end of existence.

In the history of nations as in the history of individuals there are periods when the formative ideals of life (through some hidden influence) change ; and the mode of life and evolution in consequence changes also. I remember when I was a boy wishing—like many other boys—to go to sea. I wanted to join the Navy. It was not, I am sure, that I was so very anxious to defend my country. No, there was a much simpler and more prosaic motive than that. The ships of those days with their complex rigging suggested a perfect paradise of *climbing*, and I know that it was the thought of *that* which influenced me. To be able to climb indefinitely among those ropes and spars ! How delightful ! Of course I knew perfectly well that I should not always have free access to the rigging ; but then—some day, no doubt, I should be an Admiral, and who then could prevent me ? I remember seeing myself in my mind's eye, with cocked hat on my head and spy-glass under my arm, roaming at my own sweet will up aloft, regardless of the remonstrances which might reach me from below ! Such was my childish ideal. But a time came—needless to say—when I conceived a different idea of the object of life.

It is said that John Tyndall, whose lectures on Science were so much sought after in their time, being on one occasion in New York was accosted after his discourse by a very successful American business man, who urged him to devote his scientific knowledge and ability to commercial pursuits, promising that if he did so, he, Tyndall, would easily make " a big pile." Tyndall very calmly replied, " Well, I myself thought of that once, but I soon abandoned the idea, having come to the conclusion that I had *no time to waste in making money*." The man of dollars nearly sank into the ground. Such a conception of life had never entered his head before. But to Tyndall no doubt it was obvious that if he chained himself to the commercial ideal all the joy and glory of his days would be gone.

We sometimes hear of the awful doom of some of the Russian convicts in the quarries and mines of Siberia, who are (or were) chained permanently to their wheelbarrows. It is difficult to imagine a more dreadful fate : the despair, the disgust, the deadly loathing of the accursed thing from which there is no escape day or night—which is the companion not only of the prisoner's work but of his hours of rest—with which he has to sleep, to feed, to take his recreation if he has any, and to fulfil all the offices of nature. Could anything be more crushing ? And yet, and yet . . . is it not true that we, most of us, in our various ways are chained to our wheelbarrows—is it not too often true that to these beggarly things we have for the most part chained *ourselves* ?

Let me be understood. Of course we all have (or ought to have) our work to do. We have our living to get, our families to support, our trade, our art, our profession to pursue. In that sense no doubt we are tied ; but I take it that these things are like the wheelbarrow which a man uses while he is at work. It may irk him at times, but he sticks to it with a good heart, and with a certain joy because it is the instrument of a noble purpose. That is all right. But to be chained to it, not to be able to leave it when the work of the day is done—that is indeed an ignoble slavery. I would say, then, take care that even with these things, these necessary arts of life, you preserve your independence, that even if to some degree they may confine your body they do not enslave your mind.

For it is the freedom of the mind which counts. We are all no doubt caught in the toils of the earth-life. One man is largely dominated by sensual indulgence, another by ambition, another by the pursuit of money. Well, these things are all right in themselves. Without the pleasures of the senses we should be dull mokes indeed ; without ambition much of the zest and enterprise of life would be gone ; gold, in the present order of affairs, is a very useful servant. These things are right enough—but to be *chained* to them, to be unable to think of anything else—what a fate ! The subject reminds one of a not uncommon spectacle. It is a glorious day ; the sun is bright, small white clouds float in the transparent blue—a day when you linger perforce on the road to enjoy the scene. But suddenly here comes a man painfully running all hot and dusty and mopping his head, and with no eye, clearly, for anything around him. What is the matter ? He is absorbed by one idea. He is running to catch a train ! And one cannot help wondering what *exceedingly* important business it must be for which all this glory and beauty is sacrificed, and passed by as if it did not exist.

Further we must remember that in our foolishness we very commonly chain ourselves, not only to things like sense-pleasures and ambitions which are on the edge, so to speak, of being vices ; but also to other things which are accounted virtues, and which as far as I can see are just as bad, if we once become enslaved to them. I have known people who were so exceedingly ' spiritual ' and ' good ' that one really felt quite depressed in their company ; I have known others whose sense of duty, dear things, was so strong that they seemed quite unable to *rest*, or even to allow their friends to rest ; and I have wondered whether, after all, worriting about one's duty might not be as bad—as deteriorating to oneself, as distressing to one's friends—as sinning a good solid sin. No, in this respect virtues *may* be no better than vices ; and to be chained to a wheelbarrow made of alabaster is no way preferable to being chained to one of wood. To sacrifice the immortal freedom of the mind in order to become a prey to self-regarding cares and anxieties, self-estimating virtues and vices, self-chaining duties and indulgences, is a mistake. And I warn you, it is quite useless. For the destiny of Freedom is ultimately upon every one, and if refusing it for a time you heap your life per-sistently upon one object—however blameless in itself that object may be—Beware ! For one day—and when you least expect it—the gods will send a thunderbolt upon you. One day the thing for which you have toiled and spent laborious days and sleepless nights will lie broken before you—your repu-tation will be ruined, your ambition will be dashed, your savings of years will be lost—and for the moment you will be inclined to think that your life has been in vain. But presently you will wake up and find that something quite different has happened. You will find that the thunderbolt which you thought was your ruin has been your salvation—that it has broken the chain which bound you to your wheelbarrow, and that you are free !

I think you will now see what I mean by Rest. Rest is the loosing of the chains which bind us to the whirligig of the world ; it is the passing into the centre of the Cyclone ; it is the Stilling of Thought. For (with regard to this last) it is Thought, it is the Attachment of the Mind, which binds us to outer things. The outer things themselves are all right. It is only through our thoughts that they make slaves of us.

Obtain power over your thoughts and you are free. You can then use the outer things or dismiss them at your pleasure.

There is nothing new of course in all this. It has been known for ages ; and is part of the ancient philosophy of the world.

In the Katha Upanishad you will find these words (Max Müller's translation) : " As rainwater that has fallen on a mountain ridge runs down on all sides, thus does he who sees a difference between qualities run after them on all sides." This is the figure of the man who does *not* rest. And it is a powerful likeness. The thunder shower descends on the mountain top ; torrents of water pour down the crags in every direction. Imagine the state of mind of a man—however thirsty he may be—who endeavors to pursue and intercept all these streams !

But then the Upanishad goes on : " As pure water poured into pure water remains the same, thus, O Gautama, is the Self of a thinker who knows." What a perfect image of rest ! Imagine a cistern before you with transparent glass sides and filled with pure water. And then imagine some one comes with a phial, also of pure water, and pours the contents gently into the cistern. What will happen ? Almost nothing. The pure water will glide into the pure water—" remaining the same." There will be no dislocation, no discoloration (as might happen if *muddy* water were poured in) ; there will be only perfect harmony.

I imagine here that the meaning is something like this. The cistern is the great Reservoir of the Universe which contains the pure and perfect Spirit of all life. Each one of us, and every mortal creature, represents a drop from that reservoir— a drop indeed which is also pure and perfect (though the phial in which it is contained may not always be so). When we, each of us, descend into the world and meet the great Ocean of Life which dwells there behind all mortal forms, it is like the little phial being poured into the great reservoir. If the tiny canful which is our selves is pure and unsoiled, then when it meets the world it will blend with the Spirit which informs the world perfectly harmoniously, without distress or dislocation. It will pass through and be at one with it. How can one describe such a state of affairs ? You will have the key to every person that you meet, because indeed you are conscious that the real essence of that person is the same as your own. You will have the solution of every event which happens. For every event is (and is felt to be) the touch of the great

Spirit on yours. Can any description of Rest be more perfect than that ? Pure water poured into pure water. . . . There is no need to hurry, for everything will come in its good time. There is no need to leave your place, for all you desire is close at hand.

Here is another verse (from the Vagasaneyi-Samhita Upanishad) embodying the same idea : " And he who beholds all beings in the Self, and the Self in all beings, he never turns away from It. When, to a man who understands, the Self has become all things, what sorrow, what trouble, can there be to him—having once beheld that Unity ? "—What trouble, what sorrow, indeed, when the universe has become transparent with the presences of all we love, held firm in the One enfolding Presence ?

But it will be said : " Our minds are *not* pure and transparent. More often they are muddy and soiled—soiled, if not in their real essence, yet by reason of the mortal phial in which they are contained." And that alas ! is true. If you pour a phial of muddy water into that reservoir which we described —what will you see ? You will see a queer and ugly cloud formed. And to how many of us, in our dealings with the world, does life take on just such a form—of a queer and ugly cloud ?

Now not so very long after those Upanishads were written there lived in China that great Teacher, Lao-tze ; and he too had considered these things. And he wrote—in the Tao-Teh-King—" Who is there who can make muddy water clear ? " The question sounds like a conundrum. For a moment one hesitates to answer it. Lao-tze, however, has an answer ready. He says : " But if you *leave it alone* it will become clear of itself." That muddy water of the mind, muddied by all the foolish little thoughts which like a sediment infest it—but if you leave it alone it will become clear of itself. Sometimes walking along the common road after a shower you have seen pools of water lying here and there, dirty and unsightly with the mud stirred up by the hooves of men and animals. And then returning some hours afterwards along the same road—in the evening and after the cessation of traffic—you have looked again, and lo ! each pool has cleared itself to a perfect calm, and has become a lovely mirror reflecting the trees and the clouds and the sunset and the stars.

So this mirror of the mind. Leave it alone. Let the ugly sediment of tiresome thoughts and anxieties, and of fussing over one's self-importances and duties, settle down—and presently you will look on it, and see something there which you never knew or imagined before—something more beautiful than you ever yet beheld—a reflection of the real and eternal world such is only given to the mind that rests.

Do not recklessly spill the waters of your mind in this direction and in that, lest you become like a spring lost and dissipated in the desert.
But draw them together into a little compass, and hold them still, so still;
And let them become clear, so clear—so limpid, so mirror-like;
At last the mountains and the sky shall glass themselves in peaceful beauty,
And the antelope shall descend to drink, and the lion to quench his thirst,
And Love himself shall come and bend over, and catch his own likeness in you.[1]

Yes, there is this priceless thing within us, but hoofing along the roads in the mud we fail to find it; there is this region of calm, but the cyclone of the world raging around guards us from entering it. Perhaps it is best so—best that the access to it should not be made too easy. One day, some time ago, in the course of conversation with Rabindranath Tagore in London, I asked him what impressed him most in visiting the great city. He said, "The restless incessant movement of everybody." I said, "Yes, they seem as if they were all rushing about looking for something." He replied, "It is because each person does not know of the great treasure he has within himself."

How then are we to reach this treasure and make it our own ? How are we to attain to this Stilling of the Mind, which is the secret of all power and possession ? The thing is difficult, no doubt; yet as I tried to show at the outset of this discourse, we Moderns *must* reach it; we have got to attain to it—for the penalty of failure is and must be widespread Madness.
The power to still the mind—to be *able*, mark you, when you want, to enter into the region of Rest, and to dismiss or command your Thoughts—is a condition of Health; it is a condition of all Power and Energy. For all health, whether

[1] *Towards Democracy*, p. 373.

of mind or body, resides in one's relation to the central Life within. If one cannot get into touch with *that*, then the life-forces cannot flow down into the organism. Most, perhaps all, disease arises from the disturbance of this connexion. All mere hurry, all mere running after external things (as of the man after the water-streams on the mountain-top), inevitably breaks it. Let a pond be allowed calmly under the influence of frost to crystallise, and most beautiful flowers and spears of ice will be formed ; but keep stirring the water all the time with a stick or a pole and nothing will result but an ugly brash of half-frozen stuff. The condition of the exercise of power and energy is that it should proceed from a centre of Rest within one. So convinced am I of this, that whenever I find myself hurrying over my work, I pause and say, " Now you are not producing anything good ! " and I generally find that that is true. It is curious, but I think very noticeable, that the places where people hurry most—as for instance the City of London or Wall Street, New York—are just the places where the work being done is of *least* importance (being mostly money-gambling) ; whereas if you go and look at a ploughman ploughing—doing perhaps the most important of human work—you find all his movements most deliberate and leisurely, as if indeed he had infinite time at command ; the truth being that in dealing (like a ploughman) with the earth and the horses and the weather and the things of Nature generally you can no more hurry than Nature herself hurries.

Following this line of thought it might seem that one would arrive at a hopeless paradox. If it be true that the less one hurries the better the work resulting, then it might seem that by sitting still and merely twirling one's thumbs one would arrive at the very greatest activity and efficiency ! And indeed (if understood aright) there is a truth even in this, which—like the other points I have mentioned—has been known and taught long ages ago. Says that humorous old sage, Lao-tze, whom I have already quoted : " By non-action there is nothing that cannot be done." At first this sounds like mere foolery or worse ; but afterwards thinking on it one sees there is a meaning hidden. There is a secret by which Nature and the powers of the universal life will do all for you. The Bhágavat Gita also says, " He who discovers inaction in action and action in inaction is wise among mortals."

It is worth while dwelling for a moment on these texts. We are all—as I said earlier on—involved in work belonging to our place and station ; we are tied to some degree in the bonds of action. But that fact need not imprison our inner minds. While acting even with keenness and energy along the external and necessary path before us, it is perfectly possible to hold the mind free and untied—so that the *result* of our action (which of course is not ours to command) shall remain indifferent and incapable of unduly affecting us. Similarly, when it is our part to remain externally *inactive*, we may discover that underneath this apparent inaction we may be taking part in the currents of a deeper life which are moving on to a definite end, to an end or object which in a sense is ours and in a sense is *not* ours. The lighthouse beam flies over land and sea with incredible velocity, and you think the light itself must be in swiftest movement ; but when you climb up thither you find the lamp absolutely stationary. It is only the reflection that is moving. The rider on horseback may gallop to and fro wherever he will, but it is hard to say that *he* is acting. The horse guided by the slightest indication of the man's will performs all the action that is needed. If we can get into right touch with the immense, the incalculable powers of Nature, is there anything which we may not be able to do ? " If a man worship the Self only as his true state," says the Brihad-aranyaka Upanishad, " his work cannot fail, for whatever he desires, that he obtains from the Self." What a wonderful saying, and how infallibly true ! For obviously if you succeed in identifying your true being with the great Self of the universe, then whatever you desire the great Self will also desire, and therefore every power of Nature will be at your service and will conspire to fulfil your need.

There are marvelous things here " well wrapped up " — difficult to describe, yet not impossible to experience. And they all depend upon that power of stilling Thought, that ability to pass unharmed and undismayed through the grinning legions of the lower mind into the very heart of Paradise.

The question inevitably arises, How can this power be obtained ? And there is only one answer—the same answer which has to be given for the attainment of *any* power or faculty. There is no royal road. The only way is (however imperfectly) to *do* the thing in question, to practise it. If you would learn to play cricket, the only way is to play cricket ; if you would be able to speak a language, the only way is to speak it. If you would learn to swim, the only way is to practise swimming. Or would you wish to be like the man who when his companions were bathing and bidding him come and join them, said : " Yes, I am longing to join you, but I am not going to be such a fool as to go into the water *till I know how to swim !* "

There is nothing but practice. If you want to obtain that priceless power of commanding Thought—of using it or dismissing it (for the two things go together) at will—there is no way but practice. And the practice consists in two exercises : (*a*) that of concentration—in holding the thought steadily for a time on one subject, or point of a subject ; and (*b*) that of effacement—in effacing any given thought from the mind, and determining *not* to entertain it for such and such a time. Both these exercises are difficult. Failure in practising them is certain —and may even extend over years. But the power equally certainly grows *with* practice. And ultimately there may come a time when the learner is not only able to efface from his mind any given thought (however importunate), but may even succeed in effacing, during short periods, *all* thought of any kind. When this stage is reached, the veil of illusion which surrounds all mortal things is pierced, and the entrance to the Paradise of Rest (and of universal power and knowledge) is found.

Of indirect or auxiliary methods of reaching this great conclusion, there are more than one. I think a life in the open air, if not absolutely necessary, at least most important. The gods—though sometimes out of compassion they visit the interiors of houses—are not fond of such places and the evil effluvium they find there, and avoid them as much as they can. It is not merely a question of breathing oxygen instead of carbonic acid. There is a presence and an influence in Nature and the Open which expands the mind and causes brigand cares and worries to drop off—whereas in confined places foolish and futile thoughts of all kinds swarm like microbes and cloud and conceal the soul. *Experto Crede.* It is only necessary to try this experiment in order to prove its truth.

Another thing which corresponds in some degree to living physically in the open air, is the living mentally and emotionally in the atmosphere of love. A large charity of mind, which refuses absolutely to shut itself in little secluded places of prejudice, bigotry and contempt for others, and which attains to a great and universal sympathy, helps, most obviously, to open the way to that region of calm and freedom of which we have spoken, while conversely all petty enmity, meanness and spite, conspire to imprison the soul and make its deliverance more difficult.

It is not necessary to labour these points. As we said, the way to attain is to sincerely *try* to attain, to consistently *practise* attainment. Whoever does this will find that the way will open out by degrees, as of one emerging from a vast and gloomy forest, till out of darkness the path becomes clear. For whomsoever really *tries* there is no failure ; for every effort in that region *is* success, and every onward push, however small, and however little result it may show, is really a move forward, and one step nearer the light.

II

THE NATURE OF THE SELF

THE true nature of the Self is a matter by no means easy to compass. We have all probably at some time or other attempted to fathom the deeps of personality, and been baffled. Some people say they can quite distinctly remember a moment in early childhood, about the age of *three* (though the exact period is of course only approximate) when self-consciousness—the awareness of being a little separate Self—first dawned in the mind. It was generally at some moment of childish tension—alone perhaps in a garden, or lost from the mother's protecting hand—that this happened ; and it was the beginning of a whole range of new experience. Before some such period there is in childhood strictly speaking no distinct self-consciousness. As Tennyson says (*In Memoriam* xliv) :

> The baby new to earth and sky,
> What time his tender palm is prest
> Against the circle of the breast,
> Hath never thought that " This is I."

It has consciousness truly, but no distinctive self-consciousness. It is this absence or deficiency which explains many things which at first sight seem obscure in the psychology of children and of animals. The baby (it has often been noticed) experiences little or no sense of *fear*. It does not *know* enough to be afraid ; it has never formed any image of itself, as of a thing which might be injured. It may shrink from actual pain or discomfort, but it does not *look forward*—which is of the essence of fear—to pain in the future. Fear and self-consciousness are closely interlinked. Similarly with animals, we often wonder how a horse or a cow can endure to stand out in a field all night, exposed to cold and rain, in the lethargic patient way that they exhibit. It is not that they do not *feel* the discomfort, but it is that they do not envisage *themselves* as enduring this pain and suffering for all those coming hours ; and as we know with ourselves that nine-tenths of our miseries really consist in looking forward to future miseries, so we understand that the absence or at any rate slight prevalence of self-consciousness in animals enables them to endure forms of distress which would drive us mad.

In time then the babe arrives at self-consciousness ; and, as one might expect, the growing boy or girl often becomes intensely aware of Self. His or her self-consciousness is crude, no doubt, but it has very little misgiving. If the question of the nature of the Self is propounded to the boy as a problem he has no difficulty in solving it. He says " I know well enough who *I* am : I am the boy with red hair what gave Jimmy Brown such a jolly good licking last Monday week." He knows well enough—or thinks he knows—who he is. And at a later age, though his definition may change and he may describe himself chiefly as a good cricketer or successful in certain examinations, his method is practically the same. He fixes his mind on a certain bundle of qualities and capacities which he is supposed to possess, and calls that bundle Himself. And in a more elaborate way we most of us, I imagine, do the same.

Presently, however, with more careful thought, we begin to see difficulties in this view. I see that directly I think of myself as a certain bundle of qualities—and for that matter it is of no account whether the qualities are good or bad, or in what sort of charming confusion they are mixed—I see at once that I am merely looking *at* a bundle of qualities : and that the real " I," the Self, is not that bundle, but is the being *inspecting* the same—something beyond and behind, as it were. So I now concentrate my thoughts upon that inner Something, in order to find out what it really is. I imagine perhaps an inner being, of ' astral ' or ethereal nature, and possessing a new range of much finer and more subtle qualities than the body—a being inhabiting the body and perceiving through its senses, but quite capable of surviving the tenement in which it dwells— and I think of that as the Self. But no sooner have I taken this step than I perceive that I am committing the same mistake as before. I am only contemplating a new image or picture, and " I " still remain beyond and behind that which I contemplate. No sooner do I turn my attention on the subjective being than it becomes *objective*, and the real subject retires into the background. And so on indefinitely. I am baffled ; and unable to say positively what the Self is.

Meanwhile there are people who look upon the foregoing speculations about an interior Self as merely unpractical. Being perhaps of a more materialistic type of mind they fix their attention on the body. Frankly they try to define the Self by the body and all that is connected therewith—that is by the mental as well as corporeal qualities which exhibit themselves in that connexion ; and they say, " At any rate the Self —whatever it may be—is in some way limited by the body ; each person studies the interest of his body and of the feelings, emotions and mentality directly associated with it, and you cannot get beyond that ; it isn't in human nature to do so. The Self is limited by this corporeal phenomenon and doubtless it perishes when the body perishes." But here again the conclusion, though specious at first, soon appears to be quite inadequate. For though it is possibly true that a man, if left alone in a Robinson Crusoe life on a desert island, might ultimately subside into a mere gratification of his corporeal needs and of those mental needs which were directly concerned with the body, yet we know that such a case would by no means be representative. On the contrary we know that vast numbers of people spend their lives in considering *other* people, and often so far as to sacrifice their own bodily and mental comfort and well-being. The mother spends her life thinking almost day and night about her babe and the other children—spending all her thoughts and efforts on them. You may call her selfish if you will, but her selfishness clearly extends beyond her personal body and mind, and extends to the personalities of her children around her ; her " body "—if you insist on your definition—must be held to include the bodies of all her children. And again, the husband who is toiling for the support of the family, he is thinking and working and toiling and suffering for a ' self ' which includes his wife and children. Do you mean that the whole family is his " body " ? Or a man belongs to some society, to a church or to a social league of some kind, and his activities are largely ruled by the interests of this larger group. Or he sacrifices his life—as many have been doing of late—with extraordinary bravery and heroism for the sake of the nation to which he belongs. Must we say then that the whole nation is really a part of the man's body ? Or again, he gives his life and goes to the stake for his religion. Whether his religion is right or wrong does not matter, the point is that there is that in him which can carry him far beyond his local self and the ordinary instincts of his physical organism, to dedicate his life and powers to a something of far wider circumference and scope.

Thus in the *first* of these two examples of a search for the nature of the Self we are led *inwards* from point to point, into interior and ever subtler regions of our being, and still in the end are baffled ; while in the *second* we are carried *outwards* into an ever wider and wider circumference in our quest of the Ego, and still feel that we have failed to reach its ultimate nature. We are driven in fact by these two arguments to the conclusion that that which we are seeking is indeed something very vast—something far extending around, yet also buried deep in the hidden recesses of our minds. How far, how deep, we do not know. We can only say that as far as the indications point the true self is profounder and more far-reaching than anything we have yet fathomed.

In the ordinary commonplace life we shrink to ordinary commonplace selves, but it is one of the blessings of great experiences, even though they are tragic or painful, that they throw us out into that enormously greater self to which we belong. Sometimes, in moments of inspiration, of intense enthusiasm, of revelation, such as a man feels in the midst of a battle, in moments of love and dedication to another person, and in moments of religious ecstasy, an immense world is opened up to the astonished gaze of the inner man, who sees disclosed a self stretched far beyond anything he had ever imagined. We have all had experiences more or less of that kind. I have known quite a few people, and most of you have known some, who at some time, even if only once in their lives, have experienced such an extraordinary lifting of the veil, an opening out of the back of their minds as it were, and have had such a vision of the world, that they have never afterwards forgotten it. They have seen into the heart of creation, and have perceived their union with the rest of mankind. They have had glimpses of a strange immortality belonging to them, a glimpse of their belonging to a far greater being than they have ever imagined. Just once—and a man has never forgotten it, and even if it has not recurred it has coloured all the rest of his life.

Now, this subject has been thought about—since the beginning of the world, I was going to say—but it has been thought about since the beginnings of history. Some three thousand years ago certain groups of—I hardly like to call them philosophers—but, let us say, people who were meditating and thinking upon these problems, were in the habit of locating themselves in the forests of Northern India ; and schools arose there. In the case of each school some teacher went into the woods and collected groups of disciples around him, who lived there in his company and listened to his words. Such schools were formed in very considerable numbers, and the doctrines of these teachers were gathered together, generally by their disciples, in notes, which notes were brought together into little pamphlets or tracts, forming the books which are called the ' Upanishads ' of the Indian sages. They contain some extraordinary words of wisdom, some of which I want to bring before you. The conclusions arrived at were not so much what we should call philosophy in the modern sense. They were not so much the result of the analysis of the mind and the following out of concatenations of strict argument ; but they were flashes of intuition and experience, and all through the ' Upanishads ' you find these extraordinary flashes embedded in the midst of a great deal of what we should call a rather rubbishy kind of argument, and a good deal of merely conventional Brahmanical talk of those days. But the people who wrote and spoke thus had an intuition into the heart of things which I make bold to say very few people in modern life have. These ' Upanishads,' however various their subjects, practically agree on one point —in the definition of the " self." They agree in saying that the self of each man is continuous with and in a sense identical with the Self of the universe. Now that seems an extraordinary conclusion, and one which almost staggers the modern mind to conceive of. But that is the conclusion, that is the thread which runs all through the ' Upanishads '—the identity of the self of each individual with the self of every other individual throughout mankind, and even with the selves of the animals and other creatures.

Those who have read the Khandogya Upanishad remember how in that treatise the father instructs his son Svetaketu on this very subject—pointing him out in succession the objects of Nature and on each occasion exhorting him to realise his identity with the very essence of the object " *Tat twam asi*, *That* thou art." He calls Svetaketu's attention to a tree. What is the *essence* of the tree ? When they have rejected the external characteristics—the leaves, the branches, etc.—and agreed

that the *sap* is the essence, then the father says, " *Tat twam asi*
—*That* thou art." He gives his son a crystal of salt, and asks
him what is the essence of that. The son is puzzled. Clearly
neither the form nor the transparent quality are essential. The
father says, " Put the crystal in water." Then when it is melted
he says, " Where is the crystal ? " The son replies, " I do not
know." " Dip your finger in the bowl," says the father, " and
taste." Then Svetaketu dips here and there, and everywhere
there is a salt flavour. They agree that *that* is the essence of
salt ; and the father says again, " *Tat twam asi.*" I am of course
neither defending nor criticising the scientific attitude here
adopted. I am only pointing out that this psychological identification of the observer with the object observed runs through
the Upanishads, and is I think worthy of the deepest consideration.

In the ' Bhágavat Gita,' which is a later book, the author
speaks of " him whose soul is purified, whose self is the Self
of all creatures." A phrase like that challenges opposition.
It is so bold, so sweeping, and so immense, that we hesitate to
give our adhesion to what it implies. But what does it mean
—" whose soul is purified " ? I believe that it means this,
that with most of us our souls are anything but clean or purified,
they are by no means transparent, so that all the time
we are continually deceiving ourselves and making clouds
between us and others. We are all the time grasping things
from other people, and if not in words, are mentally boasting
ourselves against others, trying to think of our own superiority
to the rest of the people around us. Sometimes we try to run
our neighbours down a little, just to show that they are not
quite equal to our level. We try to snatch from others some
things which belong to them, or take credit to ourselves for
things to which we are not fairly entitled. But all the time we
are acting so it is perfectly obvious that we are weaving veils
between ourselves and others. You cannot have dealings with
another person in a purely truthful way, and be continually
trying to cheat that person out of money, or out of his good
name and reputation. If you are doing that, however much
in the background you may be doing it, you are not looking
the person fairly in the face—there is a cloud between you all
the time. So long as your soul is not purified from all these
really absurd and ridiculous little desires and superiorities and
self-satisfactions, which make up so much of our lives, just
so long as that happens you do not and you cannot see the

truth. But when it happens to a person, as it does happen in times of great and deep and bitter experience ; when it happens that all these trumpery little objects of life are swept away ; then occasionally, with astonishment, the soul sees that It is also the soul of the others around. Even if it does not become aware of an absolute identity, it perceives that there is a deep relationship and communion between itself and others, and it comes to understand how it may really be true that to him whose soul is purified the self is literally the Self of all creatures.

Ordinary men and those who go on more intellectual and less intuitional lines will say that these ideas are really contrary to human nature and to nature generally. Yet I think that those people who say this in the name of Science are extremely un-scientific, because a very superficial glance at nature reveals that the very same thing is taking place throughout nature. Consider the madrepores, corallines, or sponges. You find, for instance, that constantly the little self of the coralline or sponge is functioning at the end of a stem and casting forth its tentacles into the water to gain food and to breathe the air out of the water. That little animalcule there, which is living in that way, imagines no doubt that it is working all for itself, and yet it is united down the stem at whose extremity it stands, with the life of the whole madrepore or sponge to which it belongs. There is the common life of the whole and the individual life of each, and while the little creature at the end of the stem is thinking (if it is conscious at all) that its whole energies are absorbed in its own maintenance, it really is feeding the common life through the stem to which it belongs, and in its turn it is being fed by that common life.

You have only to look at an ordinary tree to see the same thing going on. Each little leaf on a tree may very naturally have sufficient consciousness to believe that it is an entirely separate being maintaining itself in the sunlight and the air, withering away and dying when the winter comes on—and there is an end of it. It probably does not realise that all the time it is being supported by the sap which flows from the trunk of the tree, and that in its turn it is feeding the tree, too—that its self is the self of the whole tree. If the leaf could really understand itself, it would see that its self was deeply, intimately connected, practically one with the life of the whole tree. Therefore, I say that this Indian view is not unscientific. On the contrary, I am sure that it is thoroughly scientific.

Let us take another passage, out of the ' Svetasvatara Upanishad,' which, speaking of the self says : " He is the one God, hidden in all creatures, all pervading, the self within all, watching over all works, shadowing all creatures, the witness, the perceiver, the only one free from qualities."

And now we can return to the point where we left the argument at the beginning of this discourse. We said, you remember, that the Self is certainly no mere bundle of qualities—that the very nature of the mind forbids us thinking that. For however fine and subtle any quality or group of qualities may be, we are irresistibly compelled by the nature of the mind itself to look for the Self, not in any quality or qualities, but in the being that *perceives* those qualities. The passage I have just quoted says that being is " The one God, hidden in all creatures, all pervading, the self within all . . . the witness, the perceiver, the only one free from qualities." And the more you think about it the clearer I think you will see that this passage is correct—that there can be only *one* witness, *one* perceiver, and that is the one God hidden in all creatures, " Sarva Sakshi," the Universal Witness.

Have you ever had that curious feeling, not uncommon, especially in moments of vivid experience and emotion, that there was at the back of your mind a witness, watching everything that was going on, yet too deep for your ordinary thought to grasp ? Has it not occurred to you—in a moment say of great danger when the mind was agitated to the last degree by fears and anxieties—suddenly to become perfectly calm and collected, to realise that *nothing* can harm you, that you are identified with some great and universal being lifted far over this mortal world and unaffected by its storms ? Is it not obvious that the real Self *must* be something of this nature, a being perceiving all, but itself remaining unperceived ? For indeed if it were perceived it would fall under the head of some definable quality, and so becoming the object of thought would cease to be the subject, would cease to be the Self.

The witness is and must be " free from qualities." For since it is capable of perceiving *all* qualities it must obviously not be itself imprisoned or tied in any quality—it must either be entirely without quality, or if it have the potentiality of quality in it, it must have the potentiality of *every* quality ; but in either case it cannot be in bondage to any quality, and in either case it would appear that there can be only *one* such ultimate Witness in the universe. For if there were two or more such Witnesses, then we should be compelled to suppose them distinguished from one another by something, and that something could only be a difference of qualities, which would be contrary to our conclusion that such a Witness cannot be in bondage to any quality.

There is then I take it—as the text in question says—only one Witness, one Self, throughout the universe. It is hidden in all living things, men and animals and plants ; it pervades all creation. In every thing that has consciousness it is the Self ; it watches over all operations, it overshadows all creatures, it moves in the depths of our hearts, the perceiver, the only being that is cognisant of all and yet free from all.

Once you really appropriate this truth, and assimilate it in the depths of your mind, a vast change (you can easily imagine) will take place within you. The whole world will be transformed, and every thought and act of which you are capable will take on a different colour and complexion. Indeed the revolution will be so vast that it would be quite impossible for me within the limits of this discourse to describe it. I will however, occupy the rest of my time in dealing with some points and conclusions, and some mental changes which will flow perfectly naturally from this axiomatic change taking place at the very root of life.

"Free from qualities." We generally pride ourselves a little on our qualities. Some of us think a great deal of our good qualities, and some of us are rather ashamed of our bad ones ! I would say : " Do not trouble very much about all that. What good qualities you have—well you may be quite sure they do not really amount to much ; and what bad qualities, you may be sure they are not very important ! Do not make too much fuss about either. Do you see ? The thing is that *you*, you yourself, are not *any* of your qualities— you are the being that perceives them. The thing to see to is that they should not confuse you, bamboozle you, and hide you from the knowledge of yourself—that they should not be erected into a screen, to hide you from others, or the others from you. If you cease from running after qualities, then after a little time your soul will become purified, and you will *know* that your self is the Self of all creatures ; and when you can feel that you will know that the other things do not much matter.

Sometimes people are so awfully good that their very good-

ness hides them from other people. They really cannot be
on a level with others, and they feel that the others are far
below them. Consequently their ' selves ' are blinded or hidden
by their ' goodness.' It is a sad end to come to ! And sometimes it happens that very ' bad ' people—just because they
are so bad—do not erect any screens or veils between themselves and others. Indeed they are only too glad if others
will recognise them, or if they may be allowed to recognise
others. And so, after all, they come nearer the truth than the
very good people.

"The Self is free from qualities." That thing which is so
deep, which belongs to all, it either—as I have already said—
has *all* qualities, or it has none. You, to whom I am speaking
now, your qualities, good and bad, are all mine. I am perfectly
willing to accept them. They are all right enough and in
place—if one can only find the places for them. But I know
that in most cases they have got so confused and mixed up
that they cause great conflict and pain in the souls that harbour
them. If you attain to knowing yourself to be other than
and separate from the qualities, then you will pass below and
beyond them all. You will be able to accept *all* your qualities
and harmonise them, and your soul will be at peace. You will
be free from the domination of qualities then because you will
know that among all the multitudes of them there are none
of any importance !

If you should happen some day to reach that state of mind
in connexion with which this revelation comes, then you will
find the experience a most extraordinary one. You will become
conscious that there is no barrier in your path ; that the way
is open in all directions ; that all men and women belong to
you, are part of you. You will feel that there is a great open
mmense world around, which you had never suspected before,
which belongs to you, and the riches of which are all yours,
waiting for you. It may, of course, take centuries and thousands
of years to realise this thoroughly, but there it is. You are
just at the threshold, peeping in at the door. What did Shakespeare say ? " To thine own self be true, and it must follow
as the night the day, thou can'st not then be false to any
man." What a profound bit of philosophy in three lines !
I doubt if anywhere the basis of all human life has been expressed
more perfectly and tersely.

One of the Upanishads (the Maitráyana-Brahmana) says :
" The happiness belonging to a mind, which through deep

inwardness [1] (or understanding) has been washed clean and has entered into the Self, is a thing beyond the power of words to describe : it can only be perceived by an inner faculty." Observe the conviction, the intensity with which this joy, this happiness is described, which comes to those whose minds have been washed clean (from all the silly trumpery sediment of self-thought) and have become transparent, so that the great universal Being residing there in the depths can be perceived. What sorrow indeed, what grief, can come to such an one who has seen this vision ? It is truly a thing beyond the power of words to describe : it can only be *perceived*—and that by an inner faculty. The external apparatus of thought is of no use. Argument is of no use. But experience and direct perception are possible ; and probably all the experiences of life and of mankind through the ages are gradually deepening our powers of perception to that point where the vision will at last rise upon the inward eye.

Another text, from the Brihad-Aranyaka Upanishad (which I have already quoted in the paper on " Rest "), says : " If a man worship the Self only as his true state, his work cannot fail, for whatever he desires, that he obtains from the Self." Is that not magnificent ? If you truly realise your identity and union with the great Self who inspires and informs the world, then obviously whatever you desire the great Self will desire, and the whole world will conspire to bring it to you. " He maketh the winds his angels, and the flaming fires his ministers." [I need not say that I am not asking you to try and identify yourself with the great Self universal *in order* to get riches, " opulence," and other things of that kind which you desire ; because in that quest you will probably not succeed. The Great Self is not such a fool as to be taken in in that way. It may be true—and it *is* true—that if ye seek *first* the Kingdom of Heaven all these things shall be added unto you ; but you must seek it first, not second.]

[1] The word in the Max Müller translation is " meditation.' But that is, I think, a somewhat misleading word. It suggests to most people the turning inward of the *thinking* faculty to grope and delve in the interior of the mind. This is just what should *not* be done. Meditation in the proper sense should mean the inward deepening of *feeling* and consciousness till the region of the universal self is reached ; but *thought* should not interfere there. That should be turned on outward things to mould them into expression of the inner consciousness.

Here is a passage from *Towards Democracy* : " As space spreads everywhere, and all things move and change within it, but it moves not nor changes,

" So I am the space within the soul, of which the space without is but the similitude and mental image ;

" Comest thou to inhabit me, thou hast the entrance to all life—death shall no longer divide thee from whom thou lovest.

" I am the Sun that shines upon all creatures from within— gazest thou upon me, thou shalt be filled with joy eternal."

Yes, this great sun is there, always shining, but most of the time it is hidden from us by the clouds of which I have spoken, and we fail to see it. We complain of being out in the cold ; and in the cold, for the time being, no doubt we are ; but our return to the warmth and the light has now become possible.

Thus at last the Ego, the mortal immortal self—disclosed at first in darkness and fear and ignorance in the growing babe —*finds its true identity.* For a long period it is baffled in trying to understand what it is. It goes through a vast experience. It is tormented by the sense of separation and alienation— alienation from other people, and persecution by all the great powers and forces of the universe ; and it is pursued by a sense of its own doom. Its doom truly is irrevocable. The hour of fulfilment approaches, the veil lifts, and the soul beholds at last *its own true being.*

We are accustomed to think of the external world around us as a nasty tiresome old thing of which all we can say for certain is that it works by a " law of cussedness "—so that, which- ever way we want to go, that way seems always barred, and we only bump against blind walls without making any progress. But that uncomfortable state of affairs arises from ourselves. Once we have passed a certain barrier, which at present looks so frowning and impossible, but which fades into nothing im- mediately we have passed it—once we have found the open secret of identity—then the way is indeed open in every direction.

The world in which we live—the world into which we are tumbled as children at the first onset of self-consciousness— denies this great fact of unity. It is a world in which the principle of separation rules. Instead of a common life and union with each other, the contrary principle (especially in the later civilisations) has been the one recognised—and to such an extent that always there prevails the obsession of separation, and the conviction that each person is an isolated unit. The whole of our modern society has been founded on this delusive idea, *which is false.* You go into the markets, and every man's hand is against the others—that is the ruling principle. You go into the Law Courts where justice is, or should be, administered, and you find that the principle which denies unity is the one that prevails. The criminal (whose actions have really been determined by the society around him) is cast out, disacknowledged, and condemned to further isolation in a prison cell. ' Property ' again is the principle which rules and determines our modern civilisation—namely that which is proper to, or can be appropriated by, each person, as *against* the others. In the moral world the doom of separation comes to us in the shape of the sense of sin. For sin is separation. Sin is actually (and that is its only real meaning) the separation from others, and the non-acknowledgment of unity. And so it has come about that during all this civilisation-period the sense of sin has ruled and ranged to such an extraordinary degree. Society has been built on a false base, not true to fact or life—and has had a dim uneasy consciousness of its falseness. Meanwhile at the heart of it all—and within all the frantic external strife and warfare—there is all the time this real great life brooding. The Kingdom of Heaven, as we said before, is still within.

The word Democracy indicates something of the kind—the rule of the Demos, that is of the common life. The coming of that will transform, not only our Markets and our Law Courts and our sense of Property, and other institutions, into something really great and glorious instead of the dismal masses of rubbish which they at present are ; but it will transform our sense of Morality.

Our Morality at present consists in the idea of self-goodness —one of the most pernicious and disgusting ideas which has ever infested the human brain. If any one should follow and assimilate what I have just said about the true nature of the Self he will realise that it will never again be possible for him to congratulate himself on his own goodness or morality or superiority ; for the moment he does so he will separate himself from the universal life, and proclaim the sin of his own separation. I agree that this conclusion is for some people a most sad and disheartening one—but it cannot be helped ! A man may truly be ' good ' and ' moral ' in some real sense ;

but only on the condition that he is not aware of it. He can only *be* good when not thinking about the matter ; to be *conscious* of one's own goodness is already to have fallen !

We began by thinking of the self as just a little local self ; then we extended it to the family, the cause, the nation—ever to a larger and vaster being. At last there comes a time when we recognise—or see that we *shall* have to recognise—an inner Equality between ourselves and all others ; not of course an external equality—for that would be absurd and impossible —but an inner and profound and universal Equality. And so we come again to the mystic root-conception of Democracy.

And now it will be said : " But after all this talk you have not defined the Self, or given us any intellectual outline of what you mean by the word." No—and I do not intend to. If I could, by any sort of copybook definition, describe and show the boundaries of myself, I should obviously lose all interest in the subject. Nothing more dull could be imagined. I may be able to define and describe fairly exhaustively this inkpot on the table ; but for you or for me to give the limits and boundaries of ourselves is, I am glad to say, impossible. That does not, however, mean that we cannot *feel* and be *conscious* of ourselves, and of our relations to other selves, and to the great Whole. On the contrary I think it is clear that the more vividly we feel our organic unity with the whole, the less shall we be able to separate off the local self and enclose it within any definition. I take it that we can and do become ever more vividly conscious of our true Self, but that the mental statement of it always does and probably always will lie beyond us. All life and all our action and experience consist in the gradual manifestation of that which is within us—of our inner being. In that sense—and reading its handwriting on the outer world —we come to know the soul's true nature more and more intimately ; we enter into the mind of that great artist who beholds himself in his own creation.

INDEX

INDEX

Second birth, doctrine of, *see* Re-birth

Self-consciousness, its place in evolution, 141, 150, 225; the origin of ritual, 147, 165; a danger to the Tribe, 150; a sleep and a forgetting, 174; nurse of the practical Intellect, 174; relation to Sex, 186; to birth of language, 229; the false must die, 232; the true, 274; appearing at age of three, 295; hardly found in animals, 296

Separation, an illusion, 301, 307

Serpent and Scorpion, 28

Sex, treatment of, by Christianity, ch. xii; its connection everywhere with religion, 183; as the Old Serpent, 186; commercialized, 188; primitive views on, 247; relation to love, 249

Sex-rites, in the Jewish Temple and elsewhere, ch. xii, pp. 20, 181–3; communal and pandemic, 188; organs imaged in the Mysteries, 244

Sex-taboo, the, 184–7; a necessary stage, 187; meaning of, in Christianity, 192

Shelley quoted, 97

Sin, the sense of, its origin, 103, 141; theory of sin and sacrifice, reasonable, 110 *sq.*; natural evolution of, 114; its redeeming value, 149; as separation, 142, 227, 307

Siva, as the Sacrifice, 133

Snakes in magic, 73, 82

Sollas, W. J., quoted, 230

Soma-drink, nature of, 177

Son of Man, the, 206, 235

Spartacus and the slave-revolt, 138

Spartan friendships, 65

Spencer and Gillen quoted, 61, 195

Spirit, the Great, 95; of the Hive, 148

Spirits or Sprites, 11

Spontaneous evolution of rites and creeds, 165, 222

Spring, and the renewal of life, 70, 112

Star in the East, 24; or Sirius, 29

Sungods, 10, 20, ch. ii; and Christianity, 21

Superstitions, ch. v; of ill-luck, 14, 156, 194

Suppression of instincts, 189; of sex, harmfulness of, 196

Sympathetic magic for the crops, 75

Syphilis, 188

Systems and Creeds, delusive, 12, 101; but necessary, 103

Taboos, created by fear, 14, 61, 62, 94; on food, 193; on the Sabbath, 194; on marriage, 195; of sex, 185; due to reaction, 185; to an instinct of limitation, 193, 195; their study important, 262; final freedom from, 269

Tacitus quoted, 47

Tagore, Rabindranath, quoted, 290

Taipusam, festival in Ceylon, 264; meaning of, 265

Tammuz, or Adonis, 22

Tat twam asi, 299

Taurobolium, 43

Taylor, Richard, author of *Devil's Pulpit*, 10

Tennyson quoted, 295

Tertullian quoted, 25, 130

Testament of the twelve patriarchs, 219

Thanatomania, 14, 177

Thargelia, festival of, 118

Theocritus quoted, 65 *n.*, 71, 197

Thera, inscriptions at, 170

THE END